FOURTH EDITION

Teaching English Language Learners in Elementary School Communities

A Joinfostering Approach

Christian J. Faltis
Arizona State University

PEARSON
Merrill
Prentice Hall

D1445075

Upper Saddle River, New Jersey
Columbus, Ohio

Library of Congress Cataloging-in-Publication Data

Faltis, Christian
   Teaching English language learners in elementary school communities : a joinfostering
approach / Christian J. Faltis.-- 4th ed.
      p. cm.
   . Rev. ed. of: Joinfostering : teaching and learning in multilingual classrooms. 3rd ed. c2001.
   Includes bibliographical references and index.
   ISBN 0-13-119442-9
      1. Education, Bilingual--United States. 2. Mainstreaming in education--United States.
   3. Elementary school teachers--Training of--United States. 4. Education, Elementary--Parent
   participation--United States. I. Faltis, Christian, Joinfostering. II. Title.

LC3731.F35 2006
370.117'5'0973--dc22

2005005471

Vice President and Executive Publisher: Jeffery W. Johnston
Executive Editor: Debra A. Stollenwerk
Editorial Assistant: Mary Morrill
Production Editor: Kris Roach
Production Coordination: Tim Flem/PublishWare
Design Coordinator: Diane C. Lorenzo
Photo Coordinator: Monica Merkel
Cover Designer: Trudi Gershenov
Cover image: Corbis
Production Manager: Susan Hannahs
Director of Marketing: Ann Castel Davis
Marketing Manager: Darcy Betts Prybella
Marketing Coordinator: Tyra Poole

This book was set in ITC New Baskerville by PublishWare and was printed and bound
by R. R. Donnelley & Sons Company. The cover was printed by Phoenix Color Corp.

Photo Credits: Scott Cunningham/Merrill, pp. 1, 85, 153; Barbara Schwartz/Merrill, p. 45;
Tom Watson/Merrill, p. 111; Silver Burdett Ginn, p. 197; Todd Yarrington/Merrill, p. 223.

Pearson Education Ltd.
Pearson Education Singapore Pte. Ltd.
Pearson Education Canada, Ltd.
Pearson Education—Japan

Pearson Education Australia Pty. Limited
Pearson Education North Asia Ltd.
Pearson Educación de Mexico, S.A. de C.V.
Pearson Education Malaysia Pte. Ltd.

10 9 8 7 6 5 4 3 2 1
ISBN: 0-13-119442-9

I dedicate this book to my longtime friend and mentor,
Dr. Henry T. Trueba,
who passed away in July 2004. Your memory lives in these pages
and in the hearts of all of us who share your passion for
improving schools and society for immigrant and minority children.

Preface

This book was written with three audiences in mind: (1) education majors who are in the process of becoming classroom teachers, (2) established teachers who are interested in changing the way they teach to accommodate students who are adding English to their already-developed native language(s), and (3) teachers in dual-language, enrichment bilingual classrooms. As the number of students learning in and through English as an additional language grows substantially, grade-level classroom teachers must become better prepared to help these students join in all aspects of the classroom and school communities of practice. Moreover, as bilingual education expands to include English-speaking children along with children who are learning in and through English, there is a need for improving ways to invite children from both language groups into social and academic discourses.

It is important to understand that exemplary teaching in a multilingual classroom differs in significant ways from exemplary teaching in a classroom in which all students are fully proficient speakers of the same language. When students are learning the *language* of instruction in addition to the *content* of instruction, teaching them as if they were fully proficient speakers is both ineffective and unacceptable. Teachers must learn to adapt teaching to ensure that English learners have access to and participate in all aspects of classroom communities of practice. Doing anything less means that we are denying these students the benefits of classroom learning experiences. In other words, we are denying them their civil right to an education equal to that to which children who speak English fluently are entitled.

My experience working and teaching in bilingual and second-language education spans nearly 30 years, and I remain a strong advocate of home-language teaching in bilingual education. Over the years, however, I have come to realize that, in placing all of my energies into studying and improving bilingual education, I have effectively ignored what happens to children who are placed in all-English classrooms with teachers who are underprepared to attend to these students' social and academic learning needs. Virtually all children who enter a native-language bilingual education program stay there, on average, no more than 2 years, and most of these children receive precious little English-as-a-second-language support once they exit from the bilingual program. This means that two-thirds to three-fourths of their schooling will be in all-English-medium classrooms with all-English teachers who have little or no idea about how to help these children join in all aspects of teaching and learning! This is a social injustice. The purpose of this book is to help you interrupt and reverse this injustice.

A JOINFOSTERING FRAMEWORK

This book presents a teaching framework for English-speaking teachers who will be working in ethnically diverse classrooms with students who are learning English as an additional language. The framework is organized around principles for teaching that I refer to as *joinfostering*, which means to *foster* (plan for and implement) social and academic practices that enable students who come to class speaking a language other than the teacher's language to *join* in, to actively participate in all aspects of English-medium classroom life, and to come to identify and affiliate with new communities of practice. Joinfostering is not a cookbook of teaching behaviors for teaching and assessing English learners or dual-language learners.

Joinfostering principles provide a way for monolingual English-speaking teachers to accommodate the multiple social and language abilities that children who are becoming bilingual bring to any classroom. Joinfostering stems from the credo that public schools and the English-speaking teachers and students who teach and learn in them need to invite students for whom English is an additional language to become active members of the socioacademic communities of school practices. This credo is especially important in the present-day era of segregation and isolation that many non-English speaking communities endure. Joinfostering endorses the belief that learning, inquiring, and solving problems together benefits all children, teaching them that through interdependence they can draw on one another's multiple abilities to make positive connections with school communities of practice.

Joinfostering also derives from a set of values about people, work, and play, values regarding the need to respect and consider the needs of others, and the ability to work and play in a safe environment. In a joinfostering classroom, children's active participation in classroom practices is essential for identifying with and practicing specific kinds of classroom activities; everyone in class has something special to contribute to and connect with learning. Equally valued is the assumption that people in general are well intentioned and capable. Students from linguistically diverse backgrounds who work and play together in school successfully are more likely to grow up identifying with and believing in the value of diversity and collaboration for solving problems together. In classrooms based on joinfostering principles, children also learn to work independently, but only after they have many interactive experiences with the teacher and peers who know the language of school and use it in rich enough contexts to enable them to make meaningful connections for inquiry and problem solving. Last, there is the value of participating in classroom work. Being serious about schoolwork is valued in a joinfostering classroom because activities and work are presented and modeled as being both enjoyable and purposeful. Joinfostering, therefore, is both a way of preparing you to teach in linguistically diverse classrooms supported by values and assumptions about social justice, people, and work, as well as a description of what is possible to accomplish in linguistically diverse classrooms.

Now more than 15 years old, the term *joinfostering* evolved from an idea I had about promoting children's storybooks in which characters of the story solved problems cooperatively rather than in competition with others. I referred to this genre as *cooperation-fostering children's books* (see Faltis, 1989). I appropriated the sense of cooperation-fostering from Annemarie Palincsar's work in reciprocal teaching of comprehension-fostering reading activities (Palincsar & Brown, 1984). Since the publication of the first edition of *Joinfostering* in 1993, there have been a number of important theoretical advances and policy changes in the field of bilingual and English-as-a-second-language education that have had an impact on my thinking about what teachers need to know to teach effectively to students in a language other than their mother tongue.

NEW TO THIS EDITION

- **A sociocultural framework.** One of the most important advances included in this new edition of *Teaching English Language Learners in Elementary School Communities: A Joinfostering Approach* is that I draw primarily from a sociocultural perspective. While earlier editions focused on what happens to individual English language learners, this one shows how learners socially co-construct, with the teacher and classmates, multiple and varying identities as learners and gain new academic knowledge and literate practices. From this perspective, a major goal of teaching is to enable English learners to participate actively so that they affiliate with new academic values, rules, and goals (Edelsky & Smith, 2003; Faltis & Hudelson, 1998; Gee, 2003; Hawkins, 2004; Norton &

Toohey, 2001; Pérez, 2004; Wolfe, 1999). Moreover, I have found that there is a new and growing audience for the joinfostering approach to teaching and learning. Teachers in preparation for and those already teaching in dual-language bilingual programs can also benefit.

- **Applicable to dual-language education.** Dual-language bilingual programs are also referred to as *enrichment bilingual education; bilingual immersion; two-way immersion; two-way maintenance;* and *developmental bilingual education* (Bickle, Billings, & Hakuta, 2004; Faltis & Hudelson, 1998; Soltero, 2004). A common point among all types of dual-language programs is that teachers work not only with non-English-speaking students who are adding English, but also with English-speaking students who are adding a second language, the language of their non-English-speaking peers. Most often, dual-language bilingual programs involve the languages of Spanish and English; however, other languages served include Cantonese, French, Japanese, Korean, Mandarin, Navajo, Portuguese, and Russian (Ovando, Collier, & Combs, 2003; Soltero, 2004). Regardless of the languages involved, students in dual-language classrooms need to be invited into the discourse of school in an additional language at least part of the time they spend in school. For this reason, joinfostering principles apply equally well to dual-language classrooms. Nonetheless, the bulk of practices and strategies presented are addressed mainly to the English-medium classroom teacher.

Throughout this book, I discuss the theoretical grounds for join-fostering as principles of practice (Cochran-Smith, 1999), as opposed to principles that may or may not be related to or situated in classroom practice (for example, principles that relate to video games; see Gee, 2003). This is because theory cannot exist in isolation from practice and the values that support practice. Practices carried out by a teacher and students are always drawn from theoretical principles and values about teaching, learning, and assessment. Likewise, for theoretical principles and values to have a foundation, they must be wedded to and situated in practice activities so that learners have opportunities to participate actively in and critically with the relevant academic language and to form new affiliations with people who are proficient members of the academic language.

This book presents a great deal of the teaching and learning strategies found in exceptional and wonderful bilingual and English-as-a-second-language classrooms throughout the nation. In other words, many of the strategies and ways of teaching and learning presented here are derived largely from research-based advances that have been created and fomented in exceptional bilingual education and ESL teaching settings.

- **A new view of being a good language learner.** In this edition, I have included some key advances with respect to second-language acquisition in school settings. The idea of what a "good language learner" entails is changing from a focus on what the learner does psychologically and cognitively to a view of learners constructing new (social) identities through their affiliations with multiple communities of practice as they are socialized into academic discourses (Norton & Toohey, 2001). From this perspective, learning is not an individual enterprise, but rather a result of students coming together around specific tasks in specific situated practices. Classrooms become sites of situated cultural and language practices, with learners joining together, sometimes in conflict, to negotiate new and developing meanings and understandings. In the process of using the social languages of the classroom in socially recognized ways, to the extent that learners take on new and varying identities connected to social groups and cultural practices (Hawkins, 2004), they become good language learners (Norton & Toohey, 2001).

  This book aims to engage you in a way of teaching and assessment that goes against the grain of teaching exclusively toward tests, of having students learn predetermined facts without inquiring about them, especially when the facts relate to the persistence of social inequality and social hierarchies that sort people on the basis of class, ethnicity, gender, and language.

- **A new chapter on assessment practices.** With these goals in mind, I have added a new chapter on assessment, with an eye toward understanding the multiple roles of oral and written language assessment for gauging learning and improving instruction. Moreover, I have woven in several new examples of how you and students can engage in critical inquiry about social injustice as you progress through the book.

SPECIAL FEATURES

- **Running case episodes.** These episodes/scenarios occur throughout the text and provide realistic snapshots of three teachers who represent many teachers in schools today: Julia, a first-year, 3rd grade teacher who is learning about how to teach in a multilingual classroom; Peggy, a veteran teacher who shares views of teaching English learners that probably many teachers today have; and Rudy "Jake," a bilingual teacher whose experience and wisdom is often helpful to Julia as she grows in professional experience.

- **End-of-chapter activities and assignments.** These are designed to give teachers opportunities to think about and to practice what they are learning in the chapters.

TO THE TEACHER

This book is organized to give your students an understanding of language and cultural diversity and bilingual schooling practices before introducing them to teaching strategies for whole-class and small-group learning contexts. There are many examples to draw from in this new edition, but undoubtedly you will want to bring in your own experiences and examples to fit your particular circumstances. The book begins by introducing Julia Felix, a first-year 3rd-grade teacher who is faced with learning about teaching in a multilingual classroom. Julia teaches next door to Peggy Dimwitty, a veteran teacher whose views about teaching English learners may well represent many teachers across the United States. Julia also meets Rudy "Jake" Jacobson, a bilingual teacher whose experience and wisdom Julia finds quite helpful.

I use numerous examples associated with the theme of treatment of endangered animals—in particular, elephants. I have tried to show how Julia involves students in critical consciousness about this theme. You may wish to begin your class with a different inquiry theme and then, as you move students into the later chapters, use the theme to illustrate strategies and techniques as they are described and discussed. At the end of each chapter are activities and assignments to help students think about and practice the ideas presented in the chapter. I suggest that your students interview teachers from multilingual classrooms to learn about their experiences and to observe them at work. Finally, it is important to stress to your students that this book is more than a set of adaptations for teaching English learners; it is a commitment in practice to becoming knowledgeable, capable, and critical teachers for all students.

TO THE STUDENT

You are part of the next generation of teachers—the teachers who will be responsible for educating a diverse group of children, many of whom are immigrants, children of immigrants, and may be adding English as an additional language as they are learning academic content in your classroom. This book is an introduction to teaching in multilingual classrooms. By reading, discussing, and practicing the strategies and activities presented in this book, you will be prepared to teach and assess in a multilingual classroom.

One of the most important goals of this book is to help you develop the following stance toward teaching, learning, and children: that all children can learn in a safe schooling environment and that we are responsible for finding ways to make sure that all children learn what they need in order to become responsible, knowledgeable, curious, and critical members of society. By the time you complete this book, you should not be fearful of entering a classroom where some or all of the students are second-language learners. You should welcome the opportunity.

ACKNOWLEDGMENTS

I would like to thank all of the reviewers who read drafts and earlier editions of this book: Richard E. Baecher, Fordham University; John T. Clark, California State University, Chico; Mary Carol Combs, University of Arizona; Gail A. Cueto, Central Connecticut State University; Salvador A. Gabaldón, Tucson Unified School District; Rosalind Horowitz, University of Texas, San Antonio; Craig A. Hughes, Central Washington University; Solange A. Lopes-Murphy, James Madison University; Ana H. Macias, University of Texas, El Paso; Ramón A. Serrano, St. Cloud State University; and Paula Wolfe, University of Wisconsin, Madison. I have relied on the ideas and practices of many people who have dedicated their professional lives to improving teaching and learning for children who are becoming bilingual and biliterate in school. I have learned much from long discussions about teaching with Beatriz Arias, Karen Smith, and Carole Edelsky. I am also grateful for the ideas and support from the many teachers whose classrooms I have visited. Thanks to Annie, April, Gloria, and countless others.

I would like to acknowledge my editor, Debbie Stollenwerk, for her patience and advice about how to develop this new edition. Last, but not least, this book is better because of the keen eye and extraordinary writing craft of copyeditor Roberta "Bobbie" Dempsey and production editor Timothy Flem. Mil gracias a todos.

Christian J. Faltis

REFERENCES

Bickle, K., Billings, E., & Hakuta, K. (2004). Trends in two-way immersion research. In J. Banks & C. M. Banks (Eds.), *Handbook of research on multicultural education* (2nd ed., pp. 589–604). San Francisco: Jossey Bass.

Cochran-Smith, M. (1999). Learning to teach for social justice. In G. Griffin (Ed.), *The education of teachers* (pp. 114–140). Chicago: National Society for the Study of Education.

Edelsky, C., & Smith, K. (2003). Through the Looking Glass: Understanding Academic Work. Paper presented at the Fourth International Symposium on Bilingualism. Tempe, Arizona, May 31.

Faltis, C. (1989). Spanish language cooperation-fostering storybooks for language minority children in bilingual programs. *Journal of Educational Issues of Language Minority Students, 5,* 46–55.

Faltis, C., & Hudelson, S., (1998). *Bilingual education in elementary and secondary school communities: Toward understanding and caring.* Needham Heights, MA: Allyn & Bacon.

Gee, J. (2003). Opportunity to learning: A language-based perspective on assessment. *Assessment in Education, 10*(1), 27–46.

Hawkins, M. (2004). Researching English language and literacy development in schools. *Educational Researcher, 33*(3), 14–25.

Norton, B., & Toohey, K. (2001). Changing perspectives on good language learners. *TESOL Quarterly, 35*(2), 307–322.

Ovando, C., Collier, V., & Combs, M. C. (2003). *Bilingual education & ESL classroom: Teaching in multicultural contexts* (3rd ed.). Boston, MA: McGraw-Hill.

Palincsar, A., & Brown, A. (1984). Reciprocal teaching of comprehension-fostering and comprehension-monitoring activities. *Cognition and Instruction, 1*(2), 117–135.

Pérez, B. (Ed.) (2004). *Sociocultural contexts of language and literacy.* Mahwah, NJ: Lawrence Erlbaum Associates.

Soltero, S. (2004). *Dual language: Teaching and learning in two languages.* Boston, MA: Allyn & Bacon.

Wolfe, P. (1999). *Situated learning in a transactional, secondary, English as a second language classroom.* Unpublished doctoral dissertation. Tempe, AZ: Arizona State University.

Educator Learning Center: An Invaluable Online Resource

Merrill Education and the Association for Supervision and Curriculum Development (ASCD) invite you to take advantage of a new online resource, one that provides access to the top research and proven strategies associated with ASCD and Merrill—the Educator Learning Center. At **www.educatorlearningcenter.com**, you will find resources that will enhance your students' understanding of course topics and of current educational issues, in addition to being invaluable for further research.

HOW THE EDUCATOR LEARNING CENTER WILL HELP YOUR STUDENTS BECOME BETTER TEACHERS

With the combined resources of Merrill Education and ASCD, you and your students will find a wealth of tools and materials to better prepare them for the classroom.

Research

- More than 600 articles from the ASCD journal *Educational Leadership* discuss everyday issues faced by practicing teachers.
- A direct link on the site to Research Navigator™ gives students access to many of the leading education journals, as well as extensive content detailing the research process.
- Excerpts from Merrill Education texts give your students insights on important topics of instructional methods, diverse populations, assessment, classroom management, technology, and refining classroom practice.

Classroom Practice

- Hundreds of lesson plans and teaching strategies are categorized by content area and age range.
- Case studies and classroom video footage provide virtual field experience for student reflection.
- Computer simulations and other electronic tools keep your students abreast of today's classrooms and current technologies.

LOOK INTO THE VALUE OF EDUCATOR LEARNING CENTER YOURSELF

A 4-month subscription to Educator Learning Center is $25 but is *free* when packaged with any Merrill Education text. In order for your students to have access to this site, you must use this special value-pack ISBN number *when* placing your textbook order with the bookstore: 0-13-168664-X. Your students will then receive a copy of the text packaged with a free ASCD pincode. To preview the value of this Web site to you and your students, please go to **www.educatorlearningcenter.com** and click on "Demo."

Contents

CHAPTER 4

TEACHING FOR ACTIVE PARTICIPATION
IN A MIXED-LANGUAGE WHOLE-CLASS CONTEXT   111

CHAPTER 5

FACILITATING ACTIVE PARTICIPATION
DURING SMALL-GROUP WORK   153

CHAPTER 6

INVITING AND ENGAGING FAMILIES AND COMMUNITIES IN SCHOOLING ACTIVITIES   197

1

Expect to Have Children Who Are Learning English

The purpose of this book is to open a dialogue about making English learning inviting to children who are learning English as an additional language while they are engaged in academic activities and practices. The dialogue is framed in terms of a set of guidelines for teaching, inquiring, and doing schoolwork, referred to as *joinfostering* principles of practices (see the Preface). Learning to invite students into the ongoing stream of classroom community life requires extensive practice, knowledge, and a commitment to social justice issues that especially affect school children who are becoming bilingual. If you do not speak your students' language, and these students are required to learn academic content and to engage in literacy practices in an unfamiliar language, you must have a set of guiding principles for providing students with a safe learning environment and for helping them make sense of school and identify favorably with school practices. Your success in getting students to participate actively and critically in classroom activities so that they come to identify as classroom members depends on your ability as a teacher to plan for and use six interrelated pedagogical and social principles of practice.

1

JOINFOSTERING PRINCIPLES OF PRACTICE

Following are the six principles of practice. An abbreviated form is presented in capital letters and will be used throughout the book to indicate the particular principle(s).

1. Enable all students (through invitation and nudging) to participate actively in social and academic classroom practices (ACTIVE PARTICIPATION OF ALL STUDENTS). Active participation means that students see, feel, understand, and operate on a given experience in new ways; that they create new identities as English learners and form new affiliations with members who are proficient in academic language; and that they learn how to use oral and written language to wonder about and discuss academic topics in ways that are recognized and used by proficient members of academic communities of practice. Some key questions to consider for this principle are: What do I need to do to ensure that children who are learning to use English in school participate actively? What kinds of classroom rules for talking, moving around, and sharing information facilitate active participation? What kinds of active participation enable children to identify with academic communities of practice?

2. Socially integrate students of diverse language and social backgrounds (using a variety of whole-class and small-group strategies for socially constructing meaning) to build on the unfolding identities, prior knowledge, and interests students bring with them, and to affiliate with new communities of practice (SOCIAL INTEGRATION TO FACILITATE THE CREATION OF NEW IDENTITIES AND SOCIOACADEMIC AFFILIATIONS). Children need to see themselves and have others see them as participating members of academic communities of practice. It is through the creation of new, multiple identities and affiliations that students come to understand and personally connect with academic ideas and ways of expression embedded in communities of practice. Some important questions to consider are: How can socially integrating students of diverse backgrounds help English learners create new identities and socioacademic affiliations with classroom communities of practice? What kinds of participation structures and classroom rules for behaving, sharing, and interacting facilitate the social integration of students of diverse backgrounds? What cautions should I pay attention to when socially integrating children of diverse backgrounds?

3. Integrate language and literacy acquisition strategies (based on sociocultural learning theory about how children become bilingual) into all academic content learning activities so that as students actively participate in academic practices, create new identities as learners, and affiliate with wider communities of practice, they also gain greater proficiency in their new language (INTEGRATION OF ADDITIONAL LANGUAGE LEARNING INTO ACADEMIC LEARNING PRACTICES). One of your most important functions in school is to facilitate the active participation of children who are learning academic content through an additional language; hence, you will need to understand and be able to apply what you learn about how children acquire a second language through active and situated participation in communities of practice to all aspects of how you plan for, implement, and assess academic learning practices. Key questions for this principle are: How do the classroom communities of practice and the language used in them acquire English language learners? In what ways can the language and literacy experiences be modified to ensure active participation of English language learners with varying levels of proficiency in English? In what ways does active participation, sharing of ideas, inquiry, and the discussion of meaning promote language and literacy development in English learners?

4. Assess what your students are able to do well and where they need additional assistance, using a variety of approaches and, when needed, systems for evaluation and accountability, including performance assessment based on local standards (MULTIPLE WAYS OF ASSESSMENT TO OPTIMIZE ACADEMIC LEARNING PRACTICES, AFFILIATIONS, AND CONNECTIONS TO WIDER ACADEMIC COMMUNITIES OF PRACTICE); as an advocate for children, learning about assessment is critical for four reasons: First, you need to be able to correctly identify and place English language learners according to their language and literacy abilities. Second, you need to use assessment on a daily basis for providing the best possible learning opportunities and to show progress on curriculum and language-based standards. This means that you need to be versed in performance-based assessment as well as in assessment that is designed specifically for English learners. Third, you need to know when your students no longer require home language and/or additional language support services. (In some programs, students continue learning through their home language even though they are academically proficient in English.) Fourth, you need to understand the issues involved in assessment for accountability

purposes, especially to be able to resist efforts to have assessment drive instruction, to tie educational support monies to school achievement scores, and to deny access to English learners to higher grades based on standardized test scores designed for monolingual English speakers. Several questions to consider are: How can I learn to assess in order to assist without allowing assessment to drive what I do in class? How do certain kinds of assessments help or hinder English language learners?

5. Invite, involve, and build on the participation of families and communities in classroom, school, and neighborhood activities (PARTICIPATION OF FAMILY AND COMMUNITY). Family and community participation is highly complex, requiring extensive study of the communities served by the school. It is important to understand why mainstream, middle-class models of family and community involvement are not appropriate for most new immigrant families and communities. This being the case, it is also important to incorporate culturally responsive ways of communicating with and engaging families and communities in school practices.

6. Invite and promote critical consciousness within the classroom, the school, and the community to confront racism, social stratification, and exclusionary practices that may occur in our own classroom community life (PROMOTION OF CRITICAL CONSCIOUSNESS). As teachers, therefore, you must learn to question how and why teachers evaluate some children as differentially more able than other children, with respect to how well they participate in communities of practice, and then how children are sorted on the basis of these evaluations. Critical consciousness means that we pay attention to the ways that racism, social stratification, and exclusionary practices show up in school and society, always searching to unveil, interrupt, and repudiate them.

This book takes a stance about the importance of social justice with respect to how English language learners have been and may continue to be treated differentially in school and society. Both you and your students need to learn about how some people have wrongly treated groups and individuals based on perceptions about their ability to learn, which is closely connected to evaluative perceptions about ethnicity, language abilities, sex, and religion.

A commitment to joinfostering requires you to think about ways to make classroom practices inviting, authentic, challenging, and language-sensitive and to teach in ways that are appropriate to the sociocultural groups represented in your classroom. In addition, becoming a teacher who draws on the above principles means learning to teach against the grain of social injustice and take an active stance against educationally sponsored social stratification and other forms of exclusionary practices. To do so, you must learn how what happens in your classroom can contribute to exclusionary social hierarchies based on evaluations about who is and is not able to succeed in school communities of practice. In other words, this book is *not* about changing English learners who are members of ethnic and language minority communities into Americans. It is about inviting children into social and academic communities of learning to engage them in multiple experiences associated with school and aligned with more generalized communities of practice in society. Accordingly, what is important in learning to invite and situate English learners in social and academic communities is that you continually examine your practices not only to ensure that English learners have access to the human, material, and academic resources in your classroom communities, but also to become aware of and remove social and intellectual barriers to the participation and identity construction of English learners.

You are underway to using joinfostering principles when you learn to organize your classroom so that English learners have multiple and varied opportunities to inquire about, discuss, listen to, share, and work together and individually on interesting, relevant, and academically challenging tasks connected to larger themes and practices. You will also use the principles when you learn to assess the complexities of language and literacy in ways that help students continue their active participation as builders of knowledge and members of communities of practice. You can sense that joinfostering ideas for teaching English learners are in motion when students in your classes have a say about topics, themes, activities, ways of turn-taking, and sharing, and when they begin to affiliate with more proficient users of academic language, assiduously joining classroom practices that help create their new identities as multifaceted and able English learners.

Another clue that you are practicing joinfostering principles is that the families and communities of students who are becoming bilingual are participating at various levels in school and classroom activities. It is also important for you and your students to address social justice issues embedded in the work you do in class and for the school communities.

Learning to teach from a joinfostering perspective comes with great responsibility. When you invite English and other-language learners into the classroom community, not only *how* you teach them, but *what* you teach them and *what* they learn must be given serious consideration as well. A major function of schooling is to develop in students multiple identities as learners who inquire about what they are learning, who continue to seek answers throughout their lives, who play well with others, and who question practices that rank people by language variety, ethnicity, and skin color. This book asks you to invite your students to create multiple identities as literate problem solvers who are capable of posing and answering questions to better understand the world through the eyes of multiple academic content areas and literacies. The fact that many or all of your students are English learners means that you will need to pay extra attention to how you and they interact, make sense of texts, pose questions, and try out their new affiliations as academic language users in classroom communities of practice. You should not assume that merely inviting English learners into classroom activities is sufficient for them to create new identities and affiliations with social and academic communities of practice. There are powerful forces at work in a classroom that can relegate English learners and other minority students to marginal positions, effectively blocking them from participating fully and actively in classroom communities of practice necessary for more advanced learning in school (Kanno & Applebaum, 1995; Toohey, 1998). In each of the following chapters, you will learn not only how to organize your practices to support children's learning, but you will also learn about ways to ensure that learning resources are equitably assessable to all students as they assume multiple identities as learners and members of classroom communities of practice.

A NOTE ABOUT LABELS: MAINSTREAM TEACHERS, ENGLISH LEARNERS, AND CULTURAL GROUPS

Most of the classrooms referred to in this book are *mainstream all-English* grade-level classrooms. This book uses the term *mainstream* interchangeably with and alongside *all-English* or *English-medium* to refer to grade-level classrooms taught by English-speaking teachers who have been prepared for elementary classroom teaching in an all-English teacher education program. The reason for this usage is that the overwhelming majority of grade-level classroom teachers are white, female, and monolingual English speakers who represent mainstream values and behaviors (Banks, 2004; Gold, 1997). Thus, while the schools and classrooms that appear here may not be mainstream in terms of classroom makeup, the curriculum, the teachers, and the administrators are likely to be. Relatively few minorities are choosing teaching majors in college, prompting a number of educators to conclude that it is likely that language and cultural backgrounds of classroom teachers will become even less heterogeneous in the immediate decades to come than they are at present (Cochran-Smith, Davis, & Fries, 2004; González, J., 1997; Weiner, 2000).

From time to time, this book also refers to dual-language or two-way immersion classroom settings. These classrooms are similar to mainstream classrooms in the sense that for at least part of the day, or on alternate days, students are engaged in social and academic activities in their primary language; the rest of the time, students are learning academic content through an additional language (Soltero, 2004).

The labels used by mainstream teachers and administrators to talk about students who are adding English as a second language are problematic. There are lots of labels from which to choose: the older governmental preferred labels of *non-English proficient (NEP), limited English proficient (LEP),* and *fully English proficient (FEP);* the optimistic labels of *potentially English proficient (PEP)* and *readers and writers of English as another language (REAL);* the anemic labels of *monolinguals* and *English Immersion Students (EIS);* and the current one in vogue nationally of *English language learner (ELL).* The label *English language learner* came about in the late 1990s as a way to reduce the stigma attached to having teachers label LEP students as having limited abilities (Macías, 2000).

Some labels are more positive than others. You should know, however, that once you designate a student by a label, you set into motion a potentially vicious cycle: The label, usually based on something the "normal" population has but that the student lacks, determines the student's schooling environment. As Toohey (2000) points out, many teachers place students labeled as ESL learners in the front of the class, where they only have access to the teacher and thus are blocked off from the rich environment of interaction occurring in other parts of the room. The teacher treats students differently by engaging them in fewer exchanges and by using lower-level questions and materials. Once this happens, it is difficult, but not impossible, to break the cycle. The label then drives what happens to the child as she moves through the education system. (See Rose, 2001, for a long list of acronyms used to refer to children in California.)

To be frank, it was difficult to decide which labels to use to refer to different kinds of students and different cultural groups. Most of the labels used for students have to do with language proficiency designations. It makes some sense to talk about students in terms of their language abilities because many of the pedagogical and social interactional decisions we make include language proficiency. Thus, this book will use the labels *second-language learner* and *English learner* to refer to students who are adding a new language to their native language as they participate in school. However, the term *second language learner* doesn't work with students for whom the new language is a third or fourth language. Also, the label *English LANGUAGE learner* is redundant (Díaz-Rico, 2004). Accordingly, the term *English learner* is preferable. Periodically, this book also employs the U.S. government-sanctioned terms *limited English proficient (LEP)* and *non-English proficient (NEP)* because they are used widely in the literature in bilingual education and teaching English to speakers of other languages (TESOL), and they are designations that are closely tied to entry and exit testing. However, the terms *LEP* and *NEP* conjure up and lend credence to the notion of a deficit. Here is what the deficit theory predicts: If students are limited in their language ability, they are also likely to be limited in their intellectual ability; ergo, regardless of the amount and quality of special instruction they receive, they are likely not to achieve. As mentioned above, negative labels can lead to teaching practices that keep second-language students in lower tracks and/or that engage them in unchallenging activities. Finally, the acronyms LEP and NEP are often used as labels for the children themselves, rather than for their additional language abilities. This is a reprehensible practice.

Other labels that are highly troublesome are those for the ethnic groups included in this book: Hispanic groups, Asian groups, and Native American groups. The labels *Hispanic, Asian,* and *Native American* are admittedly imprecise, and they seriously overgeneralize and even essentialize substantial language and cultural differences and identities within each major group. On occasion, this book uses seemingly more precise labels, such as *Chinese Americans* and *Mexican Americans,* but even these are problematic because of the extensive cultural variation existing within each group (Schecter & Bayley, 2002; Suárez-Orozco & Todorova, 2003). Although the descriptions of immigrant vs. non-immigrant ethnic groups presented here are fairly specific, do not stereotype any individual member of an ethnic group based on these descriptions. There is no easy way to discuss the beliefs and practices of cultural and socioeconomic groups without speaking in rather general terms.

THE LONG-TERM CHALLENGE

Many mainstream teachers have accepted the challenge of working with social, academic, and cultural differences and abilities. However, relatively few teachers are prepared to teach children who are becoming bilingual along with monolingual children who speak the language of the teacher. For example, more than 20 years ago, a 1981 nationwide survey of public school grade-level teachers found that although half of all teachers had some experience with English learners in their classes, only 6% had taken one or more academic or nonacademic courses to learn how to effectively teach second-language students (Waggoner & O'Malley, 1985). A survey reported by Penfield (1987) showed that the majority of grade-level teachers know very little about the kinds of conditions and strategies that benefit second-language learners in their classrooms. Many teachers feared that second-language learners would do poorly in their classes because they are sorely underprepared to address these children's language and cultural needs (Penfield, 1987). In a California study on the shortage of teachers qualified to work with English learners, Gold (1997) found that the number of teachers entering the profession were increasingly monolingual English teachers with little or no experience or formal preparation in working with bilingual or English-as-a-second-language learners. A telling finding common to the studies mentioned above was that *all teachers expected the numbers of language-minority students who are becoming bilingual in their classes to increase dramatically in the coming years.* According to Samway and McKeon (1999), *one out of every two teachers* in the field can expect to teach English language learners throughout their teaching career. Zhao (2002) estimates that there is one qualified teacher for every 100 English learners in school. The ongoing challenge for elementary teachers with second-language learners—novices and veteran teachers alike—is colossal not only because of the increase in the numbers of language-minority students, especially English learners, but also because of the tendency in schools to stratify students into lower tracks based upon English language and literacy abilities (Harklau, 1994; Valdés, 2001), a pernicious form of exclusion. Once children are tracked and segregated into these kinds of divisions, it is difficult for them to "jump the tracks" and move into higher social and academic circles (Oakes, 1986).

The framework presented in this book aims specifically at providing you with classroom principles of practice for meeting the social, communicative, and educational needs of fully proficient language speakers and second-language learners alike. At the same time, the framework asks you to work toward social equality by directly challenging assumptions and practices concerning language, text, knowing, and learning that are often taken for granted or unscrupulously used to socially stratify children into high and low learning groups, effectively excluding them from participation in and benefit from a challenging curriculum. Chapter 1 examines the nature and extent of linguistic and cultural variation of school-age children in the United States, with an eye toward understanding how children in different cultures are socialized in their communities to participate using language and the extent to which they are prepared for the kinds of language and literacy events stressed in school. Of particular concern is the extent to which cultural differences affect how children learn in school and whether academic success can be more adequately explained in terms of the existence of appropriate classroom principles of practice. The chapter begins with a brief introduction to Miss Julia Felix, a first-year teacher faced with teaching in a linguistically and culturally diverse third-grade classroom, and Peggy Dimwitty, a veteran second-grade teacher who has a history of teaching English learners. In each of the subsequent chapters, we will see how Miss Felix organizes her classroom to promote learning and to facilitate the joining in of second-language children and their families through appropriate communication and social integration strategies and activities. We will also see how she learns to question certain actions and practices that create inequities for English learners.

Chapter 2 introduces you to the most prevalent instructional programs for teaching second-language learners and provides a brief historical account of the political and legal decisions that led to their development. The chapter opens with Miss Felix as she examines the cumulative folders of her 10 English learners. She discovers that the students have experienced a variety of different school programs before entering her classroom. In an effort to learn more about their experiences, Julia gathers information on bilingual education programs, including transitional bilingual education, structured English immersion education, dual language, and English-as-a-second-language pullout instruction. Peggy shares with Julia some of her thoughts on teaching English language learners. In this chapter we also learn about how English language proficiency is assessed for exiting from such programs into mainstream classrooms. Chapter 3 examines the social and physical organization of the classroom to explore ways of arranging space and furniture to support social interaction and social integration. The chapter begins with a description of how most classrooms are organized in order to contrast them with a classroom organized to reflect joinfostering principles of practice. In this chapter, we are also introduced to Rudy Jacobson, a bilingual teacher who becomes a welcome source of information and support for Julia as she navigates through the school year.

Chapters 4 and 5, the heart and soul of this book, introduce ways to incorporate second-language acquisition principles and strategies into the teaching of academic content and discourses that are taught either separately (e.g., social studies, science, or math) or as integrated thematic units. I refer to this kind of instruction as *language-inviting content teaching,* because you will learn how to interact with English learners about academic content in ways that also facilitate second-language acquisition. A major concept that will be introduced in these chapters is *community invitations,* ways of inviting and nudging students to join through identification and affiliation the multiple and varying social, language, behavioral, and academic communities of practice valued in school and society. In both chapters, you will also be treated to ways of teaching against the grain to promote critical consciousness and confront racism, inequality, and exclusionary practices often resulting from informal as well as formal assessment practices. Chapter 4 emphasizes language-sensitive content teaching and critical consciousness within the social context of whole-class participation. Key questions to keep in mind are: What can I do to enable English learners to understand their relationship to the classroom communities of practice, to enable them to see themselves as active participants in the co-construction of their identities as learners across time and space? What strategies can I use to engage students so that they not only wonder about what they are learning, but also so that they build on their knowledge in ways that lead to inquiry and sustained learning? How can I learn to use classroom language in ways that engage students to wonder about their behavior and what they are learning? Like you, Julia seeks answers to these questions and has conversations about these questions with Peggy and Rudy that guide her choices.

In Chapter 5, we turn our attention to small-group management to learn how to extend inquiry and interaction to academic learning activities that require the social integration of second-language learners with fully proficient English students, with an eye toward helping students use language in ways that reflect how more proficient members of an academic-content community make recognized connections, pose questions, and seek out answers. Important questions to consider in this chapter are: How can I use small-group work to build students' knowledge base so that they will be able to wonder and inquire more deeply about questions stemming from content they are studying? In what ways can I manage small-group learning so that English learners try out their developing language abilities to make engaging connections across readings, to their own lives, and to the social world in which they reside? How can I improve the ways I converse with children so that they learn to talk to one another in civil and socially responsible ways? In this chapter, Julia and Peggy butt heads over the value of cooperative learning and small-group work. Peggy insists that English learners speak too much of their home language and don't do their own work; Julie disagrees, arguing that how you talk with children and set up and manage small-group work makes all the difference in how students engage in learning together. We also learn that word choices can make all the difference in how children actively participate in learning activities.

Chapter 6 suggests ways to involve second-language family and community members in the classroom and the school as active participants by building bridges between the home and school communities. Along with Julia, you learn how to reach out to families and communities that the school has largely ignored. You also find out what happens to Peggy on back-to-school night, a night she will remember for a long time.

The final chapter takes a comprehensive look at multiple ways of using assessment to improve classroom learning, to communicate to students what they are doing well and what they still need to practice and learn. In this chapter you will learn how Julia carries out assessment on a regular basis, and how she deals with the pressures of standardized tests, which she believes can penalize students in her class who are still learning English if used inappropriately.

Episode One: Look Who's in Your Class

Miss Julia Felix is a first-year elementary schoolteacher, fresh out of college, who has just turned 24. She has shoulder-length, curly auburn hair that frames her face. She stands about $5\frac{1}{2}$ feet tall in tennis shoes, which she insists must not be Nikes. Julia completed a semester of student teaching in a fifth-grade class in a suburban school located in a mid-sized city near her college. She rode her Trek mountain bike to the college on warm days and drove her 1992 Citroën when she had to, and to do her student teaching. Her mentor teacher, Ms. Constantino, was a wonderfully talented woman who had been teaching in the school for almost 20 years. She believed strongly in whole-language practices and worked tirelessly to help Julia understand how her perspective about language and literacy and the values she held about children and classroom life can guide the development of meaningful activities and the use of materials in ways that foster skillful and critical language use in a safe classroom environment. Ms. Constantino placed meaning-making and inquiry-learning as the central focus of students' classroom activities. She didn't rely on spelling books or reading texts with controlled vocabulary; instead she used a wealth of children's literature, thematic units, art, photographs, and the students' own stories. In her class, students were invited to think and take pleasure in learning, to get along with and appreciate others, and to participate in learning both in and out of school. (See Edelsky, Altwerger, & Flores, 1991; and Wolfe & Poyner, 2001, for a fuller explanation of whole-language theory in practice.)

Julia has been hired to teach in one of the two third-grade classes at Bruner Elementary School, a mid-sized school in a working-class neighborhood in the inner city serving an ethnically mixed student body. To get to the school from her one-bedroom apartment, Julia has to drive about 30 minutes into the city. Anxious to begin the school year, she picks up her key and an envelope containing her class roster 3 weeks before the first day of school and rushes to inspect her new room. With the key in the doorknob, she gingerly turns the handle to the left and pulls back, opening the huge wooden door and stepping into what will be her domain for the next 9 months. It is all that she expected: a huge gray desk in the front of the room, a dark green chalkboard that covers two of the four walls, six sets of tables and chairs arranged into two rows, filing cabinets, some bookcases, three PCs, an ink jet printer, a drinking fountain next to a sink with faucets, and a bathroom. She walks directly to her desk, plops herself down in the green swivel chair, and by pushing off with her red tennis shoes, spins back and forth twice.

Rolling her chair up to the desk so that she is snuggled in tight, with her feet planted on the ground, Julia shifts her attention to the manila envelope containing the class roster. In it, she knows, are the names of the children with whom she will spend 6 hours a day, 5 days a week, for a full school year, helping them become literate, engaged learners. *I can't stand the suspense!* she thinks. Pulling her hair back, she slips the ponytail holder from her wrist and fixes it tightly at the back of her head before carefully unclasping the folder. She slips her right hand in and slowly removes the computer printout. She pauses before taking it out completely and proclaims aloud to her empty room, "May I be the best teacher that I can be for these children. I want them to be excited about learning and to see that learning can happen anywhere. Whoever these children are, if they feel challenged and good about who they are, then, I can really say I am their teacher. Okay, kids, let's check you out."

With the roster tightly held in both hands, Julia leans forward and slowly begins reading the names of the children assigned to her classroom:

1. Brown, Leon
2. Cavenaugh, Kimberly
3. Cohen, Daniel
4. Cui, Xiancoung X
5. Fernandez, Maria Eugenia X
6. Freeman, Jeffrey
7. Garcia, Aucencio X
8. Gomez, Concepcion X
9. Hamilton, Jessica
10. Isabella, Emma
11. Ochoa, Miguel X
12. O'Leary, Sean
13. Pak, Kyung X
14. Petruzzella, Gina
15. Quinn, Frank
16. Rodriguez, Gloria X
17. Rojas, Guadalupe X

18. Rosen, Paula
19. Sandoval, Katherine
20. Tran, Do Thi X
21. Vanderhoff, Lance
22. Vasquez, Jaime X
23. Willet, Amy
24. Williams, Sarah
25. Walters, Paulina
26. York, Ian
27. Zbikowski, Antonin
28. Zorroblanco, Luis

X = Limited English Proficient: This student is an English language learner who has been also assigned to special instruction.

Julia is astonished at the variety of the names on the list. Her green eyes instantly dart down to the key to learn the meaning of the X next to certain names. *Oh my God, this is incredible. Am I prepared for this?* she quickly asks herself, before going over the list again and wondering if she has pronounced all the names correctly. She pauses a few seconds, with her hands steepled under her chin, her mind drifting back to student teaching and what she studied in college that might help her accommodate the 10 students who are learning English as a second language. *What if I can't communicate with all of the students and their parents? How can I get them to do assignments if they don't speak or read or write or even understand English all that well? Where can I get my hands on some children's books that these kids can read and relate to? Wait a minute. If we all work together at this, and we help one another learn, then we can all benefit.* Then she takes a long look around the room, stands up, and reaffirms her commitment to do well in the coming year, but this time she adds to herself *sotto voce,* "I swear these kids who are learning English will be part in everything we do in class, and that along with all of the students, they will see themselves as belonging to this class. But, oh my God, I really have to learn a lot about all of the students, where they came from, about their transitions, about their communities . . . about how to help them engage, and care about the things we do in class." Speaking aloud, Julia admits, "You know what? It never occurred to me that I would have so many children who are learning English in my class. Wasn't it Alice Walker who said to live life frugally on surprise, so you can savor it as something meant especially for you? It's a good thing I did my student teaching with Ms. C.; all those strategies for getting students involved in talk and writing and doing real readings are really going to help. I can't forget what Ms. C. always said about helping students find joy in learning every day. *I need to keep that in mind. This is going to be a totally awesome year." I am a little bit scared, I have to admit,* she thought, *but I know I can do this.*

LANGUAGE AND ETHNIC DIVERSITY IN TODAY'S CLASSROOMS

Who Are the School Children?

For an increasing number of elementary schoolteachers, the typical classroom resembles the one just discovered by Julia Felix. Children who come from homes in which a language other than English is used for daily household communication, for shopping, for religious ceremonies, and for many other social situations are entering school in unprecedented numbers. Many of them are born in the United States to parents who came to this country, either as refugees or voluntary immigrants, and continue to use their native language with their children and for their daily experiences.

By the mid-1990s, the population of school-age children (ages 5–17) living in households where a language other than English is spoken, regardless of their proficiency in English, was estimated to be just under 12 million (U.S. Bureau of the Census, 1995). In 1993, the number of school-age children whose English was not sufficiently developed to effectively participate in an English-only classroom was 2,524,592, or 6.03% of all K–12 students in school across the U.S. (W-B Olsen, 1993). Without counting the children of undocumented workers from other countries, the population of children for whom English is a second language was conservatively projected to reach 3.5 million by the year 2000 and to approach 6 million by 2020 (Pallas, Natriello, & McDill, 1989) (see Figure 1.1).

In 1992, the state of California had 1,078,705 students with beginning proficiency in English as an additional language. By 1995, that number had grown to 1,262,982 (Macías, 1995). By 1997, a single school district in Los Angeles had more than 300,000 English language learners (California Department of Education, 1997). The states of Arizona, Florida, Illinois, Michigan, New Jersey, New York, Pennsylvania, and Texas combined have more than a million elementary school students who are in the process of learning English as an additional language (Waggoner, 1999). The non-English languages of English learners in California continue to be Spanish (990,801; 78%), Vietnamese (48,907; 3.9%), Cantonese (23,954; 1.9%), and Cambodian (21,765; 1.7%) (Macías, 1995). This distribution of non-English languages is also reflected in nationwide counts of speakers of languages other than English. Waggoner (1993) points out that, according to the 1990

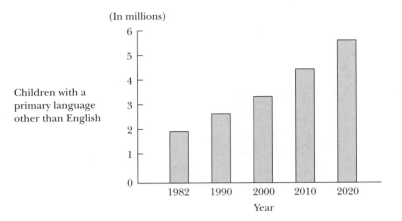

(In millions)

Figure 1.1
Projected number of children with a primary language other than English. U.S. total, 1982–2020
Source: From "The Changing Nature of the Disadvantaged Population: Current Dimensions and Future Trends" by A. Pallas, G. Natriello, and E. McDill, 1989, *Educational Research, 18,* 16–22. Reprinted by permission of the publisher.

U.S. census, "Spanish-speaking and Asian countries have replaced English-speaking countries and countries in which other European languages are spoken as the countries of birth of the largest proportion of the U.S. for-eign-born population" (p. 1).

Spanish-speaking children make up the largest and fastest-growing school-age population of second-language learners in the United States. Since 1980, nearly 1.9 million legal immigrants from Spanish-speaking countries have come to the United States to join the 15.5 million Hispanics who were already here. In 1987, the Hispanic population reached 18.8 million (U.S. Bureau of the Census, 1988); by 1993, the number had risen to 22.7 million (U.S. Bureau of the Census, 1993) and comprised the following major sub-groups:

	Number (in millions)	**Percentage**
Mexican origin	14.6 million	64.3
Puerto Rican origin	2.4 million	10.6
Central and South American origin	3.0 million	13.4
Cuban origin	1.1 million	4.7
Other Hispanic origin	1.6 million	7.0

Among Hispanic subgroups, the highest rate of growth in numbers between 1982 and 1993 occurred in the combined Central American and South

American population, which grew by nearly 50%. The next highest growth rate (35%) was experienced by other Hispanics, which the Census Bureau reported as persons "whose origins are from Spanish, or those identifying themselves generally as Spanish, Spanish-American, Hispano, Latino, etc." (U.S. Bureau of the Census, 1993). The Mexican-origin population grew by 24% and was followed by Puerto Ricans, 12%, and Cubans, 7%, who experienced the smallest growth during the period. In 2000, the Hispanic population in the United States grew to 32.8 million, with 66.1% being of Mexican origin, 14.5% of Central and South American origin, 9% of Puerto Rican origin, 4% of Cuban origin, 6.4% of other Hispanic origin (U.S. Bureau of the Census, 2001).

To indicate how much growth has occurred in the Hispanic population, the U.S. Bureau of the Census (1993) also reported that this population grew by 53% from 1980 to 1990, compared to the 9.8% growth in the general U.S. population. In major cities, where 90% of Hispanics reside (U.S. Bureau of the Census, 1993), there was a rapid increase of Hispanic residents between 1980 and 1985. Based on newer census data (Waggoner, 1999), these cities will continue to experience growth at least into the 21st century. Illinois now has the second-largest Spanish-speaking community in the United States (Suárez-Orozco & Todorova, 2003). According to the 2000 U.S. census, the Latino population in Chicago reached a total of 753,644, which represents 26% of the city's population (U.S. Bureau of the Census, 2001).

Hispanics have the highest birthrate of any major ethnic group in the United States (Hernández, 2004). Pallas, Natriello, and McDill (1989) predict that the number of Spanish-language children will increase from 4.2 million in 1980 to 18.6 million in 2020. This expected increase of 14.4 million Hispanic children, many of whom will have Spanish as their primary language, more than offsets the expected decline of nearly 6 million native-English-speaking white children over the same time period.

The second-largest population of school-age second-language learners comes from Indo-Chinese and Asian-country immigrant families (Hernández, 2004) (e.g., Chinese from Taiwan, Hong Kong, and, more recently, Mainland China; Vietnamese; Hmong; Laotians; and Cambodians). Asian-origin families began coming to the United States in large numbers in the 1960s. In 1980, three out of every five persons who identified themselves as Asian or Pacific Islander were born abroad (U.S. Bureau of the Census, 1984). The children of these two groups, virtually all of whom were born in this country, made up the remaining two-fifths. A majority of these children are being reared in the native language of their parents and caregivers and consequently enter school with little or no proficiency in English (Wallraff, 2000).

Four recent immigrant groups to the Unites States are Haitians, Russians, Arabs, and ethnic Bosnians (Banks & Banks, 2004; Carrasquillo & Rodríguez, 1996; U.S. Department of Education, 1993). Although immigrants have been coming to the United States from Haiti since the 1920s, a large number of wealthier and better-educated Haitians settled in New York and Florida in the early 1960s after the rise of François Duvalier, who seized power in 1957. In the 1970s another group came to the shores of Florida in an effort to escape the reign of terror of the new president, Jean-Claude Duvalier. These immigrants, most of whom speak Haitian Creole and are poor, are often referred to as "boat people." By the 1990s there were reported to be approximately 600,000 Haitians living legally in the United States (Carrasquillo & Rodríguez, 1996). A majority of the more recent immigrants, both legal and illegal, live in the Northeast and in Florida.

Another sizable group of immigrants to settle in the United States within the last 10 years are Russians. However, to label all immigrants coming from the former Soviet Union as Russian is inaccurate. Although they come from regions within what is now called Russia, many identify themselves by their country of origin and ethnicity. Accordingly, there are Armenians, Byelorussians, Estonians, Georgians, Kazakhs, Latvians, Lithuanians, Ukrainians, and Uzbeks. Delgado-Gaitán (1994) presents a fascinating account of how Russian immigrant families have adjusted to their new settings in northern California. According to Delgado-Gaitán, many of the more recently arrived Russian Jews have not been accepted by the older non-Jewish Russian immigrants and their communities.

New waves of Arab students from North Africa and the Middle East are showing up in public schools (Banks & Banks, 2003). Nearly all of them speak Arabic, and most practice the Islamic religion, which means that there are many religious and life-style practices that are likely to be unknown to most teachers. Carrasquillo and Rodríguez (1996) provide a number of strategies for learning about and teaching Muslim students.

Ethnic Bosnians are the most recent immigrant refugee group to settle in the United States in significant numbers. While no official count is yet available, newspaper accounts place the number as high as 20,000. However, many ethnic Bosnians returned to their homeland following the end of the war in 1999.

LANGUAGE AND LITERACY SOCIALIZATION PRACTICES

Being born into a home in which a language other than English is used for socialization is a cultural difference that can and too often does lead to negative educational consequences. For example, among Hispanics, many of whom begin school as second-language learners of English, the number of students who do not complete high school is more than twice that of native English-speaking white counterparts (Hernández, 2004; National Coalition of Advocates for Students, 1985; Olsen, 1997). It is difficult to know for sure why so many ethnic-minority children leave school before graduating, but one explanation centers on the initial difference in language between the home and the school. The Language Mismatch Hypothesis predicts that children who enter school speaking a non-English language are more likely to fail than children who speak English (see Figure 1.2). Conversely, it also predicts that the greater the match between the home language and the school language, the greater the chances are that children will succeed in school. This hypothesis blames school failure on the child's lack of school-language proficiency.

In reality, however, the Language Mismatch Hypothesis is too simplistic for two reasons: (1) it fails to account for significant numbers of minority second-language children who do succeed in school without being instructed in their native language (see Ogbu & Matute-Bianchi, 1986), and (2) it fails to account for minority second-language children who do poorly in school even though they receive instruction in their native language (National Coalition of Advocates for Students, 1985). Both reasons suggest that something more profound than initially knowing or not knowing the language of the school may be influencing the success students achieve in school.

A second hypothesis is that the *language and literacy socialization practices* in certain homes may differ substantially from those expected and reinforced

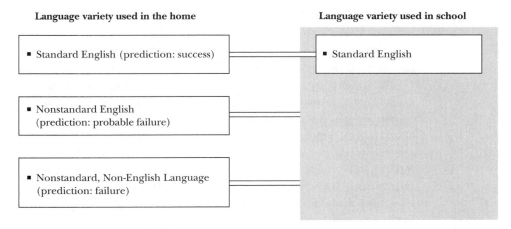

Figure 1.2
The Language Mismatch Hypothesis and predictions of school success and failure

in school, and when this occurs, the children from these homes will have difficulty in school (Banks, 2004; Beykont, 2000; Valdés, 1996). This Socialization Mismatch Hypothesis states that the victim of unsuccessful schooling is still the child whose first language and primary culture differs from that of schoolteachers and educators but attempts to explain school failure on a combination of factors, including the extent to which the school accommodates for cultural diversity and the extent to which communication between the school and the child's family and community is cultivated (Minami & Ovando, 2004; Sue & Padilla, 1986; Valdés, 1996).

The Socialization Mismatch Hypothesis draws particular attention to the different ways that children are prepared for (socialized into) the kinds of language and literacy behaviors and identities that form the foundation of classroom learning from kindergarten to 12th grade. The hypothesis is based upon two important assumptions about the relationship between language and culture: (1) that the acquisition of language and literacy uses is closely related to the process of becoming a competent member of a sociocultural group, and (2) that children learn to become competent group members by engaging in language-based activities within particular social contexts (Ochs & Schieffelin, 1982; Wills, Lintz & Mehan, 2004; Zentella, 1997).

To investigate the Socialization Mismatch Hypothesis, let us begin by examining how mainstream caregivers socialize young children to talk and to behave as literate individuals. This account will then be contrasted with the ways children in certain second-language sociocultural groups are socialized for language and literacy. The accounts presented are meant to be illustrative and characteristic rather than precise and necessarily true for all group members, because there is always individual variation within any group. Contrasting mainstream language and literacy socialization practices with those found in the home of certain language-minority families shows how fundamentally different the practices can be, and, as Heath (1989) points out, "The school teaches not only language but all skills and knowledge bases from the ethnocentric biases of mainstream language acquisition and developmental perspectives" (p. 347). An awareness of the biases toward mainstream perspectives is needed before we can begin to work toward replacing them with an appreciation for the diverse experiences that children bring to the classroom. Being a good teacher means combining information about the children we teach to produce practices that take into account these biases and that are well adapted to students and the local setting (Jacob & Jordan, 1993; Moll & González, 2004; Toohey, 2000).

LANGUAGE AND LITERACY SOCIALIZATION IN THE MAINSTREAM HOME

Mainstream children are socialized to develop and use language within a tradition of verbal interaction that places much of the responsibility for early language development on the primary caregiver. In the mainstream home, the child's natural or adopted mother serves as the primary caregiver and consequently as the child's most intimate interactional partner. Soon after a child is born, he or she is treated as a social being capable of participating in social interaction with anyone willing to make certain linguistic adjustments. It is not uncommon, for example, for parents, grandparents, and friends to carry on a "conversation" with a newborn through the nursery window as soon as he or she is brought out and placed in a crib (Heath, 1983). In this case, the parents talk for the infant, supplying what the infant may say in response to their questions.

The mother typically holds her newborn infant so that the baby faces her directly. This face-to-face position allows the mother to talk to the baby as well as to respond for the baby when the baby moves or makes a sound. The early interactional exchanges between mother and infant are precursors to the kinds of turn-taking procedures that will be reinforced in subsequent language-acquiring years.

Taking the Child's Perspective

Throughout the child's first few years, mainstream mothers consider very young children as communicative partners capable of intentional and representational speech. Treating young children as conversational partners requires mothers and other caregivers to "take the perspective of the child" (Ochs & Schieffelin, 1982). One strategy mothers use for taking the child's perspective is to modify their speech to more closely match the child's perceived verbal competence. This strategy is commonly known as using *baby talk* or *motherese* (Cross, 1977; Ferguson, 1977; Trudgill, 2000). Spoken by adults, baby talk is speech addressed to young children that has been modified in a number of ways. It is typically spoken at a slower pace than normal speech, and the pronunciation of certain key words is drawn out through variations in pitch and length. A hallmark of baby talk is the use of special terms for bodily functions, body parts, certain foods, stuffed toys, and favorite blankets (e.g., *go potty, baba, tum tum, bear bear, blankey*). Baby talk is considered to be simpler than normal speech, as utterances generally are made up of simple clauses devoid of abstract vocabulary and complex sentence structure.

A second strategy for taking the perspective of the child is to raise the child above his or her competence level by richly interpreting what he or she is attempting to express (Ochs & Schieffelin, 1982). This strategy results from the belief among mainstream caregivers that young children are capable of expressing meaning and of using language to represent ideas symbolically. Because mothers assume that the baby is attending to their talk, they interpret any utterance made by the baby in response to a question as intentional language. As such, their language needs to be interpreted verbally. Heath (1983) provides a good example to illustrate this point: "If shortly after one interpretation is given, the baby issues a contradictory signal, the mother may even comment on this shift as an attempt on the part of the child to clarify his intentions: 'Oh, you *didn't* like that, huh? I'm sorry, Mommy thought you liked that, I didn't mean to scare you'" (p. 248). Mothers continue to interpret their child's utterances until the child is able to more accurately express wants and needs, which normally begins between $2\frac{1}{2}$ and 4 years of age (Lessow-Hurley, 1990).

Both strategies for taking the child's perspective encourage the use of question-and-answer routines used in certain highly ritualized language games. One of the more popular games involving such routine is the peekaboo game (Cazden, 1983). The mother holds a blanket over her face and says "Peekaboo, where are you?" and then quickly lowers the blanket to answer "Here I am." Another early exchange pattern is the strange sound game (Heath, 1983). In this game, the mother uses a question-and-answer exchange around certain sounds that routinely appear throughout the day. For example, when the dog barks as Daddy is coming home from work, the mother may ask the child, "Who's coming?" or "Who's driving up in the driveway?" "I think it's Daddy!" In both games, the mother supplies both the question and the answer, and in this manner, models a pattern of interaction that is crucial for literacy development.

The question-and-answer routine that drives peekaboo and other verbal interaction games also underlies much of the talk that occurs in early storybook-reading activities. Storybook reading commonly begins at birth and develops into a daily bedtime and naptime ritual that often lasts beyond the preschool years (Heath, 1982). Storybooks are given as presents at baby showers, birthdays, and major religious holidays, and most mainstream caregivers enjoy reading storybooks to young children. Storybook reading is considered to be one of the most powerful means of developing literacy awareness, vocabulary and concepts, concepts of print, and a sense of story (Heath & Thomas, 1984; Teale, 1984). In addition to its role in the acquisition of fundamental literacy concepts, mainstream storybook reading inculcates the most common pattern of classroom discourse found in all grades of schooling: the three-part sequence of teacher initiation, student response, teacher evaluation (Cazden, 2001). In storybook reading, children acquire this interactional sequence as a result of *labeling* and *clarifying* exchanges with caregivers who are concerned with naming objects and clarifying meaning.

Labeling Exchanges and Clarifying Questions

The process of labeling during storybook reading depends on the use of what Mehan (1981) refers to as "known information questions." The questioner (the caregiver) already knows the information being requested of the child. Ideally, the question is posed in such a way that the child can provide an appropriate response. This enables the child to participate in a dialogue with an adult, and it allows the adult to evaluate the child's response favorably, reinforcing the value of child as knowledge-giver. Known information questions are used in many settings besides the context of storybook reading (Saville-Troike & Kleifgen, 1986).

The extent to which mainstream mothers use known information questions during storybook reading with preschool children was first explored by Ninio and Bruner (1978), who observed mothers reading with their 3- and 4-year-old children and categorized the kinds of exchanges that occurred. They found that verbal exchanges most often centered on the mother directing the child's attention to pictures in the book, followed by a request for a label of the item pointed to by the mother. Once the label was supplied, the mother responded favorably or, in the case of misinformation, gave the correct label. Ninio and Bruner categorized this labeling process into four major components: attention-getters, what-questions, labels, and feedback. Table 1.1 presents the frequency distribution of utterance types they found within each of the four major interaction components.

In addition to labeling exchanges, caregivers may also allude to the meaning of certain characters' actions and ask questions such as "Is the wolf bad? Why?" and "Why do you suppose those ducks are being so mean to the ugly duckling?" This kind of question, called a clarifying question, is typically used with children who have already learned to use connected speech. It employs the same structural format as a known information question, but because the reply is an explanation, rather than a display of knowledge, its content is relatively less predictable. In storybook reading, adults often focus the child's attention on pictures, behaviors, and story parts in order to clarify a meaning or to reinforce a value. In addition to asking for explanations of events and motivations, clarifying questions can also request that the child explain "when," "where," and "how" something happened. Adults

Table 1.1
Utterance types within the four stages of the labeling process

Stage/Example	Frequency	Stage/Example	Frequency
I. *Look*	65	III. *Label* (continued)	
Look!	61	More X.	3
Look at that.	4	They are X.	3
II. *What-questions*	85	These are the X.	3
What's that?	57	The X.	2
What are those?	8	You can see the X.	1
What are they doing?	6	That one is the X.	1
What is it?	5	Look at the X.	1
What are they?	1	It says: X.	1
What's on that page?	1	We'll call it X.	1
What's on the next one?	1	Kind of an X.	1
What's over there?	1	IV. *Feedback*	80
What else can you see there?	1	Yes.	50
What does that do?	1	Yes, I know.	8
What do you see there?	1	It is not an X.	5
What can you see?	1	That's it!	3
III. *Label*	216	Not an X.	2
X (= stressed label).	91	No, it's not an X.	2
It's an X.	34	Yes, it is an X.	1
That's an X.	28	That's charming.	1
There's an X.	12	No, it's an X, not a Y.	1
An X.	12	No, it's an X.	1
That's X.	6	Yes, they are (Xs).	1
There is X.	6	Yes, very good.	1
Lots of Xs.	5	That's not an X.	1
They are X-ing.	5		

Source: From "The Achievement and Antecedents of Labeling" by A. Ninio and J. Bruner, 1978, *Journal of Child Language, 5*(1), p. 7. Reprinted with permission of Cambridge University Press.

ask clarification questions both to other adults and to children in a variety of situations outside of literacy events.

In school, teachers constantly ask children to name objects and discuss their attributes as well as to explain and clarify the meanings of words, pictures, and behaviors. The goal of using questions in such cases is to assist students to go beyond saying what something is, to attempt to express what something means, and to support the interpretation with both facts and logical reasoning. Labeling and clarifying exchanges prepare the groundwork for similar kinds of exchanges used in classroom discourse (Gibbons, 2002).

Major Types of Narrative Discourse

Beyond their value in modeling an interactional sequence found in classroom discourse, labeling and clarifying exchanges also prepare children for the major kinds of narrative discourse associated with successful literacy experiences in school. Heath (1986a, 1986b) distinguishes among four kinds of narratives that occur in mainstream homes and that result from interactions between caregivers and their children: recounts, accounts, eventcasts, and stories.

Recounts are essentially extended versions of known information question-and-answer exchanges. Usually the first of the four narrative types to emerge in mainstream children, recounts require the child to retell experiences or information already known to both the child and the adult. Recounts are initiated either voluntarily or in response to questions from adults. The questions guide the child's telling so that events are linked together in sequence and tied to a central theme. For example, in the presence of a third party, a parent may ask the child to recount what happened on their outing to the zoo. The recount is typically opened with a question: "Can you tell Mrs. Taylor what happened at the zoo today, when we were visiting the seals?" As the child recounts the episode, the parent interjects questions to keep the child from veering off the theme and sequence. Questions also direct the child to include missing information or to clarify key information.

When children enter school, teachers regularly ask for recounts of stories read in reading books and of passages containing facts known to both the teacher and fellow students. Upon the teacher's request, students are expected to recount knowledge and experiences relying on information that has already been presented in class through readings or presentations. Moreover, as literature studies become increasingly popular in school, children ask other children to recount stories and to tell about what they understood from their readings of stories.

Accounts are narratives generated by the teller to provide new information to the listeners or new interpretations of information already known to the listeners. Children sharing with their parents special events of the day is an example of account. Because accounts provide new information or a novel interpretation, listeners judge them for both their truth value and their organizational structure. Thus, accounts that appear logical are accepted as truthful, while those told in an unorganized fashion are discounted. Adults model accounts for children when they narrate incidents occurring at work or other events that are out of the ordinary.

Accounts are generally initiated with a question, which signals that a narrative is coming. However, unlike recounts, which typically depend on a question from an adult, accounts are started with an opening by the teller: "Wanna know what happened to the kitty cat today?" Once the opening prompt has been made and acknowledged, the child is accorded the floor until the account has been given in full. Clarifying questions are usually saved until the end of the account.

Account-giving in school is rarer than recounting, but does occur in classes that encourage student interaction and engage students in multiple writing activities. In the primary grades, students are given the opportunity to tell about their personal experiences during show-and-tell time (Michaels, 1981) and in their dialogue journals. Teachers who see their children as authors and who invite children to write stories and tell about what they see, hear, feel, and like promote account-giving. In the higher grades, accounts tend to be restricted primarily to creative writing assignments, although as more and more teachers use writing across the curriculum to foster learning, account-giving has increased. In both the primary and upper elementary grades, teachers typically measure the effectiveness of accounts in terms of their logic, truth value, and organization.

Eventcasts provide an ongoing narrative of events that currently or subsequently have the attention of both teller and listeners. Eventcasting may occur as an event is happening or may precede it. An example of simultaneous eventcasting is when children talk about how to do something as they do it. Young children commonly engage in simultaneous eventcasting during their solitary play, stating aloud what they are doing. Children also eventcast when they tell how to build a model out of LEGOs® or when they describe what they will do when they go camping. Eventcasting also happens when children write out what they are doing for the day or as they devise or follow a sequence of events. Adults frequently model eventcasts as they discuss their vacation plans, telling where they will go and how long they will stay there.

Eventcasting is used by many teachers in school to preview lessons and to indicate what will be taking place throughout the day. In mathematics and science lessons, teachers use eventcasts to explain the steps needed to complete problems and experiments. When teachers place students in small groups to work cooperatively, eventcasts take the form of directions and descriptions of what students are expected to be doing at each step of the lesson. In turn, students may be asked to give eventcasts of each member's responsibility for completing the lesson. During reading lessons, students are often requested to predict the events of a story on the basis of the title and other key information. Some students also write out what is happening in stories or predict what will come next in a story.

Stories are the most familiar kind of narrative. A story is a fictional account in which some animate being (animal, object, or person) maneuvers through a string of events with goal-directed behavior (Stein, 1982). Stories have special conventions that set them apart from a simple account of facts in a sequence. Willy (1975) lists six conventions found in most stories told to young children: (1) a beginning title or formal opening phrase (e.g., "Once upon a time . . ."); (2) a formal closing phrase (e.g., "the end" or "happily every after"); (3) the use of a consistent past tense; (4) a variation in pitch or tone while storytelling; (5) the use of make-believe characters and events; and (6) the reoccurrence of certain stock character types and situations.

Children hear all kinds of stories, ranging from Bible stories and storybook adventures to their parents' tales of what it was like in the "old days." Adults entertain children with ghost stories, war stories, and stories of real events changed slightly (e.g., naming a story character after the child) to serve as lessons for the future. Children retell these stories and others from their favorite books as well.

In school, fictional stories abound in storybooks, basal readers, and social studies textbooks. Stories are often placed within nonfictional accounts to attract students to the expository prose, and students learn to analyze fictional literary stories for morals and to identify and practice certain narrative genres. And of course, students write their own stories and publish them for their classmates, family, and teacher to read.

In all four of these types of narrative, children must learn to follow and describe events both chronologically and thematically, which requires developing each event in the proper sequence and at the same time elaborating a new aspect of the theme or situation as the story unfolds (Applebee, 1978). In mainstream homes and school alike, these narrative types are developed through interactions that occur primarily around books. Children are forever being asked to label objects both in and out of books. Adults ask children to recount stories that adults have read to them. Caregivers hope that children will draw upon storybook knowledge to explain why they and others behave in a certain way. Parents enjoy hearing their children eventcast while they color in their colorbooks and build structures with their LEGOs and building blocks. In summary, caregivers engage children in lots of talk around books, preparing them for the kinds of literacy events that occur throughout school.

LANGUAGE AND LITERACY SOCIALIZATION IN LANGUAGE-MINORITY HOMES

Some or all of the four types of narratives and questioning routines found in mainstream homes and valued in school may also occur in language-minority homes. Language and literacy socialization may include many other patterns as well. To the extent that the mainstream patterns occur repeatedly and with some intensity, children in some language-minority families will succeed in school regardless of the language used for socialization purposes. This is because some children enter school with the scripts and discourse structures that are shared and reinforced by teachers (Saville-Troike & Kleifgen, 1986, p. 219). Recall that the Socialization Mismatch Hypothesis expects that children are more likely to succeed in school when the home language and literacy socialization patterns are similar to those that are used and valued in school. Let us now examine how language and literacy socialization is practiced in two language-minority groups in order to see the extent to which the patterns differ from those found in mainstream homes.

A Cautionary Note

Before beginning the following section on language-minority socialization patterns, however, it is essential to remember that the descriptions to be presented are purposefully general and that any individual member of a sociocultural group may behave differently from the pattern that may characterize the group. The descriptions are based upon ethnographic research conducted specifically to learn about the language socialization practices used in the homes of certain language-minority families through long-term participant observation and careful analysis (Spradley, 1980). As descriptions, ethnographies are not deterministic. Their goal instead is to present an accurate account of life patterns of individuals belonging to the same sociocultural group (Erickson, 1986). Other group members may behave in ways similar to those described in the ethnographies, but their behavior is never determined by their group membership. It bears repeating that these descriptions should not be used to explain why a child behaves in a particular way around literacy events.

Language and Literacy Socialization in Recently Arrived Mexican-Origin Families

In the discussion that follows, the focus is restricted to Mexican families who immigrated to the United States in the last two decades, making them relatively recent arrivals. Many of these families have established themselves within communities and are part of the work force. While the children of some of these families enter school knowing a little English, most come to school as monolingual speakers of Spanish. (For a fuller discussion of patterns of home-life, school, and work in Mexican-origin communities across the United States, see Losey, 1996; Schecter & Bayley, 2002; and Valdés, 1996.) Recent arrivals from Mexico tend to settle in communities where other family members already reside or where there are close friends, often from the same region in Mexico. As a result, many recently arrived adults and children are likely to have contact predominantly with Mexican-origin friends and workmates of similar socioeconomic and language backgrounds (Moore & Pachón, 1985). In other words, poor working-class immigrants from Mexico tend to live and interact with community members of the same kind of backgrounds (Suárez-Orozco, 1998; Suárez-Orozco & Todorova, 2003).

In terms of caregiving, young children are provided for by both family members and close friends. The responsibility for caregiving is shared among many so that young children are rarely in the company of only one adult. Young children grow up surrounded by other children and are constantly under the watchful eyes of several adults (Heath, 1986a). Children are allowed to play physically and verbally with little adult intervention. Adults talk with children primarily to praise, to scold, and to tease, and when they want to show children how something is done. Older children are immersed in the prattle of younger children and both are exposed to a rich measure of talk by an assortment of speakers who use language for many functions.

Although children grow up in a talk-filled environment, relatively little of the talk generated by adults is addressed to preschool children (Heath, 1986a). Young children are not considered to be equal conversational partners, and adults do not take the child's perspective in talking to them. While children accompany adults to most social gatherings, they are expected to talk with other children and not with adults, especially when an adult has already begun talking. Accordingly, children learn to use language with little intervention from their parents and adult relatives. The most important language instruction adults offer concerns language used for showing respect for and politeness toward elders (Heath, 1986a).

Adults ask young children for labels of objects of immediate concern, such as body parts, family members' names, and play objects. However, only rarely are children invited to label the names of objects and people in books or on television. Mothers typically do not engage in labeling exchanges with their young children, and seldom is labeling done to teach vocabulary items. Adults tend not to invite children to explain their interpretation of events to other adults. Children hear adults' interpretations of events and hear them negotiate meanings through questions, but are not invited to participate in the building of meaning or in presenting their view of the event.

Likewise, parents seldom ask questions that require children to recite the sequence of known events or to foretell their plans for the day. If parents already know the sequence for some events that the child recently experienced or will experience in the near future, they usually do not ask the child to tell about the events just for the sake of recounting or forecasting. An exception might be when a third party needs to know about a special event. In this case, the parent may ask the child to talk about the event and then will fill in information as needed. Parents do request accounts from children and ask questions about the account as it is being told. Pease-Alvarez (1991) has documented the frequent use of contingency questions (questions that occur directly in response to information just given) during account episodes. Accounts are requested most often during intimate family gatherings and concern topics ranging from daily activities to unusual accomplishments.

Children learn appropriate language and other behaviors by observing and repeating actions that parents, relatives, and friends have demonstrated in highly contextualized settings. Hence, exchanges in which the child eventcasts to an adult and vice versa seldom happen. A cooperative form of eventcasting occurs when family members exchange ideas for future plans, such as returning to Mexico or how to help a relative from Mexico get situated in the neighborhood.

Of the four narrative forms, stories figure most prominently in the lives of recently arrived Mexican-origin families. There are many kinds of stories that adults enjoy telling and young children enjoy hearing. Some stories involve fantasy and tales of witches, others tell of real events and historical figures. Adolescents spend hours telling stories and giving accounts of friends' escapades. Parents and relatives occasionally read stories to young children, but most storybook reading occurs when older siblings read aloud or when children play school with other children. Spanish-language children's books are not commonly found in the home (although Moll, 1990, disputes this, claiming that many of the Mexicans he studied in Tucson, Arizona, had Spanish-language children's books). In Mexico, children's storybooks are generally not available to the masses and many recently arrived families may have little experience with Spanish-language storybooks in the home (Faltis, 1989). Adults and older children often read *novelas* (soap-opera-type magazines), comic books, and abridged novels printed in paperback. While these reading materials contain many of the features found in storybooks, they are not the kind of stories that are told and retold to young children.

Language and Literacy Socialization in Chinese-Origin Families

This section focuses on the language and literacy learning environment of middle- and working-class post-1965 Chinese-American families. (For a more detailed account of life, language, and work patterns of the "new" Chinese in the United States, see Chang, 2004; Chen, 1981; Tsai, 1986; Tse,

2001; and Wong, 1988. Lee, 1984, provides an ethnography of East Asian student experiences.) In 1980, more than 63% of the Chinese in the United States were foreign born, and a majority lived in urban settings in California and Hawaii, which account for nearly 57% of the Chinese-American population (Wong, 1988). These patterns have changed little since 1980. More than 4.5 million Chinese reside in the five metropolitan areas of Boston, Honolulu, Los Angeles, San Francisco, and New York. New York–New Jersey and the San Francisco Bay Area have more than 300,000 Chinese each (U.S. Bureau of the Census, 1992).

In Chinese-origin families, exchanges in which caregivers request labels for items are tied primarily to the correction of errors (Chang, 2004; Heath, 1986a). Children are corrected when they misname an object that they want. Corrections occur during reading time and during creative play time. During both activities, the adult's label requests direct the child to provide the correct name of the object or attribute being focused upon.

Questions about meaning and clarification center around appropriate age- and sex-role behaviors. These questions seldom include expressions of emotional evaluation; instead their purpose is to bring attention to why it is essential to act a certain way given the child's place in the family (Heath, 1986a). Lessons about appropriate behavior often occur within the context of a written story. During storybook reading, adults ask questions and provide comments about correct behavior but almost never inquire about or interpret the emotional states of characters presented in the story.

Children are often called upon by adults to give accounts of their daily experiences. They are expected to tell new information in sequence and provide enough detail for the adults to follow without asking many questions. Recounts, which require children to tell something already known to the listener, are relatively rare because children are not ordinarily called upon to perform for adults. In fact, children are expected to remain quiet around non-intimate adults and outside the home, unless they are invited to talk (Schneider & Lee, 1990).

Eventcasts occur around activities that call for adults to model the procedure or plans for completing a task. Boys are typically engaged in fewer eventcasting episodes than girls due to the way tasks are divided between boys and girls. Girls are expected to help in the kitchen and around the house; boys run errands and look after younger children. Hence, girls are exposed to eventcasts about cooking, ironing, sewing, and cleaning, while boys, especially if the father is not at home, do routinized tasks (Heath, 1986a). Nevertheless, both boys and girls are exposed to eventcasts during family discussions of problems or when the parents are planning for outings and other sequential actions.

Adults enjoy telling and reading stories to young children. They often use book stories to tell analogous stories about special people and events from the past.

Analysis of the Differences in Socialization Practices

The ways that children are socialized for language and literacy practices clearly varies from family to family, but it is also evident that families within a particular cultural group tend to socialize their children differently from families in other cultural groups. From the discussion presented above, it can be seen that both the Mexican-origin and the Chinese-origin families exhibit socialization patterns that contrast with the mainstream pattern, though it appears that the socialization practices of Chinese-origin families are more compatible with the mainstream pattern. In fact, Schneider and Lee (1990) point out that socialization behaviors emphasized in Asian families are rewarded in school because they exemplify the desired classroom behavioral traits of being quiet, orderly, and industrious. In a similar vein, Wong Fillmore (1985) notes that mainstream teachers believe that Chinese ESL children become more attentive to classroom tasks and activities that are poorly introduced and described by the teacher.

What do the contrasts mean for the grade-level classroom teacher who has children from Mexican-origin, Asian-origin, and mainstream cultures? According to the Socialization Mismatch Hypothesis, Mexican-origin children are immediately at risk of failing academically because their socialization practices have prepared them to be competent in a set of language and literacy practices that typically are not reinforced or rewarded in school. On the contrary, the school may even discourage certain cultural literacy behaviors such as cooperative storytelling and other forms of sharing (Trueba & Delgado-Gaitán, 1983).

For the Chinese-origin children, the contrasts are less obviously drastic but are different enough to have serious consequences as children progress through school. For example, the fact that Chinese-origin children tend to be socialized to demonstrate literal interpretations and to remain quiet in the presence of adults means that these children may have less opportunity to develop social interactional skills. One dire consequence of this practice is that Asian-origin children in general are encouraged by both their parents and the school to pursue science and technical professions that are relatively less language-based than other kinds of high-level professions (Schneider & Lee, 1990). This kind of tracking into science-oriented professions has led Asian Americans to become a "middleman minority" group

(Chang, 1995; Kim, 1981; Schneider & Lee, 1990), which is allowed to rise above the professional levels of other minority groups because of a specialized skill and knowledge advantage. However, according to Blalock (1967), the middleman minority soon reaches a job ceiling resulting from a combination of dominant-group discrimination and persisting ethnic-group cultural values.

CONTEXTUALIZING THE SOCIALIZATION MISMATCH HYPOTHESIS

The Socialization Mismatch Hypothesis is a relatively context-free explanation for why certain language-minority groups succeed or fail in school. The hypothesis states that the success or failure depends primarily on the goodness of fit between the language and socialization patterns of the home and those reinforced in school. One feature the hypothesis lacks is reference to the role of context in learning. In other words, consideration needs to be given to the notion that socioacademic performance and language use are also partially dependent on the social organization of learning contexts in the classroom (Erickson, 1986). Without such reference, we would not be able to account for the variable success of certain language-minority children. For example, Philips (1982) found that Native American children were performing very poorly in classroom contexts that required individualized performance and emphasized competitive tasks. These two learning contexts were culturally unfamiliar and threatening to the children: "The notion of a single individual being structurally set apart from all others, in anything other than an observer role, and yet still a part of the group organization, is one that Indian children probably encounter for the first time in school" (Philips, 1972, p. 391).

However, as a result of long-term ethnographic study, Philips learned that the children were able to perform successfully in certain kinds of contexts, particularly those in which the obligation of individual students to perform in public was minimized. Philips attributed the variable performance of the Native American children to classroom conditions that either reinforced or denied structures of participation normally demanded in the home. Drawing on Philips's findings of context-specific performance, Erickson and Mohatt (1982) examined ways to create culturally congruent contexts for learning in classrooms containing Native American and non-Native American children. They found that all students benefited from instruction when teachers learned to vary the participant structures used to activate and evaluate student participation. Moreover, they showed that mainstream Anglo teachers were capable of learning and incorporating participation structures commonly used among the Native American families whose children attended the school.

There are many other examples of context-specific learning environments that are both meaningful and appropriate for language-minority students (e.g., Au & Kawakami, 1984; Delgado-Gaitán, 1991; Gutiérrez, 1992; Macías, 1987; Moll, 1988, 1989; Moll & Díaz, 1987). In each of these studies, as in the Philips case above, notable language and cultural differences existed between the home and the school culture, yet teachers were able to change classroom contexts for learning so that language-minority students improved their socioacademic performance. Díaz, Moll, and Mehan (1986) refer to the fact that teachers can improve learning for language-minority students despite cultural differences as *pedagogically optimistic*. They agree that a measure of school failure among language-minority students can be accounted for by the mismatch between home and school language and literacy socialization patterns, but argue that school failure is also the result of classroom organization patterns that exclude language-minority children from full participation. Thus, the pedagogical optimism expressed by Díaz, Moll, and Mehan comes from the understanding that *teachers can and must create meaningful and culturally appropriate learning environments so that all children join in, participate in, identify and affiliate with, and benefit from social and academic classroom experiences.*

Making changes in the mainstream all-English classroom environment to include rather than exclude second-language learners requires that we as teachers (1) are aware of the kinds of special instructional services that second-language learners have experienced in bilingual and English-as-a-second-language programs; (2) have an understanding of how classrooms are socially and physically arranged to support different instructional strategies; (3) have the ability to incorporate second-language participation strategies into learning activities in ways that promote active student participation, inquisitive learning, and the ability to get along with others; (4) seek culturally appropriate ways to involve the second-language community in both classroom- and school-related activities; (5) develop a stance against social injustice and for questioning practices that promote racism, inequality and exclusionary practices; and (6) have multiple ways of assessing children fairly and using the assessment to promote further learning. All six areas of knowledge and action, which are addressed in subsequent chapters, enable you to use joinfostering principles of practice for teaching and learning in linguistically and culturally diverse classrooms.

CONCLUSION

In this chapter, we were introduced to Miss Julia Felix, a first-year teacher assigned to teach a 3rd-grade class of 28 students, 10 of whom are learning English as an additional language. This kind of classroom composition is increasingly becoming the norm across the United States as new waves of immigrants and their children seek to improve living conditions. Few mainstream all-English classroom teachers are prepared to assist second-language learners in the joining-in process required for participation in, affiliation with, and benefit from learning activities. We want to break this pattern and move beyond the status quo! Part of the needed preparation hinges on our understanding of language and literacy socialization differences between language-minority and mainstream communities. As teachers of children from different cultural backgrounds, we need to understand that our particular language and literacy socialization in large part contributes to how we interpret and generate classroom activities. The more we learn about the diverse experiences and needs of our students, the better prepared we will be to question existing practices and create educationally and culturally appropriate activities for all of our students.

In addition to learning about the strengths and experiences students bring to class, it is also important to provide students with a safe learning environment where your goals as a teacher can be accomplished, and to get students to relate to and identify with you as the teacher, as well as to affiliate with the academic communities of practice valued in school. This means that students will need to take on the values you emphasize in class as you work toward achieving joinfostering goals. In the next chapter, Julia Felix discovers that the 10 second-language children assigned to her class have had distinct schooling experiences before coming to her class: Four were in bilingual education programs, two were in ESL pullout programs, and four were in classrooms with specially designed academic instruction in English (SDAIE). With Julia, we will examine the nature of these different approaches to preparing (and underpreparing) students for the transition into mainstream English-only classrooms and the historical conditions that have led to the development of educational programs for second-language learners. In addition, Julia meets Peggy Dimwitty, who holds a very different view of English learners and how to teach them.

ACTIVITIES

1. Observe interaction between a mainstream, middle-class adult caregiver and a young child for at least 15 minutes. Jot down examples of taking the child's perspective and child-raising as described in this chapter and share them with the class.

2. Ask a mother or father with a toddler (age 2 or 3) if you can tape-record them reading a favorite story

to the child. Replay the recording and look for examples of labeling as presented in Table 1.1. Share your best example of "using known information questions" with the class.

3. Select one of the following "pedagogically optimistic" studies to share with the class as a presentation: Au & Kawakami, 1984; Erickson & Mohatt, 1982; Macías, 1987; Moll, 1988, 1989; and Moll & Díaz, 1987; Moll & Gonzalez, 2004. In the presentation, point out how teachers successfully contextualized cultural differences during lessons.

4. Have each student in your class survey at least two different mainstream teachers to find out their views on and fears of teaching English learners in their classrooms. Use the survey in Figure 1.3 (on page 43) or modify it to fit your needs. As a class, tally and summarize the results for discussion.

REFERENCES

Applebee, A. (1978). *The child's concept of story.* Chicago: University of Chicago Press.

Au, K., & Kawakami, A. J. (1984). Vygotskian perspectives on discussion processes in small-group reading lessons. In P. L. Peterson, L. C. Wilkinson, & M. Hallinan (Eds.), *The social context of instruction: Group organization and group processes* (pp. 209–225). New York: Academic Press.

Banks, J. (2004). Multicultural education: Historical development, dimensions, and practice. In J. Banks & C. M. Banks (Eds.), *Handbook of research on multicultural education* (2nd ed., pp. 3–29). San Francisco: Jossey-Bass.

Banks, J., & Banks, C. M. (Eds.). (2004). *Handbook of research on multicultural education* (2nd ed.). San Francisco, CA: Jossey-Bass.

Beykont, Z. (Ed.). (2000). *Lifting every voice: Pedagogy and politics of bilingualism.* Cambridge, MA: Harvard Education Publishing Group.

Bickle, K., Billings, E., & Hakuta, K. (2004). Trends in two-way immersion research. In J. Banks & C. M. Banks (Eds.), *Handbook of research on multicultural education* (2nd ed., pp. 589–604). San Francisco: Jossey-Bass.

Blalock, H. (1967). *Toward a theory of minority relations.* New York: John Wiley and Sons.

California Department of Education. (1997). *Language census report for California public schools.* Sacramento, CA: Educational Demographics Unit, author.

Carrasquillo, A., & Rodríguez, V. (1996). *Language minority students in the mainstream classroom.* Clevedon, England: Multilingual Matters.

Cazden, C. (1983). Peekaboo as an instructional model: Discourse development at school and at home. In B. Bain (Ed.), *The sociogenesis of language and human conduct: A multidisciplinary book of readings.* New York: Plenum.

Cazden, C. (2001). *Classroom discourse: The language of teaching and learning.* Portsmouth, NH: Heinemann.

Chang, J. (1995). When they are not Asian American model students. *Focus on Diversity, 5*(3), 5–7.

Chang, J. (2004). Language and literacy in Chinese American communities. In B. Pérez

(Ed.), *Sociocultural contexts of language and literacy* (pp. 179–205). Mahwah, NJ: Lawrence Erlbaum Associates.

Chen, J. (1981). *The Chinese of America.* San Francisco: Harper & Row.

Christian, D. (1994). *Two-way bilingual education: Students learning through two languages.* Santa Cruz, CA: National Center for Research on Cultural Diversity and Second Language Learning.

Cochran-Smith, M., Davis, D., & Fries, K. (2004). Multicultural teacher education: Research, practice, and policy. In J. Banks & C. M. Banks (Eds.), *Handbook of research on multicultural education* (2nd ed., pp. 931–978). San Francisco, CA: Jossey-Bass.

Cross, T. (1977). Mothers' speech adjustments: The contributions of selected child listener variables. In C. Snow & C. Ferguson (Eds.), *Talking to children: Language input and acquisition* (pp. 151–188). New York: Cambridge University Press.

Cummins, J. (1986). Empowering minority students: A framework for intervention. *Harvard Educational Review, 56*(1), 18–36.

Delgado-Gaitán, C. (1991). Relating experience and text: Socially constituted reading activity. In M. McGroarty & C. Faltis (Eds.), *Languages in school and society: Policy and pedagogy* (pp. 512–528). Berlin: Mouton de Gruyter.

Delgado-Gaitán, C. (1994). Russian refugee families: Accommodating aspirations through education. *Anthropology and Education, 25,* 137–155.

DeVillar, R. A., & Faltis, C. (1991). *Computers and cultural diversity: Restructuring schools for socio-academic success.* Albany: State University of New York Press.

Díaz, S., Moll, L., & Mehan, H. (1986). Sociocultural resources in instruction: A context-specific approach. In California State Department of Education (Ed.), *Beyond language: Social and cultural factors in schooling language minority students* (pp. 187–230). Los Angeles: California State University, Los Angeles.

Díaz-Rico, L. (2004). *Teaching English learners: Strategies and methods.* Boston: Allyn & Bacon.

Edelsky, C., Altwerger, B., & Flores, B. (1991). Hookin' 'em in at the start in a whole language classroom. *Anthropology and Educational Quarterly, 14,* 257–281.

Erickson, F. (1986). Qualitative methods in research on teaching. In M. C. Wittrock (Ed.), *Handbook of research on teaching* (3rd ed., pp. 119–161). New York: Macmillan.

Erickson, F., & Mohatt, G. (1982). Cultural organization of participant structures in two classrooms of Indian students. In G. D. Spindler (Ed.), *Doing the ethnography of schooling* (pp. 132–174). New York: Holt, Rinehart & Winston.

Faltis, C. (1989). Spanish language cooperation-fostering storybooks for language minority children in bilingual programs. *Journal of Educational Issues of Language Minority Students, 5,* 46–55.

Faltis, C., & Hudelson, S., (1998). *Bilingual education in elementary and secondary school communties: Toward understanding and caring.* Needham Heights, MA: Allyn & Bacon.

Ferguson, C. (1977). Baby talk as a simplified register. In C. Snow & C. Ferguson (Eds.), *Talking to children: Language input and acquisition* (pp. 209–237). New York: Cambridge University Press.

Fránquiz, M., & Reyes, M. (1998). Creating inclusive learning communities through English language arts: From *Chanclas* to *Canicas. Language Arts, 75*(3), 211–220.

Gee, J. (2003). Opportunity to learning: A language-based perspective on assessment. *Assessment in Education, 10*(1), 27–46.

Gee, J. (2004). *What video games have to teach us about learning and literacy.* New York: Palgrave MacMillan.

General Accounting Office. (1987). *Bilingual education: Information on limited English proficient students.* Washington, DC: Author.

Gibbons, M. (2002). *Scaffolding language, scaffolding learning.* Portsmouth, NH: Heinemann.

Gold, N. (1997). *Teachers of LEP students: Demand, supply and shortage.* Sacramento, CA: State Department of Education.

González, J. (1997). Recruiting and training minority teachers: Student views of the preservice program. *Equity and Excellence in Education, 30*(1), 56–64.

Gutiérrez, K. D. (1992). A comparison of instructional contexts in writing process classrooms with Latino children. *Education and Urban Society, 24,* 244–262.

Harklau, L. (1994). Tracking and linguistic minority students: Consequences of ability grouping for second language learners. *Linguistics and Education, 6,* 217–244.

Heath, S. B., & Thomas, C. (1984). The achievement of preschool literacy for mother and child. In H. Goelman, A. Oberg, & F. Smith (Eds.), *Awakening to literacy* (pp. 51–72). Exeter, NH: Heinemann Educational.

Heath, S. B. (1982). What no bedtime story means: Narrative skills at home and school. *Language in Society, 11*(2), 49–76.

Heath, S. B. (1983). *Ways with words: Language, life, and work in communities and classrooms.* New York: Cambridge University Press.

Heath, S. B. (1986a). Sociocultural contexts of language development. In California State Department of Education (Ed.), *Beyond language: Social and cultural factors in schooling language minority students* (pp. 143–186). Los Angeles: California State University, Los Angeles.

Heath, S. B. (1986b). Separating 'things of the imagination' from life: Learning to read and write. In W. H. Teale & E. Sulzby (Eds.), *Emergent literacy: Writing and reading* (pp. 156–172). Norwood, NJ: Ablex.

Heath, S. B. (1989). The learner as cultural member. In M. L. Rice & R. L. Schiefelbusch (Eds.), *The teachability of language* (pp. 333–350). Baltimore, MD: Paul H. Brookes.

Heath, S. B., & Thomas, C. (1984). The achievement of preschool literacy for mother and child. In H. Goelman, A. Oberg, & F. Smith (Eds.), *Awakening to literacy* (pp. 51–72). Exeter, NH: Heinemann Educational.

Hernández, D. (2004). Children and youth in immigrant families: Demographic, social, and educational issues. In J. Banks & C. M. Banks (Eds.), *Handbook of research on multicultural education* (2nd ed., pp. 404–419). San Francisco: Jossey-Bass.

Jacob, L., & Jordan, C. (Eds.). (1993). *Minority education: Anthropological perspectives.* Norwood, NJ: Ablex.

Kanno, Y., & Applebaum, S. D. (1995). ESL students speak up: Their stories of how we are doing. *TESL Canada Journal, 12*(2), 32–49.

Kim, I. (1981). *New urban immigrants: The Korean community in New York.* Princeton, NJ: Princeton University Press.

Lee, Y. (1984). *A comparative study of East Asian American and Anglo American academic achievement: An ethnographic study.* Doctoral dissertation. Evanston, IL: Northwestern University.

Lessow-Hurley, J. (1990). *The foundations of dual language instruction.* New York: Longman.

Losey, K. (1996). *"Listen to the silences": Mexican American interaction in the composition classroom and the community.* Norwood, NJ: Ablex.

Macías, J. (1987). The hidden curriculum of Papago teachers: American Indian strategies for mitigating cultural discontinuity in early schooling. In G. Spindler & L. Spindler (Eds.), *Interpretative ethnography of education: At home and abroad* (pp. 363–380). Hillsdale, NJ: Lawrence Erlbaum Associates.

Macías, R. (1995). California LEP enrollment continues slow growth in 1995. *UC Linguistic Minority Research Institute, 5*(1), 1–2.

Macías, R. (2000). The flowering of America: Linguistic diversity in the United States. In S. McKay & S. C. Wong (Eds.), *New immigrants in the United States* (pp. 11–57). New York: Cambridge University Press.

McDermott, R. (1988). Inarticulateness. In D. Tannen (Ed.), *Linguistics in context: Connecting observation and understanding* (pp. 213–254). Norwood, NJ: Ablex.

Mehan, H. (1981). What time is it, Denise?: Asking known information questions in classroom discourse. *Theory into Practice, 18*(4), 285–294.

Merino, B., & Quintanar, R. (1988, April). *The recruitment of minority students into teaching careers: A status report of effective approaches.* Paper presented at the Far West Holmes Group Meeting, University of Colorado, Boulder.

Michaels, S. (1981). Sharing time: Children's narrative style and differential access to literacy. *Language in Society, 10*(1), 423–442.

Milk, R. (1985). The changing role of ESL in bilingual education. *TESOL Quarterly, 19*(4), 657–672.

Minami, M., & Ovando, C. (2004). Language issues in multicultural contexts. In J. Banks & C. M. Banks (Eds.), *Handbook of research on multicultural education* (2nd ed., pp. 567–588). San Francisco: Jossey-Bass.

Moll, L. (1988). Some key issues in teaching Latino students. *Language Arts, 65*(5), 465–472.

Moll, L. (1989). Teaching second language students: A Vygotskian perspective. In D. M. Johnson & D. H. Roen (Eds.), *Richness in writing: Empowering ESL students* (pp. 55–69). New York: Longman.

Moll, L. (Ed.). (1990). *Vygotsky and education.* New York: Cambridge University Press.

Moll, L., & Díaz, S. (1987). Change as the goal of educational research. *Anthropology and Education Quarterly, 18*(4), 300–311.

Moll, L., & Gonzáles, N. (2004). Engaging life: A funds of knowledge approach to multicultural education. In J. Banks & C. M. Banks (Eds.), *Handbook of research on multicultural education* (2nd ed., pp. 699–715). San Francisco: Jossey-Bass.

Moore, J., & Pachón, H. (1985). *Hispanics in the United States.* Upper Saddle River, NJ: Prentice Hall.

National Coalition of Advocates for Students. (1985). *Barriers to excellence: Our children at risk.* Boston: Author.

Ninio, A., & Bruner, J. (1978). The achievement and antecedents of labelling. *Journal of Child Language, 5*(1), 1–15.

Oakes, J. (1986). *Keeping track: How schools structure inequality.* New Haven: Yale University Press.

Ochs, E., & Schieffelin, B. (1982). Language acquisition and socialization: Three developmental stories and their implications. *Working Papers in Sociolinguistics,* Number 105. Austin, TX: Southwest Educational Development Laboratory.

Ogbu, J., & Matute-Bianchi, M. E. (1986). Understanding sociocultural factors: Knowledge, identity, and school adjustment. In California State Department of Education (Ed.), *Beyond language: Social and cultural factors in schooling language minority students* (pp. 73–142). Los

Angeles: California State University, Los Angeles.

Olsen, L. (1997). *Made in America: Immigrant students in our public schools.* New York: The New Press.

Olson, L. (1988). Study finds few minorities reach the end of "educational pipeline." *Education Week, 8*(9), 5.

Ovando, C., Collier, V., & Combs, M.C. (2003). *Bilingual education & ESL classroom: Teaching in multicultural contexts* (3rd ed.). Boston, MA: McGraw-Hill.

Pallas, A., Natriello, G., & McDill, E. (1989). The changing nature of the disadvantaged population: Current dimensions and future trends. *Educational Research, 18,* 16–22.

Pease-Alvarez, L. (1991). Home and school contexts for language development: The experience of two Mexican-American pre-schoolers. In M. McGroarty & C. Faltis (Eds.), *Languages in school and society: Policy and pedagogy* (pp. 487–509). Berlin: Mouton de Gruyter.

Penfield, J. (1987). ESL: The regular classroom teacher's perspective. *TESOL Quarterly, 21*(1), 21–39.

Philips, S. (1972). Participant structures and communicative competence: Warm Springs children in community and classroom. In C. Cazden, V. John, & D. Hymes (Eds.), *Functions of language in the classroom* (pp. 370–394). New York: Teachers College Press.

Philips, S. (1982). *The invisible culture: Communication in classroom and community on the Warm Springs Indian Reservation.* New York: Longman.

Rose, D. (2001). Acronymonia. *CATESOL News, 33*(1), 8–9.

Samway, K. D., & McKeon, D. (1999). *Myths and realities: Best practices for language minority students.* Portsmouth, NH: Heinemann.

Saville-Troike, M., & Kleifgen, J. (1986). Scripts for school: Cross-cultural communication in elementary classrooms. *Text, 6*(2), 207–221.

Schneider, B., & Lee, Y. (1990). A model for academic success: The school and home environment of East Asian students. *Education and Anthropology Quarterly, 21*(4), 358–387.

Schecter, S., & Bayley, R. (2002). *Language as cultural practice: Mexicanos en el norte.* Mahwah, NJ: Lawrence Erlbaum Associates.

Soltero, S. (2004). *Dual language: Teaching and learning in two languages.* Boston, MA: Allyn & Bacon.

Spradley, J. (1980). *Participant observation.* New York: Holt, Rinehart & Winston.

Stein, N. (1982). What's in a story? Interpreting the interpretations of story grammars. *Discourse Processes, 5,* 319–336.

Suárez-Orozco, C., & Todorova, I. (Eds.). (2003). Understanding the social worlds of immigrant youth. *New Directions for Youth Development,* Winter.

Suárez-Orozco, M. (Ed.). (1998). *Crossings: Mexican immigration in interdisciplinary perspectives.* Cambridge, MA: Harvard University Press.

Sue, S., & Padilla, A. M. (1986). Ethnic minority issues in the United States: Challenges for the educational system. In California State Department of Education (Ed.), *Beyond language: Social and cultural factors in schooling language minority students* (pp. 35–72). Los Angeles: California State University, Los Angeles.

Teale, W. (1984). Reading to young children: Its significance to literacy development. In H. Goelman, A. Oberg, & F. Smith (Eds.), *Awakening to literacy* (pp. 110–121). Exeter, NH: Heinemann Educational.

Toohey, K. (1996). Learning English as a second language in kindergarten: A community of proactive perspective. *Canadian Modern Language Review, 52,* 549–576.

Toohey, K. (1998). 'Breaking them up and taking them away': ESL students in grade one. *TESOL Quarterly, 32*(3), 61–84.

Toohey, K. (2000). *Learning English at school: Identity, social relations and classroom practice.* Clevedon, England: Multilingual Matters.

Trudgill, P. (2000). *Sociolinguistics: An introduction to language and society.* London: Penguin Books.

Trueba, H. T., & Delgado-Gaitán, C. (1983). Socialization of Mexican children for cooperation and competition: Sharing and copying. *Journal of Educational Equity and Leadership, 5*(3), 189–204.

Tsai, S. H. (1986). *The Chinese experience in America.* Bloomington: University of Indiana Press.

Tse, L. (2001). *"Why don't they learn English?": Separating fact from fallacy in the U.S. language debate.* New York: Teachers College Press.

U.S. Bureau of the Census. (1984). *The 1980 census of the population.* Washington, DC: U.S. Government Printing Office.

U.S. Bureau of the Census. (1988). *The Hispanic population in the United States: March 1986 and 1987.* Washington, DC: U.S. Government Printing Office.

U.S. Bureau of the Census. (1989). *Population estimates by race and Hispanic origin for states, metropolitan areas, and selected counties, 1980 to 1985.* Washington, DC: U.S. Government Printing Office.

U.S. Bureau of the Census. (1992). *Selected social characteristics: 1990.* Washington, DC: U.S. Government Printing Office.

U.S. Bureau of the Census. (1993). *The Hispanic population in the United States: March 1993.* Washington, DC: U.S. Government Printing Office.

U.S. Bureau of the Census. (1995). *1990 Census of the population, Volume I, characteristics of the populations.* Washington, DC: U.S. Government Printing Office.

U.S. Bureau of the Census. (2001). *The Hispanic population in the United States: March 1993.* Washington, DC: U.S. Government Printing Office.

U.S. Department of Education. (1993). *Descriptive study of services to limited English proficient students.* Washington, DC: Planning and Evaluation Service.

Valdés, G. (1996). *Con respeto: Bridging the distance between culturally diverse families and schools: An ethnographic portrait.* New York: Teachers College Press.

Valdés, G. (2001). *Learning and not learning English: Latino students in American schools.* New York: Teachers College Press.

W-B Olsen, Roger E. (1993). *Enrollment statistics of limited English proficient students in the United States (1985–1993).* Alexandria, VA: TESOL.

Waggoner, D. (1993). 1993 census shows dramatic change in the foreign-born population in the US. *NABE News, 16*(7), 1, 18–20.

Waggoner, D. (1999). Who are secondary newcomer and linguistically different youth? In C. Faltis & P. Wolfe (Eds.), *So much to say: Adolescents, bilingualism, and ESL in the secondary school* (pp. 1–14). New York: Teachers College Press.

Waggoner, D., & O'Malley, J. M. (1985). Teachers of limited English proficient children in the United States. *NABE Journal, 9*(3), 25–42.

Wallraff, B. (2000). What global language? *Atlantic Monthly, 286*(5), 52–66.

Weiner, L. (2000). Research in the 90s: Implications for urban teacher preparation. *Review of Educational Research, 70*(3), 369–406.

Wills, J., Lintz, A., & Mehan, H. (2004). Ethnographic studies of multicultural education in U.S. classrooms and schools. In J. Banks & C. M. Banks (Eds.), *Handbook of research on multicultural education* (2nd ed., pp. 163–183). San Francisco: Jossey-Bass.

Willy, T. (1975). *Oral aspects in the primitive fiction of newly literate children.* ERIC document No. ED 112 381.

Wink, J. (2001). Labels often reflect educators' beliefs and practices. *BEOutreach,* 28–29.

Wolfe, P. (1999). *Situated learning in a transactional, secondary, English as a second language classroom.* Unpublished doctoral dissertation. Tempe, AZ: Arizona State University.

Wolfe, P., & Poyner, L. (2001). Politics and the pendulum: An alternative understanding of the case of whole language as educational innovation. *Educational Researcher, 30*(1), 15–20.

Wong, S. C. (1988). The language situation of Chinese Americans. In S. L. McKay & S. C. Wong (Eds.), *Language diversity: Problem or resource?* (pp. 193–228). New York: Newbury House.

Wong Fillmore, L. (1985). When does teacher talk work as input? In S. Gass & C. Madden (Eds.), *Input in second language acquisition* (pp. 17–50). Rowley, MA: Newbury House.

Zentella, A. C. (1997). *Growing up bilingual: Puerto Rican children in New York.* Malden, MA: Blackwell.

Zhao, Y. (2002, August 5). *Wave of pupils lacking English strains schools. The New York Times,* p. A1.

All-English Teachers Questionnaire

1. School (optional): _____ Grade you currently teach: _____

2. Prior coursework/workshops in teaching English as a second language (ESL)—course title and date taken:

3. Number of students in your classroom who are adding English:

   How much time does each student spend with you each day? Each week?

4. What is their country of origin? What language do they affiliate with at home? At school? What kinds of schooling experiences did they have in their home language prior to coming to your class? What kinds of reading and writing abilities have they acquired in their home language?

5. Rank the following programmatic approach to preparing students who are adding English in K-8 grade-level classrooms:

   a. Grade-level classes only (structured English immersion or submersion with little or no home language support in class)

   b. Grade-level classes plus an ESL support class (ESL pullout)

   c. Home language instruction plus an ESL support class where only students of the same home language learn together

   d. An immersion classroom segregated for ESL students only

   e. A dual-language classroom for English speakers to learn through another language, together with speakers of the other language, who are learning through English

6. Why do you feel your top choice is the best way to prepare ESL students for the mainstream grade-level classroom?

7. What are some of the difficulties you see in implementing the approach you have selected?

8. What criteria does your school use to determine when English learners are ready for grade-level, English-only classrooms?

9. When do *you* think they should be placed in a grade-level, English-only classroom? In other words, what abilities do you think English learners should possess before they are placed in an all-English grade-level classroom?

10. What frustrates you most in teaching English learners along with learners who are fully proficient in English?

11. In your opinion, how much of an English learner's school day should be spent with the ESL teacher? With a grade-level teacher, either bilingual or monolingual English speaker?

12. If you don't speak a language other than English, how do you communicate with the parents of English learners about their progress/problems in your classroom?

13. Which of the following would help you most in dealing more effectively with English learners in your class? (Choose only 3.)

    _____ Better communication between ESL teachers and grade-level teachers

    _____ More time to adapt lessons/tasks to English learners

    _____ Strategies/techniques on how to teach English learners

    _____ More familiarity with appropriate materials for English learners

    _____ Information about cultures represented by English learners

    _____ Materials prepared by the ESL teacher for English learners in your class

    _____ Ways to increase active participation of English learners

    _____ How to recognize and remove barriers that marginalize English learners

Figure 1.3
Mainstream teachers questionnaire

Pathways to English-medium and Dual-language Classrooms

OVERVIEW

Section 1703(f) of the Equal Educational Opportunity Act of 1974 states that schools with limited-English-proficiency students are required by federal law to "take appropriate action to overcome language barriers that impede equal participation by its students in its instructional programs." Furthermore, the *Lau* Remedies state that Section 1703(f) applies to school districts having 20 or more English learners (Avila & Godoy, 1979; Crawford, 1999). In this chapter, we will review some of the major legal policies enacted to protect language-minority students from inferior schooling practices, and we will examine the kinds of options and obligations schools have in addressing the special needs of English learners, especially in the era of No Child Left Behind (2001). Moreover, we will learn about the criteria that schools use for placing second-language learners in special language programs, for reclassifying them once in a program, and for determining when they are no longer eligible to receive such services.

Episode Two: Finding Out About Bilingual and ESL Programs

In the main office, Julia Felix asks the secretary, Mrs. Flores, if she can take a look at the cumulative files of the 10 English-as-a-second-language students assigned to her class. Obligingly, Mrs. Flores, with more than 10 years experience in the main office, goes directly from her front desk to a row of locked, green filing cabinets, next to the vice-principal's office. Bending down, she opens the proper drawers and searches for the files. Fortunately, all of the files are in their places, with information from last year's teachers. Julia carefully packs the folders into her large straw purse, thanks Mrs. Flores with a full smile, and walks eagerly back to her new classroom. Once again at her desk, Julia neatly and gingerly spreads out the folders across her desk and begins perusing through them, one by one. She remembers Mrs. C telling her not to pay too much attention to what's in the folders. That way, there is less of a chance of forming a wrong impression of a student before actually getting to know the student. In Julia's social mind, she simply wants some meaningful information that might give her clues about where to start. *I know it is not a good idea to form opinions about the children when I have almost no history or current information about them, but it would be cool to know at least something about who they might be.* She immediately notices several terms present in each folder that are not entirely new to her: *NEP, LEP, Transitional Bilingual Program, Language Assessment Scales, IDEA Test,* and *ESL Pullout Program. Let me see. NEP means non-English-proficient,* she says to herself. *I don't like this way of referring to children—NEPs and LEPs. How come some of the students have been in bilingual programs and others only have ESL support?* She also wonders how long each day students will get special ESL support now that they are in her class, and how long will they continue to receive that help. *Do the ESL teachers who work with the students also speak, read, and write their language?* Julia figures that bilingual programs are for students who come to school speaking Spanish. She surmises that the *Language Assessment Scales* and the *IDEA* test are the language assessments used to determine program eligibility, but having never administered them, she is not sure what language abilities they test for or what kind of useful information they might provide. *This is like totally bizarre. There is no way that I am going to start out my year without finding out a lot more about this stuff.*

Where can Julia turn for help in finding answers to these questions? Her first thought is to ask the principal, recollecting that the principal had mentioned something about special programs when she was interviewing Julia for the position. *I remember that the principal seemed to have a pretty good grasp on who the kids are that attend this school, and oh yeah, outside of her office, she keeps a variety of materials for and by children written in different languages. Surely, that is a propitious sign.* Returning to the main office, she makes an appointment for early afternoon to see Mrs. Turner, the principal. Mrs. Turner is a special kind of a principal. She believes strongly in knowing and working with the community served by the school, and she makes an attempt to get to know every student in the school. She has been an elementary teacher for 13 years, and was one of the first bilingual (Spanish–English) teachers in her school district. She became a principal 5 years ago when the school began changing rapidly from an all-English speaking school to a multilingual one for newcomers and immigrant families.

The visit with Mrs. Turner turns out to be very informative, and Julia senses that Mrs. Turner has a good heart. Julia learns that the district has operated a bilingual/ESL program for the last 10 years, and that in the last 5 years, the number and variety of students served by the programs across the district has tripled. Mrs. Turner talks about the criteria for entry into a bilingual/ESL program, about the major kinds of services offered, and generally about how and when children are exited from the program. At this point, Julia learns that all of the English learners assigned to her class will continue to receive some home language and ESL instruction, most likely for the entire year, as all of them still need additional proficiency in English. Julia asks why the students aren't in bilingual classes for the entire day so they can keep up with the class work while they are acquiring English. Mrs. Turner laments that there just aren't enough bilingual teachers proficient in the languages we need beyond the 2nd grade. On a brighter note, she adds that most of the English learners assigned to her class are good readers and writers in their home language, and they enjoy participating with other students.

Julia is a bit puzzled and asks, "That's interesting. How does being able to read and write well in their first language make a difference?" Julia's preparation coursework for teaching included almost nothing about bilingual children and biliteracy.

"Oh, it makes a whole lot of difference," replies Mrs. Turner. "There's a longstanding axiom in education that children only learn to read and write once. Children who have learned to read and write in their home language will probably do just fine in your class, uh, you know, they've got the fundamentals down. Most importantly, they get what's going on . . . when they have a good idea what reading and writing are for; they figure things out."

"That's good to hear, I'll have to watch for that," says Julia. *I better get myself a new notebook so that I can observe and take notes on how the children read and write and stuff in their home language.* "But what about the children who aren't such good readers and writers in the language they speak and understand?" Julia asks.

Mrs. Turner pauses to think and then says in a more serious tone, "In simple terms, you *have to* get them to experience what reading and writing are all about. And, I expect that the children will have extra help with a bilingual teacher who speaks their language whenever possible—and for sure, with an ESL teacher. What is really important is to ensure that *these children have multiple opportunities to use their developing English for meaningful communication with other children in the classroom.* I know all of the teachers in our bilingual program, and they work really hard at helping the children become creative, productive, and curious learners. It is up to you to continue that work so that these children can come to see themselves as smart and capable learners, both in their home language and while they are learning English." Mrs. Turner brings the discussion to an end by suggesting to Julia that she spend some time learning about bilingual education to get a better picture of how bilingual programs work and what kinds of experiences the English learners in her class most likely will and won't have had. She also points out to Julia that she needs to begin to see herself as a language facilitator to her English learners, in the sense that what she does in class can promote their language and literacy acquisition while they engage in learning academic content.

The principal's suggestion piques Julia's curiosity about bilingual/ESL programs, prompting questions not only about their history, but also how and why they work. *I hate being in the dark about the different kinds of bilingual programs and all the terminology.* That very afternoon, Julia decides to detour from her normal route home and stop at the library to check out some books on bilingual and ESL education in the United States. What follows is a summary of what Julia gleaned from her readings on bilingual and ESL education.

A BRIEF ACCOUNT OF BILINGUAL EDUCATION IN THE UNITED STATES

The Bilingual Education Act of 1968

Broad support for bilingual education began in 1968 with the signing of the Bilingual Education Act (BEA). Prior to 1968, few school districts serving large numbers of non-English-speaking children considered implementing bilingual education to prepare these children for English-only schooling. Nearly all non-English-speaking children attending public schools were submerged in English-only classrooms, left on their own to either sink or swim. Unfortunately, many of these children sank long before finishing high school. In the mid-1960s, bilingual education began to receive national recognition because of its success with Cuban refugee children at the Coral Way School in Dade County, Florida (Mackey & Beebe, 1977). The Coral Way bilingual program soon spread to other elementary and secondary schools in Dade County, and by the late 1960s, several cities in the Southwest began to locally support bilingual education programs (Malakoff & Hakuta, 1990).

As the decade of the 1960s came to a close, the federal government was ready to accept bilingual education as a means to combat school failure among the nation's poor, many of whom were non-English-speaking children. The acceptance of bilingual education was fueled by a number of social and political events that began to surface around the mid-1960s (Judd, 1978). First, bilingual education had been effective in Dade County with Cuban refugee children. Second, research conducted in the early and mid-1960s supported a positive relationship between bilingualism and intelligence (Jacobs & Pierce, 1966; Lambert & Peal, 1962). Third, there was a strong national move toward cultural pluralism accompanied by ethnic revitalization, both of which were fueled by the Civil Rights movement. Fourth, President Lyndon Johnson believed strongly that the way to win the War on Poverty was through increasing educational spending. Fifth, the Elementary and Secondary Education Act of 1965 had already paved the way for federal intervention in schooling efforts targeted for poor, low-achieving students. Sixth, to combat the spread of communism from Cuba, the United States stepped up its involvement in Central and South America, resulting in the need for increased numbers of bilingual government employees. Seventh, a renewed interest in foreign language instruction developed as a result of the launching of *Sputnik*. Eighth, the 1960 census data indicated that the Spanish-surnamed population had increased by more than 50%—from 2.3 million in 1950 to nearly 3.5 million in 1960. The data also indicated that Spanish-speaking children were faring poorly in school and that education was a primary concern of Hispanics. Last, a number of powerful Hispanic interest groups had begun to support specific instructional programs, such as bilingual education, ESL, and the teaching of Hispanic culture.

So, in January 1967, when Texas Senator Ralph Yarborough introduced a four-and-a-half-page bill, known as the Bilingual Education Act, for consideration as the Title VII amendment to the Elementary and Secondary Education Act of 1965, the social and political tone of the nation was ripe for its passage. Senator Yarborough's original bill was intended to provide assistance to local education agencies for setting up bilingual programs for low-income, native Spanish-speaking children for whom English was a foreign language. By mid-year, however, there was considerable pressure placed on the Senator to expand the assistance to all low-income, non-English-speaking groups in the United States, which he did in order to pass the bill through the Senate. President Lyndon Johnson signed the bill into law on January 2, 1968, making bilingual education a federal policy for the first time in the history of the United States.

The BEA defined bilingual education as a federal policy "to provide financial assistance to local educational agencies to carry out new and imaginative elementary and secondary school programs" to meet the special educational needs of "children who are educationally disadvantaged because of their inability to speak English" (PL 90-247, Sec. 702). While the BEA of 1968 did not specifically mandate or define the kinds of programs that schools should use, grants were awarded only to applicants who (1) developed and operated bilingual programs for low-income, non-English-speaking students, (2) made efforts to attract and retain bilingual teachers, and (3) established communication between the home and the school.

Bilingual Education in the 1970s

The 1970s produced several important changes to the original BEA policy. The first major change was initiated in 1970, when the Office of Civil Rights sent a formal memorandum to school districts serving LEP students (Malakoff & Hakuta, 1990). The memorandum spelled out the conditions of Title VI of the Civil Rights Act of 1964 in relation to students of English as a second language, noting that a Title VI review team had found "a number of practices which have the effect of denying equality of educational opportunity to Spanish-surnamed pupils" and that these practices "have the effect of discrimination on the basis of national origin" (Pottinger, 1970). The memorandum also specified that the school district must take affirmative steps to rectify language deficiencies in cases where "the inability to speak and understand English excludes national origin minority group children from effective participation in the educational program" (Pottinger, 1970, p. 595). The memorandum did not specify what the "affirmative steps" should be nor did it make any mention whatsoever of teaching students in their native language (Malakoff & Hakuta, 1990).

The Office of Civil Rights memorandum set the stage for a series of major legal battles over the legal obligation of school districts receiving federal funds to comply with Title VI guidelines. The single most important legal decision came from the case known as *Lau v. Nichols*. In 1970, a class-action suit filed by Chinese parents in San Francisco on behalf of their children claimed that the children were being denied equal educational opportunity. The school district had identified 2,856 non-English-speaking children, but provided ESL instruction to fewer than half of them. The school district did not dispute the number of students in need of special attention nor that it had attempted to serve the needs of this population. The issue of the suit was whether non-English-speaking children were able to receive an equal education in an English-only mainstream classroom and whether the school district had a legal obligation to provide special instructional programs to meet the needs of these children. The federal district court ruled in favor of the school district, finding that, because the non-English-speaking children were receiving the same curriculum in the same classrooms as English-speaking children, they were being treated no differently and thus were not being discriminated against by the school district. Accordingly, the court ruled that the school district was under no obligation to provide special services to non-English-speaking students. Instead, the court encouraged the school district to address the program as an educational rather than a legal obligation to the students (August & García, 1988). The ruling was appealed to the Ninth Circuit District Court of Appeals, which upheld the lower court's decision on January 8, 1973. But the dispute did not end there. The case was appealed to and eventually decided upon by the Supreme Court in the following year.

In 1972, a federal district court in New Mexico had addressed the same legal issues in a case involving Mexican-American children in the Portales Municipal School district. In *Serna v. Portales Municipal Schools* (1972), however, the court found that non-English-speaking Mexican-American children were being treated *differently* when they received the same curriculum as native English-speaking children and thus were being discriminated against (Malakoff & Hakuta, 1990). In response to the ruling, the school district submitted a non-bilingual plan as a remedy to the problem, but the court rejected it, based on expert testimony presented at the court hearing. The school district appealed to the Tenth Circuit Court of Appeals, which in 1974 ruled in favor of the plaintiffs, finding that the students' Title VI rights had been violated and that as a result they had a right to bilingual education.

Also in 1974, the Supreme Court handed down the *Lau v. Nichols* decision in favor of the students and their parents. The Supreme Court justices avoided the constitutional question of equal protection (the 14th Amendment), and instead, as in *Serna v. Portales Municipal Schools,* relied heavily on Title VI of the Civil Rights Act of 1964 and the Office of Civil Rights memorandum issued in 1970. The court found that guidelines outlined in the 1970 Office of Civil Rights memorandum "clearly indicate that affirmative efforts to give special training for non-English-speaking pupils are required by Title VI as a condition to federal aid to public schools" (Pottinger, 1970, p. 569). Moreover, the court found that students with limited knowledge of English who are submersed in mainstream classes are "effectively foreclosed from any meaningful education" (Pottinger, 1970, p. 566).

The *Lau* decision did not impose any particular educational remedy, such as (native language) bilingual education or English-as-a-second-language instruction. Instead, the court recommended that school districts take into account the numbers of students involved when making decisions concerning an appropriate remedy, suggesting that a remedy may differ from setting to setting.

For those school districts wishing to establish or continue with federally funded bilingual education programs, there were new guidelines to follow under the 1974 amendment to the BEA, which in effect provided the first governmental definition of bilingual education, choosing to define it in transitional terms as "instruction given in, and study of English, and to the extent necessary to allow a child to progress effectively through the education system, the native language" (Schneider, 1976, pp. 436–437).

In the same year, following the *Lau* decision, Congress legislated the Supreme Court ruling into the Equal Educational Opportunity Act (EEOA) of 1974. The major effect of this new legislation was to extend the *Lau* decision to all public school districts, not just those receiving federal funds. As of 1974, a school district with students who are speakers of languages other than English in any one of its schools is required to "take appropriate action to overcome language barriers that impede equal participation by its students in its instructional programs" (20 U.S.C. Sec. 1703(f)). Section 1703(f) of the EEOA was especially significant because it addressed the issue of "discriminatory effect" vs. "discriminatory intent" (Malakoff & Hakuta, 1990), declaring that schools could be in violation of Title VI of the Civil Rights Act if second-language students were not receiving some sort of special instructional remedy (discriminatory effect) *even if no substantial intent to discriminate was found*. Following the pattern of earlier legislation, however, the EEOA did not single out any particular instructional remedy as appropriate, leaving the choice between transitional bilingual education and English-as-a-second-language programs up to the local districts. Moreover, in the ensuing years, the power of the Section 1703(f) has become increasingly diluted as the courts have continually ruled that local districts would not be subject to taking "appropriate action" without first having the opportunity for due process; that is, to be heard on a case-by-case basis (McFadden, 1983).

Also in 1974, in the wake of the *Lau* decision, the Department of Health, Education, and Welfare appointed a task force to establish guidelines for implementing the decision. The guidelines, issued in 1975 under the name *Lau Remedies*, directed school districts having 20 or more students of the same language group having a primary language other than English (1) to establish a means for identifying all students whose primary language is not English, (2) to evaluate the English-language proficiency of these students, and (3) to provide them with appropriate bilingual education programs.

Unfortunately, because the guidelines were applied only to districts found to be out of compliance with Title VI or the EEOA, their application has not been widespread (Malakoff & Hakuta, 1990). Moreover, Avila and Godoy (1979) point out that when cases are brought to trial, the courts are inclined to examine the guidelines in terms of the ratio between the number of English learners and the total school population. Thus, a large school system may not be required to implement a bilingual program for its students who are speakers of languages other than English even though the number of these students exceeds the minimum specified in the *Lau* Remedies. Nonetheless, the Remedies remain in effect today, and together with Section 1703(f) of the EEOA of 1974, they continue to be a major force in supporting the rights of second-language students to have access to bilingual education programs under certain circumstances.

Bilingual Education in the 1980s

By the early 1980s bilingual education increasingly was coming under fire from anti-bilingual-education forces, including certain members of the Republican Party (August & García, 1988, p. 84; Padilla, 1990). The Office of Planning, Budget, and Evaluation sponsored a report by Baker and de Kanter (1981) to review the effectiveness of bilingual education as compared to English-only approaches (structured immersion and English-as-a-second-language programs). Baker and de Kanter found that second-language children receiving English-only approaches performed as well in English and other content areas as students in bilingual education programs. The Baker and de Kanter report concluded that bilingual education, which is, in the short run, more costly to school districts, should not be the only approach for remedying the needs of second-language learners. (This study has been fiercely contested on the grounds that it was poorly designed, methodologically flawed, and extremely biased. See Hakuta, 1986, pp. 220–222; Willig, 1985, 1987; and Yates & Ortiz, 1983, for criticisms of the study.)

The Baker and de Kanter report set the tone for some significant changes in bilingual education policy in the 1980s. In 1984, the BEA was amended to more strictly define the nature of transitional bilingual education programs and to allow school districts more flexibility in the kinds of educational remedies from which to choose. Transitional bilingual education programs were now required to have a structured English language component, one that was tied directly to eligibility testing and subject to approval by experts in the field. Prior to 1984, an English language component had been required, but there were no controls on the kinds of programs that school districts could use. Under the 1984 amendment to the BEA, special alternative instructional programs not requiring the use of a child's native language were now allowed, and even encouraged, for certain populations. However, the special alternative programs had several guidelines to follow to receive Title VII funding: (1) They needed to have specifically designed curricula; (2) they had to be appropriate for the language and educational needs of the students; and (3) they had to provide structured English language instruction to enable a child to achieve competence in English. The amended BEA of 1984 also established an Office of Bilingual Education and Minority Language Affairs and appointed a director to oversee it.

A major policy change to the BEA occurred in 1988. The amended act requires that federal monies to support bilingual education programs be divided between transitional bilingual education programs (75%) and special alternative instruction programs (25%). This represents the greatest percentage of federal support for non-native language instruction programs to date. The 1988 BEA also limits the amount of time that a student can spend in a transitional bilingual or a special alternative instruction program to 3 years. Students can be enrolled for a fourth or fifth year "only if teachers and school personnel familiar with the students' overall academic progress have conducted an evaluation. The results of the evaluation must be made available to students' parents. The fourth and fifth year emphasis must be on English acquisition" (August & García, 1988, p. 92). This particular requirement calls special attention to the exit criteria used to declare students ineligible for special instructional services. Finally, the 1988 BEA obliges schools to make every effort to provide information to students' parents in a language they understand—a requirement that is specifically addressed in the joinfostering framework.

Several important court cases involving bilingual education were decided throughout the 1980s. In *Castañeda v. Pickard* (1981), the Fifth Circuit Court of Appeals once again found that schools must address the special language needs of students who are adding English as a second language. But the central issue of this Arizona case was really whether the court has the authority to direct a school to use a specific educational remedy. The plaintiffs argued for transitional bilingual education as the "appropriate action" for students of Mexican or Yaqui ancestry, citing Section 1703(f) of the Equal Educational Opportunity Act of 1974. The court responded that Section 1703(f) did not require any particular form of remedy, and so the task of determining the appropriateness of a given program for a given school district was up to the particular judge presiding over the case. However, in an unprecedented move, the court presented three criteria that judges should use for determining the "appropriateness" of a particular remedy in subsequent cases:

1. The program must be based on sound educational theory;
2. the program must be implemented in an effective manner; and

3. the program, after a period of "reasonable implementation," must produce results to substantiate that language barriers are being overcome (August & García, 1988).

Criterion number two was especially significant because it spoke to the need for capable educational personnel, materials, and other relevant support needed to ensure effective program implementation. In other words, for whatever program model a school district chooses to address the needs of second-language students, the district must provide evidence that the staff and materials are suitable for the program. An unanticipated result of *Castañeda v. Pickard,* therefore, was support for the idea that teaching staff working in bilingual and ESL programs must be specialists in bilingual and second-language teaching and learning. Implicit in this ruling was the need to create new state-approved credential and endorsement programs for ESL teachers and to upgrade professional coursework in existing bilingual teacher education programs to reflect the changing role of ESL instruction in bilingual education. (See Faltis, 1993b, for an overview of practices in bilingual/ESL K–12 instruction, and McKnight & Antinuez, 1999, for a description of nationwide ESL endorsement and credential program requirements.)

Teacher abilities were also a major concern in *Keyes v. School District No. 1* (1983). The suit was originally filed in 1969 as a class action of minority parents on behalf of their children attending the Denver Public Schools, which segregated them on the basis of their ethnic background. The plaintiffs won their case in 1974 but, at the urging of the Congress of Hispanic Educators, they returned to court to argue that years of segregation and inferior education required a special remedy above and beyond the school district's desegregation efforts. In late 1983, the court, following the three criteria presented in the *Castañeda v. Pickard* decision, ruled in favor of the plaintiffs, stating that the school district had failed to develop an educationally sound program for its language-minority students and that teachers in the existing programs were pedagogically underprepared.

The issue of teacher preparation in transitional bilingual and special alternative instruction programs was again brought up in a class-action suit known as *Teresa P. et al. v. Berkeley Unified School District* (1989). In this case the plaintiffs alleged that the rights of students who were adding English as a second language were being violated by the Berkeley, California, USD because the students were being taught by teachers who did not have bilingual or ESL teaching credentials. However, at the heart of the case was the plaintiffs' assertion that English learners were being exited too quickly from the bilingual programs and that students placed in the district's English-only (ESL) program were being denied comprehensible instruction precisely because teachers lacked the necessary preparation in second-language methodology. The court ruled that Berkeley's programs for ESL students satisfied Section 1703(f) of the Equal Education Opportunity Act of 1974. Ruling in favor of the defendants, the court found that Berkeley's English-only (ESL) program was no less effective than the native-language transitional program in developing students' English-language proficiency. Moreover, the court found that federal standards concerning the effective delivery of programs outlined in *Castañeda v. Pickard* did not require teachers of ESL students to have special credentials.

Teresa P. v. Berkeley USD may have serious consequences for both native-language bilingual and ESL instruction in the future. If school districts decide to follow the ruling, the quality of instruction provided to second-language learners in both bilingual and ESL classrooms will probably diminish, because greater numbers of poorly prepared teachers will be teaching in bilingual and ESL classrooms. (See Sánchez & Walker de Felix, 1986, for an account of how untrained and inept teachers were routinely placed in ESL classrooms.) Consequently, fewer students will be exiting with higher levels of English proficiency. Moreover, because the ruling concludes that bilingual education is no more effective than English-only instruction, and the latter is hailed as less expensive than the former, it is likely that more school districts will apply for Title VII money under the 1988 provision that set aside 25% of funding for special alternative instruction programs. Finally, as non-native-language approaches to bilingual education gain in popularity, it is possible that the next amendment to Title VII will increase the percentage of support for special alternative instruction programs and decrease support for transitional bilingual education.

What is especially troubling about the *Teresa P.* case is that the judge relied on one so-called "expert" witness for ruling that ESL was an "effective educational remedy," and that witness was a school district official. As Haas and Poynor (2003) point out, it is disingenuous of the court to allow as an expert witness the very people who for decades have been neglectful in providing quality education for language-minority students.

Bilingual Education in the 1990s

There have been many changes in funding patterns, legal decisions, and public opinion since the birth of bilingual education. While funding did not significantly diminish in the 1970s and 1980s, it is clear that the proportion of funding for non-bilingual special alternative instruction (English-only) programs has increased significantly, from zero to 25%. At the same time, the proportion of funding for native-language bilingual instruction has decreased from 100% to 75%. The shift in funding emphasis is also showing up in the number of English learners being served by bilingual education programs as compared with ESL students in non-bilingual programs. A study conducted by the National Education Association (Rodríguez, 1990) found that in the 1989 academic year, bilingual education programs served only an estimated 5.6% of all students who were speakers of languages other than English. The rest were presumably served either by special English instruction (ESL) or provided no help at all (submersion). The number of students served by bilingual programs has decreased considerably from 1980, when Stein (1986) estimated that bilingual programs served approximately 10% of all students in need of bilingual education.

The legal system has consistently decided in favor of English learners' right to equal educational opportunities but has repeatedly resisted handing down a ruling that prescribes a particular remedy as more appropriate than another. The effect of leaving the decision up to the district has been that many districts are choosing bilingual education programs over other forms of instruction. But the pressure has been great to switch to English-only remedies. As of 1988, only 22 states even allowed native-language use for instruction in bilingual programs (August & García, 1988). In the late 1980s, a newly formed group calling itself "U.S. English" began to mount a large-scale attack on any attempt to use languages other than English for schooling and governmental affairs. (See Rossell, 1989, as an example of anti-bilingual education research and propaganda.) This group is also responsible for introducing and passing official English-language amendments in several states having large bilingual populations.

Public opinion generally favors bilingual education over English-only special instruction for language-minority children (Hakuta, 1986). Yet there are reports of increasing numbers of non-English-speaking parents specifically requesting English-as-a-second-language programs rather than native-language bilingual programs. For example, Spanish-speaking parents at a school in urban Phoenix, Arizona, which in 1995 had an ESL program, were vociferously opposed to starting up a Spanish–English bilingual program because most of the bilingual teachers were not native speakers of Spanish and, according to the parents, had inadequate proficiency in Spanish to teach content and literacy in that language.

As we move into the 21st century, it appears certain that fewer students who are speakers of languages other than English will receive native-language bilingual instruction than ever before. The states of California, Arizona, and Massachusetts have already passed referenda prohibiting any type of bilingual or native-language instruction. It remains to be seen, however, what role the courts, especially the higher courts, will have in reversing this apparent trend. The matter of whether English-only instruction is an "appropriate remedy" for educating language-minority students or whether other approaches are more suitable under certain conditions will surely continue to be contested as a civil rights issue in the years to come (Haas & Poyner, 2003).

In the first half of the 1990s, bilingual education witnessed a rash of pro-English-only propaganda aimed at obliterating the use of languages other than English in the schools (Crawford, 1999). Several of the major Republican candidates for the 1996 presidential election, for example, were openly opposed to bilingual education and the use of non-English languages in public places. In a similar vein, states' rights advocates have continually argued that states should be able to determine for themselves how to educate children who enter school not speaking English.

Bilingual education advocates have mounted an equally energetic counterattack to convince educators and the public that learning through the native language is an effective and equitable means for schooling large numbers of language-minority students. Ramírez, Yuen, and Ramey (1991) and Rosier and Holm (1980) found long-term benefits of late-exit bilingual programs. Christian (1994) has also found language and academic benefits for two-way bilingual education programs. Moreover, the Office of Bilingual Education and Minority Language Affairs, under the direction of Eugene García from 1993 to 1995, made the granting of Title VII monies to schools and school districts contingent upon *schoolwide* plans for the incorporation of English learners into all aspects of schooling. This reform is very much in line with joinfostering principles. That is, the entire school has to show how it is involved in the education of English learners, in helping them join in the schooling activities and receive the benefits that schools, as opposed to special programs, have to offer them. One significant result of this reform in Title VII is that all teachers may need to be prepared to work with children who are learning English as an additional language. In a recent court case in Arizona, *Flores v. the State of Arizona* (2001), where bilingual education has been outlawed in favor of English-only instruction, the United States District Court of Arizona found in favor of the plaintiff and held the State of Arizona responsible for providing training in English immersion teaching strategies to all teachers in the state.

In spite of strong evidence that good bilingual programs are effective for enabling students to continue learning in their native language and for learning English, the push to eradicate the use of languages other than English for teaching picked up tremendous steam in late 1990s. In 1998, Californians passed Proposition 227, which requires school districts to teach

ESL students "overwhelmingly in English, bans the use of languages other than English for instruction, and limits ESL instruction to one year" (Crawford, 1999, p. 301). Individual parents, however, can request a waiver from this requirement, and ask for native language instruction. Proposition 227 was spearheaded by millionaire monolingual businessman, Ron Unz, who believes that 1 year of special immersion into English (with an ESL teacher) is enough time for students to be ready for participating in English-medium regular classrooms. Early in 1999, the school districts of Hayward, Berkeley, and Oakland applied as districts for a waiver from the requirements of Proposition 227, in an effort to reinstate their bilingual programs. Supporters of 227 immediately sued the districts and took the matter to court. In September of the same year, the 1st District Court of Appeal ruled in favor of the Unz initiative saying that only individual parents, not an entire school district, can seek a waiver ("Court limits," 1999).

Unz and his group, English for the Children, also set up an operation in Tucson, Arizona, and in 2001, voters passed a referendum, Proposition 203, to eliminate bilingual education in Arizona as well. Bilingual education continues to be under attack, especially in the No Child Left Behind era, and it will undoubtedly remain so to the extent that speaking a language other than English is considered by the dominant power group to be unAmerican.

Under President George W. Bush, the Elementary and Secondary Education Act was reauthorized under a new name, the No Child Left Behind Act of 2001 (Public Law 107–110). Under this new reauthorization, the Bilingual Education Act or Title VII was renamed the English Language Acquisition, Language Enhancement, and Academic Achievement Act, which became known as Title III. Moreover, the Office of Bilingual Education and Minority Language Affairs (OBEMLA) was given the new name of the Office of English Language Acquisition, Language Enhancement, and Academic Achievement for Limited English Proficient Students, bringing to a close a period in U.S. history when the legal term *bilingual education* was used in U.S. law and government offices. Although the codified term of *bilingual education* is no longer used under Title III, bilingual education programs continue to be offered nationwide.

PROGRAM DESIGNS

The preceding section on the history of bilingual education in the United States mentioned transitional bilingual education and special alternative (non-native) language instruction programs. This section will look more closely at the meaning of these program types as well as at the various ways that program designs can be distinguished.

There are lots of ways to organize a discussion on the bilingual education program types (Hornberger, 1991). A reasonable starting distinction is whether the program leads to *additive* or *subtractive* bilingualism (August & García, 1988; Soltero, 2004). The distinction has to do with one of the goals of bilingual education: to add a second language while learning in it or to minimize the use and importance of the first language while learning in the second. Additive bilingualism is the result of programs that honor and use the student's native language for language arts, literacy, and subject matter instruction along with English for all or most of schooling. In an additive bilingual program, there is an effort to develop in students high levels of proficiency in two languages—the student's native language and English. Additive bilingualism is based on the theory of "less English initially means more English later." The "less equals more" argument derives from the idea that students who acquire high levels of literacy and develop content and discourse knowledge in their native language before acquiring English will not only acquire high levels of English, but will also be able to participate well in English settings because they have the academic base to do so (Cummins, 1979). The best, and most researched example of additive bilingualism is dual-language bilingual education, in which both English speakers and speakers of another language become bilingual and biliterate together (Bickle, Billings, & Hakuta, 2004; Cloud, Genesee, & Hamayan, 2000; Soltero, 2004).

Subtractive bilingualism, in contrast, results from programs that provide minimal instruction in the student's native language and do so for a limited amount of time. In this case, the goal is to get students to become English proficient as quickly as possible without developing the native language in the process. One of the eventual results of subtractive bilingualism, therefore, is monolingualism. Businessman Ron Unz and his supporters favor subtractive bilingualism. He believes that if families wish to maintain their native language, they should be doing that at home or in church, but not at school. In school, students should learn English only, even if it means losing their native language.

Additive and subtractive bilingual programs can be further distinguished by the manner in which language is distributed during and for instruction. Jacobson (1990) differentiates bilingual instructional methodology in terms of whether the two languages of instruction are used concurrently or separately, yielding eight types of bilingual instructional methodology:

Concurrent Language Models	**Separate Language Models**
Preview-Review	Content
Concurrent Translation	Person
Code-Switching	Time
New Concurrent Approach	Place

Generally speaking, separate language model methodology is found most often in additive-oriented bilingual programs; concurrent language methodology, in subtractive-oriented programs. The reason is that separate model programs aim toward a distribution of the two languages for distinct purposes, and thus tend to use the native language for longer periods of time and for a wider range of functions than do concurrent language models.

Concurrent Language Models

Preview-Review. In the preview-review instructional model, the teacher previews and reviews subject matter content in one language (usually the native language) and interacts with students during the main part of the lesson (including practice activities) in the other language (Delgado-Gaitán, 1991; Moll & Díaz, 1985). So, for instance, if you were in a Spanish-English bilingual class talking with students about Thanksgiving and how Native Americans are often misrepresented during this holiday, you would talk about the major ideas and encourage students to discuss major ideas in Spanish. Then you might have them work in small groups to read a variety of stories about Native Americans in English and discuss in English with their fellow students the ways Native American children and the community are portrayed in books. Finally, you would lead a discussion about the major points presented in the preview and relate them to what students learned in their small groups. This review phase would be conducted in Spanish.

Concurrent Translation. Concurrent translation occurs when the teacher presents information in one language and then translates it word for word into the other language. Ostensibly, the purpose of concurrent translation is to ensure that all the students in the class understand what is being said. However, because students usually ignore the second language and wait instead for information to be provided in their native language (Saville & Troike, 1971), they are less likely to develop high levels of English-language proficiency when instruction is presented through this model, and their native language is likely to suffer as well. Consider this: When teachers use concurrent translation to interact with students at any point of a lesson, they are taking twice as much time, and students are paying attention only half of the time. For this reason alone, the detriment of concurrent translation outweighs the benefit of student comprehension. There are other, better ways to invite students into the discourse of the lesson without resorting to translation all the time.

Code-Switching. Code-switching occurs when the teacher alternates from one language to the other within a sentence or between several sentences of the same thought. This type of language alternation, known as *intralingual code-switching*, reflects a back-and-forth switching strategy used for informal interaction among some bilingual adolescents and adults in U.S. bilingual communities (Faltis, 1989; Zentella, 1997) and thus may be useful for learning subject matter content because it ties in to community language practices. Code-switching looks something like this:

(Spanish to English) *Andale, Gerardo,* why don't you tie your shoe, *porque si no, te vas a caer.* [Hey, Gerardo, why don't you tie your shoe, because if you don't, you'll fall.]

(English to Spanish) Okay, class, *quiero que escuchen* really hard right now because I am going to explain *cómo vamos a hacer el dibujo.* [Okay, class, I want you to listen really hard right now because I am going to explain how we are going to do the drawing.]

If language development is the primary goal of instruction, however, this language alternation approach may be totally inappropriate, as students are rarely exposed to full ideas in one language or the other. They need opportunities to hear, read, use, and write both languages for extended stretches of meaning to acquire high levels of proficiency.

New Concurrent Approach.   One approach to language switching that does aim to provide bilingual students with extended use of both languages in a way that promotes dual language and content learning is the New Concurrent Approach (Jacobson, 1982), a non-translation bilingual methodology that systematically incorporates the reasons proficient bilingual speakers switch languages. An NCA teacher learns to alternate from one language to the other between thought units and in response to consciously identified sociolinguistic cues (Faltis, 1989). NCA teachers can also incorporate critical reasons for language switching in order to engage students in politically oriented discussions. Here is an example of using NCA to engage students in a bilingual discussion about war—in this case, the Gulf War (Morgan, 1992/93).

After a general discussion about the Bosnian War and how war can change people's lives, the teacher asked her 6th-grade students to consider the Gulf War, in which the United States attacked Iraq to stop the Iraqi military advancement in Kuwait:

Teacher: *¿Cómo cambiaría el mundo si Saddam Hussein controlara el mundo? ¿Tendríamos los mismos derechos?* [How would the world change if Saddam Hussein controlled the world? Would we have the same rights?]

Student 1: *Sería totalmente diferente, pero yo no creo que la guerra contra Saddam sea justa. No es justo bombardear Iraq.* [It would be completely different, but I don't think that the war against Saddam was fair. It isn't fair to bomb Iraq.]

Student 2: *Sí es justo porque Saddam invadó a Kuwait.* [Yes, it is fair because Saddam invaded Kuwait.]

Teacher: What do you think, class? Did Saddam invade Kuwait? Was there a reason for the invasion? Was the United States right to attack Iraq?

Student 3: (to Student 1) What would you do if a robber came to your house and attacked your family and stole your property? Wouldn't you try to stop him?

Student 2: I agree. We have to protect what is ours.

Student 1: Yes, but the United States was protecting oil, not people.

Teacher: *Ahora llegamos al problema: ¿Estaban los Estados Unidos protejiendo su fuente de petroleo o estaban ayudando a su amigo Kuwait?* [Now we are getting to the problem: Was the United States protecting its oil source or was it helping its friend Kuwait?]

Student 1: *Ya sabemos que Kuwait tiene mucho petroleo. ¿Por qué no se mete los Estados Unidos en otras guerras, y no más en ésta?* [We already know that Kuwait has lots of oil. Why doesn't the United States get involved in other wars, not only this one?]

In this NCA exchange, the students follow the teacher's lead and stay in the language she speaks. They and the teacher switch from one language to the other as they carry on a discussion of ideas. One feature to notice is that the students are listening to and speaking both languages about equally.

Separate Language Models

Content. One way to separate languages for instruction is to assign one language for certain academic subjects and the other language for the rest. The decision can be made on a content-free basis by randomly assigning each of the languages to a particular set of subjects or on a content-sensitive basis where each language is judged to be more appropriate for teaching certain subjects. (See Wong Fillmore & Valadez, 1986, pp. 660–664, for a discussion of the issues involved in separating languages by content.) Some bilingual educators believe that language arts, mathematics, and social studies should first be taught in the students' native language, and that art, science, and music should be taught in the students' new language. However, as elementary school teaching becomes increasingly integrated and less focused on discrete subject matter areas, language separation by content seems out of touch.

Person. Some bilingual programs separate language teaching by having two individuals in the classroom; one speaks in one language, and the second speaks in the other. There are several ways of organizing for this kind of separation-by-person bilingual instruction. Team teaching and use of a teacher's aide are the two most common practices. The goal in classes where two adults consistently teach in different languages is to accustom students to use the language of the adult to whom they are speaking and/or listening.

Time.   The two languages of a bilingual program can also be separated by time so that one language is used on one day and the other is used on the next day. This is called *the alternate-days approach.* Or the teacher can designate one language for morning use and the other for afternoon use. Ordinarily, language use separated by time factors is achieved by posting signs at the classroom door so that when students enter, they are reminded as to which language will be used that day or during a certain block of time.

Place.   The physical location of the classroom may also signal to students which language will be used for instruction. In certain bilingual programs, the classrooms in which native-language and English-medium classwork occur are physically separated. This means that students change classrooms for the native-language and English parts of the school day once English is introduced into the curriculum. In this manner, students learn to associate language use with a particular physical setting. Occasionally, when separate classrooms are unavailable, clearly marked activity centers serve the same purpose (Jacobson, 1990).

Additive Bilingual Education

In the United States, there is basically only one type of additive bilingual program: bilingual maintenance education, also known as *bilingual immersion education* (Lindholm, 1990) or *two-way* or *dual-language bilingual education* (Bickle, Billings, & Hakuta, 2004; Christian, 1994; Soltero, 2004). In bilingual maintenance programs, non-English-speaking students receive instruction in their home language along with English, and fully English-proficient students receive instruction in English along with the second language of English learners. Bilingual maintenance programs typically maintain a strict separation of language use according to time, content, place, and/or teacher (Bickle, Billings, & Hakuta, 2004). Typically, after an initial year or two of total minority-language instruction, the two languages are distributed so that the minority language is used 60% of the time up to the 4th grade, and then the two languages are used for equal amounts of time through the 6th grade. After the 6th grade, the minority language may be offered as a subject up through 12th grade. Figure 2.1 presents a graphic representation of the percentage of time spent in the two languages over time in a program

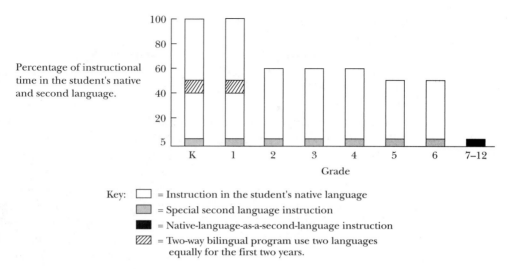

Percentage of instructional time in the student's native and second language.

Key: ☐ = Instruction in the student's native language
        ▨ = Special second language instruction
        ■ = Native-language-as-a-second-language instruction
        ▨ = Two-way bilingual program use two languages
             equally for the first two years.

Figure 2.1
Bilingual maintenance education programs

such as the one described above. Bilingual maintenance programs, which are extraordinarily rare in the United States, promote cultural pluralism, language enrichment, and language restoration (Baker, 1988, p. 47). Krashen and Biber (1988) describe several exemplary bilingual maintenance programs in California. Bickle, Billings, & Hakuta (2004) discuss recent emerging results of two-way immersion programs nationwide. Lindholm-Leavy (2000) and Christian, Montone, Lindholm, & Carranza (1997) provide a directory and profile of bilingual maintenance and dual-language programs throughout the United States. Cloud, Genesee, & Hamayan (2000) and Soltero (2004) present an overview of dual-language programs, with principles and practices found in high-quality programs. However, it is worth pointing out that Valdés (1997) raises a number of issues about the quality of language instruction in the minority language, the effects of dual-language immersion on intergroup relations, and how dual-language programs figure into the relationship between language and power.

Subtractive Bilingual Programs

The overwhelming majority of bilingual education programs throughout the United States, however, lead to subtractive bilingualism in conformance with assimilationist goals. Subtractive bilingual programs "are designed to help students make the transition from one language to another; that is, they take monolinguals and produce monolinguals" (Malakoff & Hakuta, 1990, p. 39).

The most commonly practiced subtractive educational program is transitional bilingual education. Following the definition spelled out in the 1974 amendment to Title VII, this kind of program uses the native language for some or all subject matter instruction, usually for no more than three academic years, while the student is acquiring English as a second language. In other words, the native language is used temporarily as a bridge to English.

Programs that use the native language for part of instruction for less than 2 years are called *early-exit transitional programs* (Ramírez & Merino, 1990). Students in these programs may continue to have structured English instruction even after they no longer receive native-language instruction, usually for an additional year. Thus, a student entering the program in kindergarten would be exited at the end of 1st or 2nd grade. Programs that offer native-language instruction from kindergarten through the upper elementary grades are called *late-exit transitional programs* (Ramírez & Merino, 1990). Students stay in late-exit programs even after they have learned enough English to succeed academically in a mainstream classroom. In both types of programs, students who fall too far behind in academic achievement after being placed in a mainstream classroom for the entire day may be reclassified as limited English proficient and become eligible again for English-as-a-second-language instruction for up to 2 years. See Figures 2.2 and 2.3 for a graphic representation of early-exit and late-exit transitional bilingual education programs.

Transitional bilingual education is primarily practiced in schools serving large numbers of English learners who speak and understand the same minority language (Faltis & Hudelson, 1998). Such programs can be designed

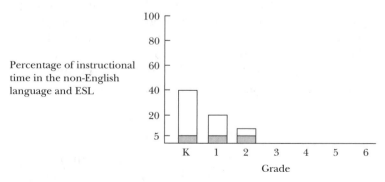

Figure 2.2
Early-exit
transitional bilingual
education programs

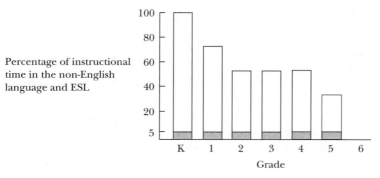

Figure 2.3
Late-exit transitional
bilingual education
programs

Key: ☐ = Instruction in the student's native language
      ▨ = English-as-a-second-language instruction

so that the two languages are used separately or concurrently for instruction. However, even in programs organized to separate language use according to content, time, person, and/or place, there is little to prevent teachers from using both languages concurrently (usually by translating back and forth) in an effort to reach all students in the class (Faltis, 1990). Moreover, given the tremendous push to use English and the major objectives of transitional programs, teachers tend to use more English than the native language, regardless of whether the two languages are allocated for concurrent or separate use (Halcón, 1983; Milk, 1986).

Four other common programs that lead to subtractive bilingualism, or eventual monolingualism, are *submersion, ESL pullout, ESL push in,* and *Structured English Immersion (SEI).* In a submersion program, students are placed in mainstream classrooms and are given no special assistance or English-language instruction. Teachers may try to help by assigning a buddy to work with individual students, but by and large, no other adjustments are made. Students are expected to sink or swim. In ESL pullout programs, second-language students leave their mainstream classes at certain times during the day to receive structured ESL instruction in a separate classroom (Richard-Amato, 1988). The instruction ranges from 15 to 50 minutes daily. ESL pullout programs are frequently used in schools where native-language bilingual instruction is difficult to implement; for example, in schools serving second-language students from different language backgrounds or where there are a small number of second-language students. Teachers in ESL pullout programs may or may not have an endorsement or certification to teach ESL to children. Such endorsement usually entails at least 12 credits of college-level courses in the areas of ESL methodology, second-language curriculum and materials development, second-language acquisition theory, and second-language testing and assessment. Few states offer certification in teaching English as a second language because this specialty is generally not recognized as a discipline.

A more recent English medium approach to helping English learners who find themselves placed in mainstream all-English classrooms is *ESL push in*. The idea here is to keep English learners in the mainstream class and have an ESL teacher or aide come into the class on a daily basis to work with ESL students on specific class assignments. This approach has more support than pullout programs because the ESL teachers work more closely with the regular classroom teacher. Moreover, the students remain in the mainstream class for the entire day.

A less common subtractive program that is slowly gaining in popularity is *structured English immersion* (Ovando, Collier, & Combs, 2003; Soltero, 2004), which is roughly modeled after the Canadian French-immersion programs for middle-class language-majority students (English speakers in Quebec). In the Canadian model, language-majority students who volunteer for the program receive all or part of their instruction in French for the first few years of schooling, and then at least 50% of their studies are conducted in English, their home language, up through secondary school (Genesee, 1987), and the goal is high bilingualism and biliteracy. In contrast, in the U.S. model, minority students who are limited English proficient are assigned to self-contained classrooms in which English is the only language of instruction. When students exit from the program, usually within one year of SEI, they enter mainstream classrooms where the remainder of their education is conducted through the English language. (See Hernández-Chávez, 1984, for a critical comparison of Canadian immersion with American SEI.) Although most structured immersion teachers are monolingual English speakers, a few are only functionally bilingual, but they tend to avoid using the students' home language in class for anything other than emergencies (Soltero, 2004). Home language use among students may be tolerated initially, but students are openly encouraged to use English for classroom interaction. Structured immersion students are taught the same subject matter content as their fully English-proficient peers in regular classrooms; however, much of the content is highly structured, lacking in rich language and literacy uses. Structured immersion teachers may adjust their vocabulary, discourse, and pacing to enhance comprehension so that students can understand the material and participate in classroom activities, but often the result is a watered-down curriculum that denies students high-quality education (Valdés, 2001).

Structured English immersion education is designed primarily for early elementary grades. At the higher grades of elementary school and at the secondary level, a variation of structured English immersion has developed under the name of *sheltered content teaching* (Echevarria & Graves, 2003; Faltis, 1993a). Only English learners attend sheltered content classes, where they do not have to compete with native speakers of English. Such classes enable English learners to study important subject matter because teachers use comprehension-oriented teaching methodology and teach students study skill strategies to prepare them for mainstream classes.

Finally, it is worth mentioning that a growing trend in states with large numbers of immigrant students from different language backgrounds is the introduction of Newcomer Centers, in which students who are new to U.S. schools and English are provided with instruction in English and support for navigating school. Typically students are assigned to Newcomer Centers for between 6 weeks and 6 months (Boyson & Short, 2003; Chang, 1990; Constantino & Lavadenz, 1993; Friedlander, 1991; McDonnell & Hill, 1993). The purpose of these centers is to ease newcomer students' transition into English and U.S. schooling practices and routines.

ENTRY, RECLASSIFICATION, AND EXIT CRITERIA

Let us now turn to the questions of who is eligible for special language instructional services, how and how often language proficiency is assessed, and when and how a student becomes ineligible for special language instruction services once the services have begun. Getting in and out of special language programs is largely determined by tests. Accordingly, it is important for us to learn how language test scores are used to determine program eligibility as well as program ineligibility. A more extensive discussion on assessment and evaluation is presented in Chapter 7.

You need to join forces with bilingual and ESL teachers as advocates for English learners to ensure that they are not exited from special language programs before they are ready for all-English instruction (Cazden, 1986; O'Malley & Pierce, 1996). The following section examines the kinds of procedures and tests that are commonly used for identifying eligible students, for assessing their language proficiency, for reclassifying them once they are in a program, and finally, for exiting them from the program. All of the tests that we examine are worthy of criticism; they can hardly be called authentic assessments of how students use language for communication with a variety of audiences. Nonetheless, we will learn about them and then look for other ways of making sense about how well students use language for oral and written communication.

Determining Program Eligibility

The *Lau* Remedies of 1974 made the identification of students whose primary language is not English and the evaluation of their English-language proficiency mandatory in all school districts. The first step in determining program eligibility is to identify students whose first language is not English. Most school districts in multilingual cities administer a survey to parents upon the enrollment of children in school. The survey commonly contains four questions:

1. Was your child's first language a language other than English?
2. Is a language other than English spoken in the home?
3. Is the language most often spoken by your child a language other than English?
4. Do you speak a language other than English to your child most of the time?

A parent's answer of "yes" to any of these four questions indicates that the student's primary home language is not English. Once this has been determined, the next step is to find out whether the student has limited English proficiency and thus, whether he or she is eligible for bilingual or English-only special language instruction.

The criteria for entering a special instructional program vary from state to state, but most states determine entry eligibility on the basis of oral English proficiency test scores, English reading test scores, and home language reading test scores (Canales, 1992; O'Malley & Pierce, 1996). The three most popular oral English proficiency tests are the Language Assessment Scales (LAS), the Bilingual Syntax Measure II (BSM), and the Language Assessment Battery (LAB). Other frequently used tests are the Basic Inventory of Natural Language (BINL) and the Individualized Developmental English Activities (IDEA) Placement Test (Samway & McKeon, 1999). A new assessment test for English learners gaining popularity nationwide is the Stanford English Language Proficiency (SELP) test developed by Harcourt Brace (2003). This test assesses oral and written abilities using pictures and language text and has versions for primary, elementary, middle, and high school students. The SELP test claims to be aligned with NCLB standards. The most commonly used standardized English reading tests are the Comprehensive Test of Basic Skills (CTBS) and the California Achievement Test (CAT). When available, schools most often choose the following non-English language standardized reading tests: the Spanish version of LAS and the Spanish version of BSM (Cardoza, 1986). Increasingly, schools are using a combination of proficiency and alternative assessment procedures to gauge language development and content learning (O'Malley & Pierce, 1996).

To get an idea of what oral English proficiency tests propose to measure and how they distinguish levels of proficiency, we will examine three popular tests, the LAS, the BSM, and the IDEA test, in greater detail. (For a review of all of the tests mentioned as well as many others, see Alderson, Krahnke, & Stansfield, 1987; and Samway & McKeon, 1999). All three of these tests have updated versions.

The Language Assessment Scales.   The LAS is an individually administered test that was developed by Edward DeAvila and Sharon Duncan in the late 1970s (McGroarty, 1987). There are two versions: LAS I for grades 2 through 5, and LAS II for grade 6 and up. Both versions measure oral language skills in English and in Spanish based on a student's performance on four linguistic subsystems, which include the sound system, vocabulary, syntax, and pragmatics (the ability to complete certain tasks in the language). Computer-based versions of the LAS are currently available. The sound system is assessed by having students indicate whether minimal pairs of words sound the same or different (30 items) and by having them repeat certain sounds of the language (36 items). Vocabulary is tested by having the student name items pictured in the test (20 items). Syntax is measured through two subscales—oral comprehension and oral production of a story presented on an audiocassette. The assessment of pragmatic ability is optional and consists of 10 questions that draw out the student's ability to use language for describing and narrating without the use of story props.

Students are assigned to one of five proficiency levels on the basis of total correct responses that are converted to weighted scores.

Level 1 indicates that the student is non-English-proficient (NEP). Level 2 is also non-English-proficient with some isolated language abilities. Level 3 students are designated as limited-English-proficient (LEP), while levels 4 and 5 mean that students are fully English proficient (FEP) and highly articulate, respectively. After reviewing the LAS tests, MacSwan (2000) asserts that "the test is so poorly designed that literally no conclusions regarding a child's linguistic abilities may be drawn" from any particular score.

The Bilingual Syntax Measure.   The BSM has two versions, one for K through 2 (BSM I) and one for grades 3 through 12 (BSM II). Developed by Marina Burt, Heidi Dulay, and Eduardo Hernández-Chávez in the mid- and late 1970s, both versions are individually administered (Cziko, 1987; Hayes-Brown, 1987). The BSM provides a direct measure of syntactic proficiency in Spanish or English by stimulating natural conversation through a structured interview. The student and the examiner engage in a conversation about a story depicted by the test's cartoon characters. Students are asked a total of 25 questions based on seven cartoon drawings. The examiner writes down each student response in the test booklet and later scores them as correct or incorrect according to whether the student has produced to target form in an obligatory instance.

The number of correct responses is used to determine proficiency level assignment. For BSM I there are five levels (Cziko, 1987): Level 1 (no English or Spanish); Level 2 (receptive English or Spanish only); Level 3 (survival English or Spanish); Level 4 (intermediate English or Spanish); and Level 5 (fully English or Spanish proficient—FEP). Levels 1 through 4 are considered to indicate limited English proficiency. BSM II has six levels (Hayes-Brown, 1987). As in BSM I, students scoring in Levels 1 through 4 are classified as limited-English-proficient (LEP). Level 5 can indicate either full English proficiency (FEP) or high limited English or Spanish proficiency, depending on school district policy (Hayes-Brown, 1987). Level 6 indicates native-like proficiency in English or Spanish.

The IDEA Placement Test.   The IPT was developed by Wanda Ballard and Phyllis Tighe in 1982. The test is designed to assess oral proficiency in English or Spanish for grades K through 6. Both the English and the Spanish versions consist of 83 items divided among the areas of vocabulary, syntax, comprehension, and verbal expression spread over seven proficiency levels (McCollum, 1987). Thirty-five items require students to respond to questions about figure drawings. The rest of the items measure the student's ability to (a) discriminate between minimal pairs, (b) respond to verbal commands, (c) retell a short story, (d) describe a common object, and (e) identify the main idea from a passage that is read to the student.

The IPT has seven levels of oral proficiency attainment, Levels A/B to F. Each level corresponds to a series of structured English-language lessons provided through the IDEA Language Program. Students answering fewer than 50% of the 12 items on Level B are automatically placed in Level A to work on language activities designed specifically for that level. For any level above Level B, students are assigned to the corresponding level when they are unable to answer correctly at least 80% of the items at that level (McCollum, 1987). The IPT uses NEP/LEP/FEP designations, and students are placed in bilingual or ESL programs if they are classified as either NEP or LEP. However, proficiency designations are tied directly to grade-level considerations so that higher levels are required for each of the designations as students progress through the grades. For example, 2nd-grade students who score at Level D might be considered to be fully English proficient. The same students in the 6th grade would need to complete Level F to be classified as FEP; Level D students could still be considered to be LEP.

All three of these tests are old (originally from the 1970s and 1980s) and, frankly, provide little information that is useful to teachers who are interested in how well children can use English to write and talk about things that interest them and about school-related topics. In addition to being old and less than useful, these test are problematic and limited in the following ways:

1. All three tests assume that children will perform in English when called on to do so. Children from different cultures respond differently to requests to answer questions to which the answers are already known. There are also differences in how children from different cultures respond to questions posed by unfamiliar adults. These tests, which are based on performance, do not take into account the effect of possible cultural differences in response. So, for example, if a child chooses not to label certain items or not to create a narrative from a sequence of pictures, the child may be labeled "not proficient." It may be, however, that the child has chosen not to talk because the test asks the child to use language in ways that violate the norms of the child's home and community.

2. Often the tests require specific answers for the child to receive credit for a response. If the child answers using words other than those expected, she or he may not receive credit for doing so and may again be mislabeled. For example, the IDEA test uses a picture of a man in a white coat holding a pair of scissors and asks the child looking at the picture: Who cuts your hair? The only acceptable answer is "a barber." However, many children from Mexican families answer "my father, my mother," because in their families hair is cut at home, not in a shop.

3. Given the ways that the tests are scored, some children may be labeled as not proficient either in English or their native language. (See Mac-Swan, 2000, for a discussion of this egregious and apparently widespread practice.) For example, many children who have to take the IDEA test and the LAS simply refuse to play the game and instead give no answer or respond with noncredited answers. These children often end up being mislabeled as "semilingual," having limited proficiency in both English and their native language.

4. The tests are based on monolingual norms of reference. Many children who are placed in bilingual classrooms have grown up in bilingual homes and communities in which two languages are heard and used for communication. The proficiency they acquire in the two languages and the ways in which they use their languages may be qualitatively and quantitatively different from that of monolingual speakers of each language. Accordingly, comparisons made between a bilingual

child's language abilities in two languages with monolinguals' use of each language may be inappropriate (Faltis & Hudelson, 1998; Grosjean, 1982).

In summary, these tests assess things that really don't count as speaking and writing in school settings. They assess how well children can respond to and pick out things that the test developers thought represented language proficiency. None of the tests present language as a whole system, one that cannot be fragmented into minimal pairs, sentence patterns, and recall formats. If you have to use any of these tests or ones like them (e.g., the BINL or the SELP), use them judiciously; look for additional, alternative ways of assessing language ability; inquire about home language abilities; and pay lots of attention to how children use language within diverse settings. In Chapter 7, you will be presented with a wide range of alternatives for assessing oral and written language abilities.

Reclassification and Exit Criteria

Reclassification refers to the practice of regularly assessing students to determine continued eligibility for language-related instructional assistance. Reclassification is used primarily in late-exit and maintenance bilingual programs. Accordingly, a student could be reclassified as fully English proficient (FEP) and still remain in the bilingual program as high up in grade level as the program goes. In transitional early-exit bilingual programs as well as in English-only programs, reclassifying a student as FEP usually means that the student is ready to exit out of the special program. In this manner, exiting and reclassification are not distinguished in a majority of cases (Cardoza, 1986).

Assessing students to determine continued eligibility is usually done once a year, in the final weeks of school. Most school districts assess English oral language proficiency as a part of their exit criteria, and most use the same tests employed for entry eligibility. The cutoff scores used for program exit are usually those recommended by the test publisher. When standardized English tests are used for exit purposes, there is considerable variation across states as to the cutoff percentile score used for discontinuing program eligibility (Ovando, Collier, & Combs, 2003). New York, for example, uses the 40th percentile. Arizona exits LEP students from programs when they score at or above the 36th percentile on a standardized English test. In Texas, students are exited from the program when they score between the 23rd and the 40th percentile on a standardized English test.

In addition to English oral proficiency testing, many school districts that have bilingual and/or ESL programs rely on other information to determine when to exit a student out of a program. Some districts, for example, make exit decisions for students in bilingual and ESL programs based on the following criteria: (1) teacher evaluation of the student's oral English-language proficiency; (2) assessment of oral English-language proficiency as measured by state-designated proficiency tests (LAS, BSM, IDEA; BINL or SELP); (3) assessment of writing ability as measured by teacher-scored writing samples or standardized tests; (4) assessment of English-language arts (spelling, punctuation, and reading comprehension); and (5) consultation with parents to ensure that final classification is appropriate. Most states that have multiple exit criteria, however, rely primarily on the first three areas of assessment (Samway & McKeon, 1999). Few states assess home language literacy as part of the exit battery of tests.

It is important to note that in recent years several states have begun to raise the cutoff scores for exit criteria based on the finding that nearly 40% of elementary students in programs with low exit cutoff scores required remediation after being placed in mainstream classes. In contrast, fewer than 20% of students in programs with exit cutoff scores at or above the 40th percentile required additional language remediation (Lee, 1989; Nadeau & Miramontes, 1988). The reason for raising the exit cutoff scores is to ensure that students are not exited prematurely, before they have developed the requisite language proficiency to progress in an English-only instructional setting.

In addition to standardized tests, many teachers have begun to use alternative assessment strategies for both fully proficient English-speaking and English-learning students. Chapter 7 presents an overview of alternative assessment, with suggestions on how to use multiple assessment plans and strategies to improve your teaching and students' learning.

The Teacher Next Door

After reading about bilingual education and English-as-a-second-language programs for English learners, Julia wonders even more deeply about what she will need to do in her class to ensure that her English learners will be able to participate in and benefit from classroom activities when she only speaks English. Back in her classroom, Julia thinks about ways that she can support the primary languages of children who are learning in and through English for most of their school day. One of the first actions she plans to take is to collect as many good children's books written in the languages of her English learners so that she can have them available for pleasure reading throughout the year.

As Julia is moving her two bookcases, someone knocks at the door. A woman saunters into her classroom and introduces herself, extending her hand to Julia. She is wearing a red baseball cap and a tee shirt that proclaims, "If you can read this, thank a teacher."

"I see that you are the new kid on the block. Name's Peggy, in case you are interested. My class is right next door. I am getting it ready for the next group of kids, second-graders. Oh Lord, I have a bunch of little guys from all over the Third World, those poor countries. I tell you, it is getting more like the United Nations at this school. Half of my students can't even talk English good."

"Well, nice to meet you too, I'm Julia Felix." *No, it is not nice. I can't believe what I just heard.* "Well, I happen to believe there's something *absolutely special* about every child, and having children from so many places; it makes for a more interesting learning environment," Julia replies as she steps forward to shake Peggy's hand. Peggy, with short reddish hair, and a bit on the plump side, is in her forties and has been teaching primary school for more than 15 years at this school. Julia continues unintimidated, "I have 10 students who are still learning English, and from what I have gathered about their schooling experiences, it is up to me to, you know, be creative and engaging, to make sure that they feel a part of everything that goes on in my class."

"Don't get me wrong, but most of these immigrant kids don't really want to learn English; they just hang on to their own culture stuff," Peg asserts. "Sometimes it really burns me that they talk their language, and I can't understand them. The Mexicans are the worst. What they really need is a strong dose of English because their parents don't seem to help much in that area," she declares with conviction.

"Wait a minute," replies Julia, somewhat stunned at Peggy's brutal candor, "there is nothing wrong with children speaking their own language while they are learning English. In fact, I have just been reading about the benefits of building a strong first language—how it really helps with learning English. That's the way I understand it." *Oh my God, is there an elephant in the room or what?*

"Humph, well, you'll see soon enough, young lady. You give 'em an inch and before you know it, they will claim they don't understand anything you say to them in English. You mark my words, when you get *my* students in your class, they will speak English only. I don't put up with that nonsense. Listen, Julie, is it? You're new and don't understand about how to deal with these immigrant kids. If you want any help on classroom management or reading programs, just let me know. I have loads of materials from Success for All and Steck-Vaughn. Come on over, but right now, I have to skedaddle. I am getting my nails done at 11:00. See you soon."

"It's *Julia,* not Julie. Thanks for your offer. I am sure I will see you around," says Julia, who is relieved to have Peggy leave. *I wouldn't subject my students to that stuff if you paid me. I can hardly believe what I just heard from that wicked woman. That is so wrong. I bet she is not a friend to bilingual education. At least, I know that my classroom will be a safe and fair place for children to learn, and if using their first language helps them, then I am going to encourage them in any way I can,* Julia thinks to herself.

CONCLUSION

This chapter presented a short history of the legal and political events that have influenced the development of bilingual and other forms of special language instruction for students who enter school speaking a language other than English. You were introduced to the ways in which bilingual education programs vary in terms of whether the home language is being maintained or lost and whether the languages of instruction are used concurrently or separately. Also presented were the various non-native-language instructional programs that serve increasing numbers of children who are learning English as an additional language. Knowing about these programs helps you gain an appreciation of the time and effort it takes to acquire enough English along with academic knowledge to be able to function without assistance in a grade-level all-English classroom. Finally, you read about the entry and exit criteria used in bilingual and English-as-a-second-language programs throughout the United States. Of particular importance to grade-level teachers is an understanding of the criteria used to determine when a student is ready for all-English instruction without continuation of special English-language instruction. You may have to join forces with other teachers to make sure that stu-

dents are not being pulled out of bilingual programs too quickly. Likewise, you need to be vigilant that they are not kept in an ESL program for too long, and that alternative ways of assessing readiness for all-English classes are taken into consideration. These may be battles you choose to fight.

In the case of Julia Felix, all 10 of the English learners in her class will continue to receive some kind of English-language help for 1 hour daily until the end of the school year, at which time their English proficiency and achievement will be evaluated for reclassification. Moreover, Julia will be making adjustments in her class to engage the students in myriad activities organized to ensure their participation using language and literacy to learn and inquire about what they are learning. Knowing this, and having reviewed the history and types of bilingual programs, Julia is now ready to begin organizing her classroom to ensure that she provides an optimal learning environment for all of her students, regardless of their oral and written English-language proficiency. Accordingly, in the next chapter, you will learn ways to organize the social and physical environment of classrooms in line with joinfostering principles.

ACTIVITIES

1. Read "Anatomy of the English-only Movement" online at **http://ourworld.compuserv.com/homepages/JWCRAWFORD/** **anatomy.htm** and "Language Politics in the USA: The Paradox of Bilingual Education" online at **http://ourworld.compuserv.com/**

homepages/**JWCRAWFORD**/ **paradox.htm**. Also visit the Web site of U.S. English at **www.us-english.org**. Divide the class into two groups to present a debate about the merits of English-only versus native-language approaches to bilingual education.

2. Observe and describe a bilingual classroom in which the teacher and students use a non-English language. Observe the class at least twice for no less than 1 hour each time. Note how students are physically arranged, whether student materials are displayed on the walls, and whether the teacher and the students primarily use one language or two for teaching and communication. Interview the teacher about his or her views on native-language instruction and concurrent vs. separate language use for teaching. Remember that any time you set foot on school grounds you need to check in at the main office before going to the classroom in which you plan to observe.

3. Observe and describe an English-as-a-second-language classroom, an ESL pullout class or a structured English Immersion classroom, following the instructions in activity 2. Talk with several of the students and ask them about their likes and dislikes, their hobbies, and their families. Find out whether and how their interests and hobbies are used as topics for learning in their classrooms. Remember that any time you set foot on school grounds you need

to check in at the main office before going to the classroom in which you plan to observe.

4. Explain the difference between an ESL credential and an ESL endorsement. If your state offers either or both or some variation of either (e.g., Structured English Immersion, English Language Development), summarize and compare the kinds of required coursework needed to obtain them. If your state offers a bilingual teaching credential, summarize the required coursework and then compare and contrast it with the ESL coursework. Write to a neighboring state's department of education and inquire about their ESL credential/endorsement and bilingual credential requirements. You might wish to consult Kreidler (1987), McKnight & Antinuez (1999) and ERIC document No. ED 400-86-0019 for some initial information and comparison data.

5. Following the lessons presented in Jacobson (1990), write out new lessons, using any content area to demonstrate the major ways of allocating language for instruction concurrently or separately. This activity requires individuals with fluency in two languages.

6. Invite the language testing specialist from your local school district to give an in-class demonstration of the kinds of assessment and other criteria used for bilingual or ESL program entry, reclassification, and exit.

7. Read Valdés (1997) about reservations she has concerning dual-language immersion bilingual programs. Provide an original summary of her main cautions and share with the entire class.

REFERENCES

Alderson, J. C., Krahnke, K. J., & Stansfield, C. W. (Eds.). (1987). *Reviews of English language proficiency tests.* Washington, DC: TESOL.

August, D., & García, E. (1988). *Language minority education in the United States.* Springfield, IL: Charles C. Thomas.

Avila, J. G., & Godoy, R. (1979). Bilingual/bicultural education and the law. In National Dissemination and Assessment Center (Ed.), *Language development in a bilingual setting* (pp. 15–33). Los Angeles: California State University.

Baker, C. (1988). *Key issues in bilingualism and bilingual education.* Clevedon, England: Multilingual Matters.

Baker, K. A., & de Kanter, A. A. (1981). *Effectiveness of bilingual education: A review of the literature.* Washington, DC: Office of Planning, Budget and Evaluation, U.S. Department of Education.

Bickle, K., Billings, E., & Hakuta, K. (2004). Trends in two-way immersion research. In J. Banks & C. M. Banks (Eds.), *Handbook of research on multicultural education* (2nd ed., pp. 589–604). San Francisco: Jossey-Bass.

Boyson, B., & Short, D. (2003). *Secondary school newcomer programs in the United States, Research Report #12.* Santa Cruz, CA: Center for Research on Education, Diversity & Excellence.

Canales, J. (1992). Innovative practices in the identification of LEP students. *Proceedings of the second National Research Symposium on limited English proficient student issues: Focus on evaluation and measurement,* Vol. 2 (pp. 89–122). Washington, DC: U.S. Department of Education.

Cardoza, D. (1986). The identification and reclassification of limited English proficient students: A study of entry and exit classification procedures. *NABE Journal, 11*(1), 21–45.

Castañeda v. Pickard, 648 F. 2d 989 (5th Circuit), 1981.

Cazden, C. (1986). ESL teachers as language advocates for children. In P. Rigg & D. S. Enright (Eds.). *Children and ESL: Integrating perspectives* (pp. 7–21). Washington, DC: TESOL.

Chang, H. (1990). *Newcomer programs: Innovative efforts to meet the educational challenges of immigrant students.* San Francisco, CA: California Tomorrow.

Christian, D. (1994). *Two-way bilingual education: Students learning through two languages.* Washington, DC: Center for Applied Logistics.

Christian, D., Montone, C., Lindholm, K., & Carranza, I. (1997). *Profiles in two-way immersion education.* Washington, DC: Center for Applied Linguistics.

Cloud, N., Genesee, F., & Hamayan, E. (2000). *Dual language instruction: A handbook for enriched education.* Boston: Heinle & Heinle.

Constantino, R., & Lavadenz, M. (1993). Newcomer schools: First impressions. *Peabody Journal of Education, 69*(1), 82–101.

Court limits bilingual education. (1999, September 28). *The San Francisco Chronicle*, pp. A17, A24.

Crawford, J. (1999). *Bilingual education: History, politics, theory and practice*. Los Angeles: Bilingual Education Services.

Cummins, J. (1979). Linguistic interdependence of the educational development of bilingual children. *Review of Educational Research, 19*, 222–251.

Cziko, G. (1987). Bilingual syntax measure I. In J. C. Alderson, K. J. Krahnke, & C. W. Stanfield, (Eds.), *Reviews of English language proficiency tests* (pp. 12–14). Washington, DC: TESOL.

Daniels, H. A. (1990). *Not only English: Affirming America's multicultural heritage*. Urbana, IL: NCTE.

Delgado-Gaitán, C. (1991). Relating experience and text: Socially constituted reading activity. In M. McGroarty & C. Faltis (Eds.), *Languages in school and society: Policy and pedagogy* (pp. 512–528). Berlin: Mouton de Gruyter.

Echevarria, J., & Graves, A. (2003). *Sheltered content instruction: Teaching English language learners with diverse abilities*. Boston, MA: Allyn & Bacon.

Faltis, C. (1989). Code-switching and bilingual schooling: An examination of Jacobson's new concurrent approach. *Journal of Multilingual and Multicultural Development, 10*(2), 117–127.

Faltis, C. (1990). New directions in bilingual research design: The study of interactive decision making. In R. Jacobson & C. Faltis (Eds.), *Language distribution issues in bilingual schooling* (pp. 45–57). Clevedon, England: Multilingual Matters.

Faltis, C. (1993a). Critical issues in the use of sheltered content teaching in high school bilingual programs. *Peabody Journal of Education, 69*(1), 136–151.

Faltis, C. (1993b). From kindergarten to high school: Teaching and learning English as a second language in the U.S. In S. Silberstein (Ed.), *State of the art TESOL essays: Celebrating 25 years of the discipline* (pp. 91–114). Alexandria, VA: TESOL.

Faltis, C., & Hudelson, S. (1998). *Bilingual education in elementary and secondary school communities*. Needham Heights, MA: Allyn & Bacon.

Feinberg, R. (2000). Newcomer schools: Salvation or segregated oblivion for immigrant students? *Theory into Practice, 39*(4), 20–227.

Flores v. State of Arizona, 48 Federal Supplement 2d 937 (D. Ariz. 2001).

French, R. (1992). Portfolio assessment and LEP students. In *Proceedings of the second National Research Symposium on limited English proficient student issues: Focus on evaluation and measurement*, Vol. 1 (pp. 249–272). Washington, DC: U.S. Department of Education.

Friedlander, M. (1991). *The newcomer program: Helping immigrant students succeed in U.S. schools*. Washington, DC: National Clearinghouse for Bilingual Education.

Genesee, F. (1987). *Learning through two languages: Studies of immersion and bilingual education*. New York: Newbury House.

Gottlieb, M. (1995). Nurturing student learning through portfolios. *TESOL Journal, 5*(1), 12–14.

Grosjean, F. (1982). *Life with two languages: An introduction to bilingualism*. Cambridge: Harvard University Press.

Haas, E., & Poyner, L. (2003). What does "sound educational theory" mean for the rights of English language learners? A review of case law and statutes from *Lau* to *Valeria G.* Savannah, GA: Education Law Association 49th Annual Conference paper.

Hakuta, K. (1986). *Mirror of language: The debate on bilingualism.* New York: Basic Books.

Halcón, J. J. (1983). A structural profile of basic Title VII (Spanish–English) bilingual bicultural education programs. *NABE Journal, 7*(3), 55–73.

Harcourt-Brace Assessment. (2003). *Stanford English language proficiency test.* San Antonio, TX: Author.

Hayes-Brown, Z. (1987). Bilingual syntax measure II. In J. C. Alderson, K. J. Krahnke, & C. W. Stanfield, (Eds.), *Reviews of English language proficiency tests* (pp. 14–17). Washington, DC: TESOL.

Hernández-Chávez, E. (1984). The inadequacy of English immersion education as an educational approach for language minority students in the United States. In California State Department of Education (Ed.), *Studies on immersion education* (pp. 144–183). Sacramento, CA: California State Department of Education.

Hornberger, N. (1991). Extending enrichment bilingual education: Revisiting typologies and redirecting policy. In O. García (Ed.), *Bilingual education: Focusschrift in honor of Joshua A. Fishman* (pp. 215–234). Philadelphia: John Benjamins.

Jacobs, J. F., & Pierce, M. L. (1966). Bilingualism and creativity. *Elementary English, 43,* 1390–1400.

Jacobson, R. (1982). The implementation of a bilingual instructional model—The new concurrent approach. In R. Padilla (Ed.), *Ethnoperspectives in bilingual education research,* Vol. III (pp. 14–29). Ypsilanti, MI: Eastern Michigan University.

Jacobson, R. (1990). Allocating two languages as a key feature of a bilingual methodology. In R. Jacobson & C. Faltis (Eds.), *Language distribution issues in bilingual schooling* (pp. 3–17). Clevedon, England: Multilingual Matters.

Judd, E. L. (1978). *Factors affecting the passage of the Bilingual Education Act of 1967.* Doctoral dissertation. New York University.

Keyes v. School District No. 1, 576 Federal Supplement 1503, 1516–1518 (District of Colorado, 1983).

Krashen, S., & Biber, D. (1988). *On course: Bilingual education's success in California.* Sacramento, CA: California Association for Bilingual Education.

Kreidler, C. (1987). *ESL teacher education.* Washington, DC: Center for Applied Linguistics.

Lambert, W. E., & Peal, E. (1962). The relationship of bilingualism to intelligence. *Psychological Monographs, 76,* 1–23.

Lau v. Nichols, 414 U.S. 563 (1974).

Lee, E. (1989). Chinese American fluent English proficient students and school achievement. *NABE Journal, 13*(2), 95–111.

Lindholm-Leary, K., (2000). *Biliteracy for a global society: An idea book on dual language education.* Washington, DC: The George Washington University.

Lindholm, K. (1990). Bilingual immersion education: Criteria for program development. In A. M. Padilla, H. H. Fairchild, & C. M. Valadez (Eds.), *Bilingual education: Issues and strategies* (pp. 91–105). Newbury Park, CA: Sage.

Mackey, W. F., & Beebe, V. N. (1977). *Bilingual schools for a bicultural community: Miami's adaptation to the Cuban refugees.* Rowley, MA: Newbury House.

MacSwan, J. (2000). The threshold hypothesis, semilingualism, and other contributions to a deficit view of linguistic minorities. *Hispanic Journal of Behavioral Sciences, 22*(1), 3–45.

Malakoff, M., & Hakuta, K. (1990). History of language minority education in the United States. In A. M. Padilla, H. H. Fairchild, & C. M. Valadez (Eds.),

Bilingual education: Issues and strategies (pp. 27–44). Newbury Park, CA: Sage.

McCollum, P. (1987). IDEA oral language proficiency test. In J. C. Alderson, K. J. Krahnke, & C. W. Stanfield, (Eds.), *Reviews of English language proficiency tests* (pp. 37–39). Washington, DC: TESOL.

McDonnell, L., & Hill, P. (1993). *Newcomers in American schools: Meeting the educational needs of immigrant youth.* Santa Monica, CA: RAND.

McFadden, B. J. (1983). Bilingual education and the law. *Journal of Law and Education, 12*(1), 1–27.

McGroarty, M. (1987). Language assessment scales. In J. C. Alderson, K. J. Krahnke, & C. W. Stanfield, (Eds.), *Reviews of English language proficiency tests* (pp. 51–53). Washington, DC: TESOL.

McKnight, A., & Antinuez, B. (1999). State survey of legislative requirements for educating limited English proficient students. Washington, DC: National Clearinghouse for Bilingual Education.

Milk, R. (1986). The issue of language separation in bilingual methodology. In E. García & B. Flores (Eds.), *Language and literacy research in bilingual education* (pp. 67–86). Tempe, AZ: Arizona State University Press.

Moll, L., & Díaz, E. (1985). *Ethnographic pedagogy: Promoting effective bilingual instruction.* In E. García & R. Padilla (Eds.), *Advances in bilingual education research* (pp. 127–149), Tucson, AZ: University of Arizona Press.

Morgan, B. (1992/93). Teaching the Gulf War in an ESL classroom. *TESOL Journal, 2*(2), 13–17.

Nadeau, A., & Miramontes, O. (1988). The reclassification of limited English proficient students: Assessing the inter-relationship of selected variables. *NABE Journal, 12*(3), 219–242.

O'Malley, J. M., & Pierce, L. V. (1996). *Authentic assessment for English language learners.* New York: Longman.

Ovando, C., Collier, V., & Combs, M. C. (2003). Bilingual and ESL classrooms: Teaching in multicultural contexts. Boston, MA: Allyn & Bacon.

Padilla, A. M. (1990). Bilingual education: Issues and perspectives. In A. M. Padilla, H. H. Fairchild, & C. M. Valadez (Eds.), *Bilingual education: Issues and strategies* (pp. 15–26). Newbury Park, CA: Sage.

Pottinger, J. S. (1970). Memorandum, Department of Health, Education, and Welfare, May 25, 1970.

Public Law No. 107–110. 115 Statute 1425 (No Child Left Behind).

Ramírez, J. D., & Merino, B. (1990). Classroom talk in English immersion, early-exit and late-exit transitional bilingual education programs. In R. Jacobson & C. Faltis (Eds.), *Language distribution issues in bilingual schooling* (pp. 61–103). Clevedon, England: Multilingual Matters.

Ramírez, J. D., Yuen, S. D., & Ramey, D. R. (1991). *Longitudinal study of structured English immersion strategy, early-exit and late-exit transitional bilingual education programs for language-minority children. Final report to the U.S. Department of Education. Executive Summary and Vols. I and II.* San Mateo, CA: Aguirre International.

Richard-Amato, P. (1988). *Making it happen: Interaction in the second language classroom.* New York: Longman.

Rodríguez, R. (1990, July 1). Escasez de maestros bilingües en una etapa crítica [A paucity of bilingual teachers in a critical period]. Los Angeles: *La Opinión,* 5.

Rosier, P., & Holm, W. (1980). *The Rock Point experience: A longitudinal study of Navajo school programs.* Washington, DC: Center for Applied Linguistics.

Rossell, C. H. (1989). The effectiveness of educational alternatives for limited English proficient children. In G. Imhoff (Ed.), *The social and cultural context of instruction in two languages: From conflict and controversy to cooperative reorganization of schools.* New York: Transaction Books.

Samway, K. D., & McKeon, D. (1999). *Myths and realities: Best practices for language minority students.* Portsmouth, NH: Heinemann.

Sánchez, K., & Walker de Felix, J. (1986). Second language teachers' abilities: Some equity concerns. *Journal of Educational Equity and Leadership, 6*(4), 313–321.

Saville, M., & Troike, R. C. (1971). *Handbook of bilingual education.* Washington, DC: TESOL.

Schneider, S. G. (1976). *Revolution, reaction or reform: The 1974 Bilingual Education Act.* New York: Las Americas.

Serna v. Portales Municipal Schools, 351 Federal Supplement, 1279 (D.N.M. 1972). Affidavit, 499 F.2d 1147 (10th Circuit 1974).

Smolen, L., Newman, C., Wathen, T., & Lee, D. (1995). Developing student self-assessment strategies. *TESOL Journal, 5*(1), 22–27.

Soltero, D. (2004). *Dual language: Teaching and learning in two languages.* Boston: Allyn & Bacon.

Stein, C. B. (1986). *Sink or swim, the politics of bilingual education.* New York: Praeger.

Teresa P. et al. v. Berkeley Unified School District et al. (1989). U.S. District Court Case for the Northern District of California, Case No. C-87-2396-DLJ.

Valdés, G. (1997). Dual-language immersion programs: A cautionary note concerning the education of language-minority students. *Harvard Educational Review, 67*(3), 391–427.

Walton, A. L. (1989). *Exit criteria for limited English proficient students: A memorandum to the honorable members of the Board of Regents, The University of the State of New York, Albany.* Albany, NY: The State Department of Education.

Willig, A. (1985). A meta-analysis of selected studies on the effectiveness of bilingual education. *Review of Educational Research, 55,* 269–317.

Willig, A. (1987). Examining bilingual education research through meta-analysis and narrative review: A response to Baker. *Review of Educational Research, 55,* 363–376.

Wong Fillmore, L., & Valadez, C. (1986). Teaching bilingual learners. In M. C. Wittrock (Ed.), *Handbook of research on teaching* (3rd ed., pp. 648–685). New York: Macmillan.

Yates, J. R., & Ortiz, A. A. (1983). Baker-de Kanter review: Inappropriate conclusions on the efficacy of bilingual education. *NABE Journal, 7*(3), 75–84.

Zentella, C. (1997). *Growing up bilingual.* Oxford, England: Blackwell.`

3

Arranging the All-English Classroom Environment for Active Participation and Social Integration

OVERVIEW

The bulk of what and how children learn in school takes place inside the four walls of the classroom. Within this physical setting, the teacher is solely responsible for organizing the environment so that students have multiple opportunities to participate and have some control over the selection of topics, the ways of interacting with peers, and the audiences with whom they talk and write. In linguistically diverse all-English classrooms, this responsibility is especially important because English learners can easily be left out of decisions about topic selection, interaction exchanges, and types of audiences. English learners need to hear and use English to talk about topics that interest them and to participate in academic discourses to develop high levels of social and academic proficiency in English (Faltis & Hudelson, 1998). As teachers, we need to organize the classroom environment so that second-language students have opportunities for social interaction about many topics with the teacher, their native English-speaking classmates, and among themselves in the three major social and academic learning contexts that support language (including literacy) and content learning:

1. Teacher-led whole-class teaching, interaction, and inquiry

2. Teacher-led small-group teaching, interaction, and inquiry

3. Teacher-delegated small-group projects in which students interact and work together on their own

Organizing the classroom so that students experience these three major social and learning contexts helps ensure that not only are we meeting a wide range of cultural preferences and individual learning needs, but also that we are paying attention to the distribution of resources students need to participate actively across all three contexts. Accomplishing this goal requires an agreed-upon set of classroom norms for interaction, classroom movement, and sharing ideas and a physical arrangement of the classroom that permits students to interact, move around, and share ideas by talking, writing, listening, reading, and working to-

gether. The focus of this chapter will be on how to organize the social environment—how students participate in social and academic learning—and to support the physical environment—the classroom furniture, pathways, learning space, and distribution of learning resources and materials—so that students can successfully be a part of all three social contexts and, in addition, have opportunities for individual reading, writing, and thinking about ideas and information presented and discussed in small-group work (Charney, 1992; Ostrow, 1995). Let's begin by looking into Julia's classroom as she prepares it for her opening day.

Episode Three: Social Interaction, Sharing, and the Physical Environment

With the start of the school year less than 2 weeks away, Julia anxiously begins the process of organizing and decorating her classroom. She has somewhat of an idea of how she wants it to be, but she's having trouble figuring out exactly how to arrange the furniture to match the images. Moreover, as a new teacher she is a little worried that her plans are going to diverge too much from what teachers in neighboring classrooms have already done: These teachers have either placed student desks in rows or have placed chairs at a table so there is no room for students to sit comfortably on the floor during certain times of the day. The teacher's desk, now Julia's, is located in the front of the room, slightly off to the side. The computers are placed against the wall in the back of the room, one right next to the other. *This is pretty much how someone left her room from the year before! This arrangement doesn't feel right at all,* Julia thinks to herself, *and I'm going to figure out how to fix it so that it represents what I have in mind.* She desires a more integrated classroom, one in which students will be moving around the room throughout the day, at times working in pairs and small groups, and at other times as a whole class. She also wants to have ample space set aside for individual reading, writing, thinking, and practice time, places where students can settle in for comfortable learning and when necessary feel a sense of personal ownership of their work space. *In my class, students will be engaged in a wide range of reading and writing and talking activities, that's for sure. I also plan to have an author's corner where I read them the best children's stories I can find . . . and where they read and share their stories with the class.*

Julia has a passion for art. Since she was very young, she has loved drawing, oil painting, and working on crafts. In college, Julia made a little extra money selling silver jewelry, mostly earrings and bracelets and, on occasion, a painting or two. Now she wants artwork and decorations to abound in her classroom. She wants them to be unconventional and for the most part to be works that the students create. In her student-teaching classroom, there were all kinds of odd, but appealing *objets d'art* around the room, and the children loved that. In her room, Julia wants designs and pictures hanging from the ceiling, posters dotting the walls, and special locations devoted to highlighting storybooks, community and inquiry projects, and multicultural events. But most of all, she wants the room to be a setting that offers purpose for learning, captures students' interests, and allows for both planned and spontaneous uses of language and literacy throughout the day. *There is ample space for me to display a few posters and some of my paintings, but I want to reserve most of the space I have to highlight the students' work.*

Julia decides that one of her first tasks should be to consider how to arrange the desks, including her own, as well as the few tables and chairs so that students can move around freely, interact verbally, and collaborate socially. *This is going to be quite cumbersome to re-arrange all these desks. I wish I had tables instead. But then, I would still need some help moving them. Let's see. . . .* She plans to tackle the decorations and related stuff later, after she figures out how to arrange the room. She remembers talking about how to arrange the classroom with her cooperating teacher during her student teaching experience, but didn't accord it much importance at the time. She recalls her cooperating teacher mentioning how important it is to begin by visualizing which parts of the room will be used for student activities and which parts will be associated with teacher space. *I need to figure out how to see this place the way the kids might, from their eyes.* So before attempting to move anything, she goes to the chalkboard and begins sketching out a diagram of her room, including all of the fixed and movable furniture.

Just as Julia is about to finish the drawing, she hears an unfamiliar voice coming from the side classroom door. In the doorframe stands a tall man with short brown hair, long sideburns, and wire-rimmed glasses. His black tee shirt says *Carpe Diem* with translations of that expression in 10 different languages. "How's it going? I'm Rudy Jacobson; I'm a bilingual teacher. Thought I'd stop by and introduce myself. Most people call me Jake." *Hmmm, this guy looks pretty cool. My room is a mess. But who cares? I am going to re-design it to my liking.* Jake is beginning his fourth year as a bilingual teacher at Bruner Elementary. Reared in an English-speaking family in northern California, Jake also speaks and writes Spanish fluently and knows enough words and phrases in Vietnamese and Chinese to interact a bit with students who speak these languages. Jake lived in Mexico as a child, attending schools in Hermosillo, Sonora, and Mexico City up to the sixth grade before returning to the States.

With the back of her left hand, Julia wipes her forehead and wisps several strands of her auburn hair away. She simultaneously extends her right hand to Jake and says, "A pleasure to meet you, Jake. I'm Julia Felix. Your class is down by the cafeteria, isn't it?" *I hope I have this right, or am I thinking of some other teacher I met in the main office?* "Did you know that I have a bunch of bilingual students in my class, 10 to be exact?"

"Sure do, and you know what? They're all extraordinary children; they'll add a lot to your class," Jake replies. "Little Aucenio knows more about baseball than I do, and Xiacoung can draw animals with incredible detail." *This girl has got to be new; she looks like she is right off the college boat. She is going to have her work cut out for her with so many kids who are still learning English.*

"Have you ever taught in a class with children who are becoming bilingual and biliterate, right before your eyes?" Jake queries, almost singing the end of his question.

"Uh, not exactly, but I think my personal stance about teaching and learning is sufficiently strong to guide me while I learn what I need to know," she replies, feeling somewhat defensive.

Jake senses her discomfort. "That's encouraging to hear." *I hope she believes me about these kids. She seems to be genuinely concerned, but I am gonna wait and see. She might end up being like Peggy next door.* He cautions Julia that it may take a little time for the children to become attuned and adjusted to an all-English class after having spent the summer speaking and playing almost exclusively in the language they affiliate with most outside of school. Explaining that a "silent period" is common among second-language children and that the period varies for each child, Jake assures Julia that if she pays attention to how well children are attending to lessons throughout the day, she will see that they will join in and participate right along with their peers.

Turning toward the door, Jake bids Julia good-bye and wishes her well with a thumbs-up sign: "I look forward to working with you, Julia. If there's anything I can do for you, let me know." *I really mean that, Julia.*

Julia senses that Jake, cocky as he might be, will probably be a valuable source of help during the year. *I can't let him leave without picking his brain a bit about how to arrange my room. This guy seems to really know lots about working with kids that are learning English, and his approach seems to resonate well with mine.*

"That's really thoughtful—thanks, Jake. You're totally lucky to be able to understand and talk with most of the kids." *Well here it goes.* "Hey, before you leave, ah, any chance that you could help me out a bit? I'm in a quandary about how to organize the furniture—you know, the desks, computers, and bookcases — in my classroom. It's important to me that the children get to talk, you know, ask questions, and write lots each day. Plus, I want them to work in small groups throughout the day. But the thing is that I also want to be able to teach to the class as a whole group lots of times as well because I like to use PowerPoint™ and pictures and stuff like that."

Julia goes on to explain some of her ideas and concerns about how she wants to arrange the classroom and about how she plans to place the English learners with native English students for small-group work. She also mentions that she needs special places for her African Emperor scorpion (nonpoisonous) and her two guinea pigs, Marcel and Norman. *I wonder if he thinks I'm a little weird for having these pets.*

"Wow, I can't wait to meet all your animals." *They ought to liven up the classroom.* "Tell you what, Julia, I can see that your classroom is going to be an exciting place for your students to participate in learning. It sounds to me like you know what you're doing. All I would say is when you think about where you're going to place the furniture and desks and stuff, try to think about pathways and where the learning materials might go." *Kids need space to move around and also to feel connected to a place in the room.* "Also, it is easy for the class to become unmanageable — out of control — if you don't have some way to let the kids know what's cool to do and what not to do when they are talking, sharing, walking around, and working together. The kids need to have an agreed-upon way of being students so that they can talk, move around and try out language without being disruptive and disrespectful to you and their classmates. One of the rules I insist upon is that you can't say to other students that they can't share or contribute ideas. And about the critters, I'd put them where they'll be easy to watch."

My thoughts, too, Julia thought.

Jake decides to stay a few minutes longer to exchange ideas with Julia about how to organize her classroom in line with what she has planned for her students. Together they conclude that whatever physical arrangement Julia ultimately designs, it must be supported by social norms of participation that allow her and the students to share in the decisions about opportunities for social interaction, movement, and the development of topics for learning. Jake and Julia say good-bye for now, but you can be sure that they will talk again. They each silently hope for that too. Let's learn about their ideas now, but first, let's contrast them with what many elementary classrooms in the United States look like. This will help us affirm what we don't want our classrooms to be like!

THE ORGANIZATION OF MANY U.S. CLASSROOMS

The physical and social arrangement of classroom life in the majority of American public schools has been remarkably consistent across time and space. Today's classrooms hardly vary at all from classrooms found in the beginning of the last century. Classrooms in the city are extraordinarily similar in their physical layout and social organization to classrooms in rural areas. The social and physical patterns of interaction of classrooms in big schools resemble those found in classrooms in small schools. The classrooms that the children of the wealthy attend are organized and run pretty much the same way as those attended by the children of the poor. Life in bilingual classrooms is virtually indistinguishable from what takes place in all-English classrooms.

In the following two sections, we will discover how most classrooms are arranged for instruction by paying attention to the ways talk, movement, sharing, and literacy are managed in the classroom. The amount and quality of social interaction, physical movement and authentic literacy activities in the classroom are a reliable indication of how teachers organize classrooms for learning. For example, if teachers do virtually all of the talking, and student talk and writing is restricted to short, factual responses from their desk spaces, we can assume that the physical environment is organized to block two-way communication between the teacher and the students and among the students. Whenever possible, direct reference will be made to the physical arrangement of the classroom; when this information is not available, we will be drawing inferences about how classrooms are organized on the basis of the nature of classroom talk.

All-English Classrooms

Furst and Amidon (1962) were among the first to conduct a nationwide study on social interaction in U.S. classrooms. They observed social interaction in 160 1st- through 6th-grade classrooms in low-socioeconomic urban, middle-socioeconomic urban, and suburban elementary schools. They found that most teachers taught to the entire class and that teachers did most of the talking. Within whole-class instruction, the student talk that did occur was brief and usually related to what the teacher had already presented. One of the more interesting findings was that student talk during whole-class instruction tended to decline as students progressed through the grades, decreasing from a high of 39% in the primary grades to 27% in the upper elementary grades. Furst and Amidon also reported that the prevailing interaction pattern characteristic of the upper elementary grades was fairly well established by the 3rd grade. Accordingly, in the 3rd grade they found a marked increase in teacher talk and corresponding decrease in student-generated ideas. The nature of teacher talk also changed, with a greater proportion of it now devoted to giving instructions. Students also received less teacher praise for their contributions, which by this time were expected to be short and already known by the teacher. In short, students talk quantitatively and qualitatively less.

Some 20 years later, Sirotnik (1983), in an equally ambitious nationwide study involving 129 elementary school all-English classrooms, found that students spent about 70% of their time in class listening to the teacher, who taught mostly to the class as a whole group. Verbal interaction with students in this setting most frequently entailed asking for and answering known information, factual questions. Nearly all of the classrooms had a combination of fixed and movable chairs, but students were almost never observed talking or working together on learning tasks. Fewer than half of the classrooms had separate learning centers that had been arranged by the teacher. Although a majority of the classrooms had some alteration of the physical environment, the alteration mainly consisted of having plants, area rugs, and unusual bulletin boards. Summarizing the findings, Sirotnik (1983) offered the following dismal image of the typical all-English elementary classroom:

> Consider again the model classroom picture presented here: a lot of teacher talk and a lot of student listening, unless students are responding to teachers' questions or working on written assignments; almost invariably closed and factual questions; little corrective feedback and no guidance; and predominately total class instructional configurations around traditional activities—all in a virtually affectless environment. (p. 29)

Both this and the depiction of the typical all-English classroom given by Furst and Amidon are prime examples of what Paulo Freire (1970) refers to as the *banking concept* of education, in which the teacher as holder of knowledge presents information as deposits to students. Both depictions exemplify a pedagogical pattern that has persisted in U.S. education since the turn of the last century. According to Kliebard (1989), who refers to this preferred pattern as *recitation education*, it is a manner of instruction based on the control of knowledge through a pattern of social interaction that restricts student talk. It occurs primarily in classrooms where teachers decide which, when, and how much students will talk. Kliebard suggests that the reason the recitation mode of instruction is so persistent in U.S. classrooms has to do with the need for keeping order. As Kliebard (1989) explains:

> The teacher as question-asker and the student as responder is a way of ensuring teacher dominance in the classroom situation. If students asked the questions or if they addressed one another rather than the teacher or if they engaged independently in discovery practices, the risk of disorder would be introduced, and the structure of school organization will not tolerate that kind of risk. (p. 10)

In recitation-oriented classrooms, teaching is perceived as unidirectional, from the teacher to the students, and students are essentially denied the use of language to mediate social and academic learning. This environment is especially detrimental to English learners for three reasons: First, it denies them access to language that is geared to their needs; second, it restricts the context of learning to the teacher-led whole class; and third, because interaction occurs mainly with the teacher, English learners may come to speak like their teachers, rather than like classroom peers. Figure 3.1 illustrates a recitation-oriented classroom.

To summarize up to this point, many all-English classrooms are typically arranged so that the bulk of teaching occurs in a whole-class "no talking" environment (Enright & McCloskey, 1985). The arrangement of furniture and space in this prevailing environment is easy to imagine. Student desks, though movable, are placed in stationary positions, facing forward toward the front of the class, often for the duration of the year. There is well-defined "teacher space" and "student space." Teacher space consists of a U-shaped area covering about one-third of the classroom; it includes the teacher's desk, perhaps an extra table, a bookshelf, and a storage area. Student space is the part of the classroom containing the students' desks and perhaps the computer area. Students are expected to do most of their seatwork in this space. Moving into teacher space or out of student space (e.g., to go to the bathroom, to sharpen a pencil, to consult a resource book) ordinarily requires permission from the teacher. The rule is for students to stay at their own desks or seats; they are not to move unless the teacher gives permission. Moreover, social interaction within the student space is teacher-controlled. Student-to-student communicative exchanges within the student space are discouraged because, as Kliebard (1989) reminds us, this would increase the risk of creating disorder in the classroom. Accordingly, another rule operating in this kind of environment is for students not to copy one another's written or spoken language.

Another well-established use for student space within the all-English classroom just described is to have students work individually, especially immediately following whole-class instruction (DeVillar & Faltis, 1991). This practice has come into favor over the past 20 years ostensibly as a means to address individual differences in learning aptitudes and learning styles. Goodlad (1984) reported, however, that teachers rarely customize learning materials for individual seatwork, because all tasks assigned to students for individual completion were essentially identical. Thus, individualized instruction amounts to little more than seatwork in which students complete prefabricated worksheets and other forms of ersatz busywork. More important, however, is the fact that individualized instruction requires students to

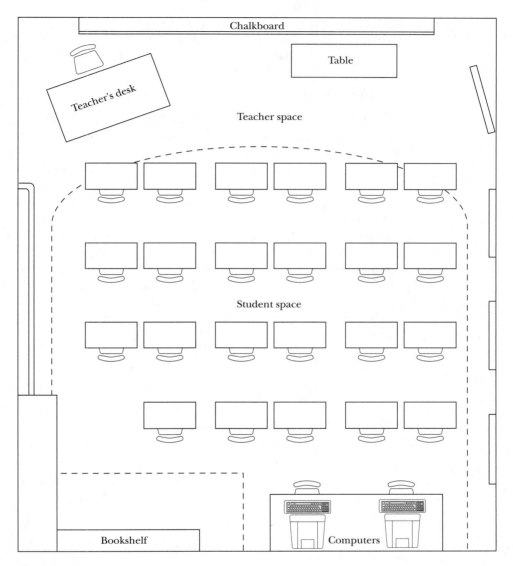

Figure 3.1
Teacher space and student space in a recitation-oriented classroom

be working alone at their seats or desks. Accordingly, this particular practice offers little opportunity for communicative exchange of information for students who are learning English as a second language. Taken together, these practices and classroom rules deny English learners access to a wide range of ongoing activity, information, resources for learning, and opportunities for participation, all of which are necessary for students to identify with and become members of classroom communities of practice.

Bilingual/English-as-a-Second-Language Classrooms

So far, we have considered only the typical all-English classroom. What about bilingual and English-as-a-second-language classrooms, where conscious attention is paid to assisting English-language development while students learn academic content? Are these classrooms arranged any differently to accommodate the language and cultural needs of the students in them? Ramírez and Merino (1990) investigated the nature of classroom interaction in three types of bilingual education program models: (a) structured English immersion, (b) early-exit transitional bilingual, and (c) late-exit transitional bilingual. (See Chapter 2 for descriptions of these program types.) Using a systematic observation instrument, they observed social interaction in 103 1st- and 2nd-grade classrooms at eight sites in California, Florida, New Jersey, New York, and Texas. Their findings indicated the following patterns of interaction and classroom organization across programs and grades:

1. Instruction was conducted mainly in large groups, typically in a whole-class setting
2. Teachers generated two to three times more talk than students
3. More than 75% of student-initiated utterances were made in response to teacher initiations
4. Student interactions with teachers were mainly for the purpose of providing expected responses
5. Less than 10% of student-initiated language was in the form of a free response or a free comment, not controlled by the teacher

These findings are strikingly similar to the patterns of little student talk and the use of whole-group instruction generally found in all-English mainstream classrooms. Ramírez and Merino (1990) suggest that students' language abilities coupled with cultural rules governing the appropriateness of talk could have contributed to the low incidence of student talk. However, it seems more plausible that the physical and social arrangements of the classrooms were largely responsible for the limited occurrence of authentic communication among students of varying language proficiency.

In summary, the majority of both all-English and bilingual/ESL classrooms are essentially one-dimensional, teacher-controlled social and physical learning environments. In this kind of environment, students have little say in determining classroom content or in using authentic language to communicate ideas with the teacher or peers. Students are expected to stay at the desks and not share ideas or materials with peers. Teachers typically rely on the whole class as the chief physical environment for teaching, virtually excluding the contexts of teacher-led small-group teaching and small-group learning from their teaching repertoire. Thus, neither the all-English nor the bilingual/ESL classrooms appear to accommodate socially or physically the language and/or educational needs of students in the process of acquiring English as a second language. This way of organizing classrooms for learning is the rule rather than the exception.

PLANNING A CLASSROOM TO PROMOTE JOINFOSTERING PRINCIPLES OF PRACTICE

In a classroom organized to promote joinfostering principles of practice, the social and physical environment must allow students of varying English-language proficiency to interact meaningfully with the teacher and with peers (ACTIVE PARTICIPATION; SOCIAL INTEGRATION TO FACILITATE THE CREATION OF NEW IDENTITIES AND SOCIOACADEMIC AFFILIATIONS). The pattern of studentless talk found in most classrooms is often a direct result of a social environment that curbs student participation and a physical arrangement that divides the room into teacher space and individual student space, with restrictions placed on student movement and student sharing. In this kind of classroom environment, there are few opportunities for students to exchange ideas or to present different points of view. In short, students are prohibited from communicating authentically about topics that matter to them or from engaging in practices that enable them to identify and affiliate with members of a community of practice. This pattern may also prevent some students from interacting in ways that are culturally familiar to them (Trueba & Delgado-Gaitán, 1983).

In planning a classroom based on joinfostering principles, we need to consider the social and physical environments in tandem, because each contributes to the efficacy of the other. The social environment concerns the ways students participate in social interaction throughout the day. Organizing the classroom so that at times students talk and work among themselves requires certain social rules of behavior and a physical environment arranged in such a way that students can move around, share ideas and materials, and collaborate without interrupting the work of others. Let's discuss the social rules of classroom behavior first and then examine ways to reinforce them through the physical arrangement of furniture, paths, and learning materials.

In the typical all-English classroom, the social organization of the classroom into rows and/or tables of students being taught as a whole group supports a participation structure in which the teacher has exclusive rights over who is granted permission to move and talk and what they are allowed to say (Au & Mason, 1981). In this arrangement, students who wish to move out of their assigned space or respond to the teacher's question must raise their hands and wait until the teacher calls on them, reinforcing competition among students (Kohn, 1986). While this type of management strategy has a justifiable place in whole-group instruction, it is not appropriate for managing student interaction and collaboration in other social contexts for learning.

The Balance of Rights of Participation

In classrooms organized around joinfostering principles of practice, we need to consider three dimensions used to differentiate access to classroom participation. The three dimensions of control, which can occur in any of the three pedagogical contexts that support language and content affiliation and learning, are as follows (Au & Mason, 1981):

1. *Control of turn-taking:* The teacher can allow more than one student to speak contemporaneously, rather than limiting the floor to one student at a time.

2. *Control of topic:* The teacher can allow the students to have a say in the topic to be studied, discussed, or written about, rather than insisting that they talk or write about a prescribed topic.

3. *Control of talk and writing audiences:* The teacher can allow the students to talk among themselves, to share ideas and works, and write to a variety of audiences, rather than insisting that they address their talk and written work only to the teacher.

Within any social context of classroom learning, a *balance of rights* of participation occurs when neither the teacher nor the students control more than two dimensions at any one time (Au & Mason, 1981). For example, in small-group literature study, a teacher may insist that students talk or write only about the story or story-related ideas (teacher control of topic). The students, however, may be allowed to talk freely and share ideas with one another throughout the story (student control of talk opportunities) without having to raise their hands and bid for an individual turn (student control of turn-taking). Talking freely supports the integration of listening and talking or what Heath (1985) refers to as the "tie-in" strategy of developing new language abilities. It also enables students to try out new language in a safe environment, with peers. Sharing ideas with peers also encourages the construction of identities of belonging to school communities of practice.

In a whole-group setting, a teacher may require students to raise their hands before talking (teacher control of turn-taking), but encourage them to bring their own experiences into the discussion or the writing activity (teacher-student shared control of topic), and at key points in the lesson ask them to share ideas in pairs (teacher-student control of talk and writing audiences). Bringing in past experiences is what Heath (1985) calls the "tie-back" strategy for making new classwork meaningful and relevant. The tie-back strategy also helps students try out new ways of using language for learning content, and in doing so, to identify as members of academic communities of practice.

Both of these participation examples achieve a balance between speaking and turn-taking rights of the teacher and the students. However, if either the teacher or the students have exclusive control over all three dimensions, we can no longer speak of a balance of rights for participation. Once this happens, all meaningful interaction between the teacher and the students ceases, as do opportunities for capitalizing on tie-in and tie-back learning strategies that encourage identity formation and the appropriation of new voices for participation in academic communities of practice. Students need opportunities to interact, share ideas, try on new voices, move around the room, and practice classroom language and literacy practices.

Support for Language Participation During Content Learning

A balance of rights provides support for active participation, identity formation, and content learning in ways that are not so obvious. For instance, allowing and encouraging more than one student to talk at a time essentially means that students are talking to one another and perhaps to the teacher, using language that more closely resembles occurring communicative exchanges associated with the academic community of practice. For example, if students are talking about math problems or commenting on an author's point of view, this amounts to practice using language and information that already belongs to a community of practice. When students engage in this kind of talk, they are affiliating with the community of practice (Lave & Wenger, 1991). In addition, when students are talking to one another, they also have a chance to take turns listening to one another and thus to tie in

JOIN
FOSTERING

several language abilities at once. In both cases, the result is greater participation in multiple academic language uses, with students trying on new and varying identities as language users and academic learners (INTEGRATION OF ADDITIONAL LANGUAGE LEARNING INTO ACADEMIC LEARNING PRACTICES). Being able to decide on and control the topic of a conversation can also facilitate second-language acquisition (Ellis, 1984). Topics that are initiated by students rather than by the teacher are often of greater interest to students and are more likely to have genuine purposes because students can tie back to prior experiences. For example, a teacher may generate some interest on the topic of earthquakes when it comes up in a chapter in science, but after experiencing one, students will have a multitude of questions. When students are truly interested in the topic, the language and interaction that occurs around it are immediately more meaningful, leading students to identify themselves as academic learners and to participate actively using a wide range of language abilities and literacy practices (ACTIVE PARTICIPATION; SOCIAL INTEGRATION TO FACILITATE THE CREATION OF NEW IDENTITIES AND SOCIOACADEMIC AFFILIATIONS; INTEGRATION OF ADDITIONAL LANGUAGE LEARNING INTO ACADEMIC LEARNING PRACTICES).

JOIN
FOSTERING

A balance of rights also encourages discourse types that expose second-language students to multiple uses of language during content learning. For example, when students are allowed to talk among themselves to accomplish a goal, they are using "share discourse" (Enright & McCloskey, 1988). Share discourse occurs frequently in classrooms rife with collaboration. Pease-Alvarez and Vásquez (1990) attest to the power of share discourse in their study on the value of social interaction for learning to use computers to enhance learning. They found that language-minority students who talked about ways to use the computer and who wrote personal messages to one another on the computer showed substantial gains in both language development and computer knowledge. Fránquiz and de la Luz Reyes (1998) also stress the importance of enabling children of diverse language and ethnic background to share experiences as a way to promote "heteroglossia," multiple ways of using language to share ideas about the world (Bakhtin, 1981). Promoting share discourse means too that children in your classroom not only share ideas, but also that they share materials as they use language. In many classrooms, children helping other children with tasks is prohibited. For English learners, sharing ideas and copying and repeating what others say and write is an important means for practicing and trying out the new language they are learning.

Another type of discourse that is practiced when students are allowed to talk freely in class is "fact discourse" (Enright & McCloskey, 1988), which involves language that is used in the discovery and creation of new knowledge. An example of fact discourse is language that would be learned in collecting information and then preparing a classroom newscast about a topic decided upon by the students. Last, when students are encouraged to exchange ideas, their imaginations are also inspired. Language that is used in the service of imagination to create and organize new ideas is "thought discourse" (Enright & McCloskey, 1988). Students meeting to decide on ways to help the flood victims or how to design a Web page for a project they are working on are examples of thought discourse. These examples are possible only in classrooms where joinfostering is supported by a balance of rights of participation between the students and the teacher, and where children are encouraged to help one another as they help one another by sharing, imagining, and trying out new language. A more complete discussion on the relationship between interaction, identity formation, and second-language participation in classroom communities of practice is presented in Chapters 4 and 5.

Classroom Norms for Participation Across Contexts

In a classroom designed to promote joinfostering principles of practice, students need to feel that talking, sharing, and collaboration are acceptable ways of behavior. If we as teachers wish to achieve a balance-of-rights classroom atmosphere, we must establish a set of rules or *norms* of participation that guide our own and the students' behavior within the three major pedagogical contexts (teacher-led large group, teacher-led small group, and teacher-delegated small group). Cohen (1986) defines a norm as a rule for how students ought to behave in classroom life. In the three social contexts for learning, students must learn norms of participation that require them to listen to their teacher and other students, to give others a chance to talk, to ask for others' opinions, and to make meaningful contributions during both large- and small-group work.

Examples of norms of participation that support the balance of rights hypothesis are:

1. Listen when the teacher or your classmates are talking to you.
2. Give your classmates a chance to talk. No put-downs.
3. Ask your classmates for their ideas.
4. Don't say you can't play (Paley, 1992).
5. Try to figure things out for yourself. When you can't, ask the teacher or a classmate for help.

6. Respect your classmates' needs for collaboration.

7. Learn how to share your materials during group work.

These norms of behavior are general enough to be applicable to multiple ways of organizing participation within a balance-of-rights perspective. Moreover, the norms reflect the conviction that learning occurs through both social and individual efforts and thus are likely to be culturally relevant to a wide range of student backgrounds. Once you have established a set of classroom rules to support joinfostering principles, it is helpful to talk with students about them and remind them as the need arises. You can also explicitly model classroom rules for your students, using both positive and negative examples. (See Enright & McCloskey, 1988, pp. 72–78, and Ostrow, 1995 for additional information on developing socially oriented classroom rules.) Although there is really no need to post the rules on a wall, some teachers like to do this at the beginning of the school year, for reference purposes.

The Physical Arrangement of the Classroom

As we have already stated, the social environment of the classroom needs to be reinforced by a physical arrangement that allows students to talk and collaborate for part of the day and to learn in a whole-class setting or individually the rest of the time. This requires the thoughtful organization of furniture, of space for movement, and of learning materials (Nations & Boyett, 2002).

Regardless of the dimension and size of your classroom, arranging the physical environment to reinforce the social needs is a difficult task that is never complete. The arrangement at the beginning of the school year will not necessarily accommodate the wide range of tasks and supporting group activities coming later in the year (Loughlin & Suina, 1982). Given that the physical arrangement of the classroom is temporary, let's start by considering how to arrange the furniture so that students can experience all three social contexts for learning. This means that we will need to set up an arrangement that allows us to teach to the whole class and to small groups part of the time as well as allowing students to collaborate in small groups and work individually part of the time. Moreover, it means that students will have to be able to move to, from, and around the spaces that we arrange for them without disrupting the general flow of instruction (Ostrow, 1995).

Learning to Revisualize Classroom Space.   A first step in arranging the physical environment to enable all three social learning contexts is to learn how to visualize classroom space (Loughlin & Suina, 1982). Many teachers see the classroom only as teacher space and student space and thus overlook valuable learning space. The way we look at classrooms is partly a function of our own experiences as students and partly a result of our preparation for teaching. For example, a common practice in teacher preparation programs is to have students conduct micro-teaching lessons in front of the room so that they can demonstrate effective teaching behaviors. Moreover, teaching in the teacher zone is abundantly reinforced when students go out into the schools to do practica for their methods courses. Both of these practices hamper the way that we visualize the use of space.

In a joinfostering classroom, teaching and learning should take place in many areas of the classroom: in the corners, in group areas, in a converted storage closet, at learning centers, at the back of the room, around the piano, on the carpet, under the window, on an old couch, around the computer screen, and at students' desks (Clayton, 2001). A primary goal of arranging a joinfostering classroom is to visualize and then create multiple learning areas in places that are not necessarily bordered only by the corners of the classroom and still maintain a functional whole-class environment.

A good place to start is to make a floor plan of the classroom showing the size and location of all of the built-in features. Next, by sketching in all of the furniture as close to scale as possible, we can begin to get a realistic picture of spaces, pathways, and room for activities. Once we have the finished floor plan in hand, we are ready to consider the following basic questions:

1. What learning spaces are available for students? Are there both small and large activity spaces?
2. Which spaces are occasionally used by the students? Which are seldom used? Which are never used?
3. Where are the crowded areas of the classroom?
4. Which spaces serve as pathways for movement?
5. Which spaces are used by students to relax?
6. Which spaces are used for noisy activities? Which are used for quiet activities?

Answers to these questions reveal where and under what conditions students spend most of their time in class, which areas they use occasionally, and which areas are never used at all. In other words, the answers tell us whether, in general, the physical arrangement supports the variety and kinds of communication and social integration features we wish to incorporate into the daily routines of our classroom.

A general picture of the physical arrangement also helps you think about the places that we have or have not provided for student activities. If the picture that emerges is one in which the majority of student activities occur either in a large-group area or individually at student desks, and that space has not been arranged to allow for variation in the amount of student interaction, then clearly students are not engaging in the kinds of activities that support two-way communication and social integration!

In a joinfostering classroom, students need certain places to talk, listen, read, and write together in a host of activities and certain other places to work alone. Accordingly, it is important to bear in mind the noise level that an activity will probably generate (small-group work is noisy!) as well as the amount of traffic in and out of the learning space. Noisy activity centers and places with lots of student traffic should be located a good distance from learning activity space designed for quieter activities (Nations & Boyett, 2002). In addition, it is a good idea to locate small animals away from noisy areas. These requirements need to be considered as furniture is arranged and learning activity spaces and pathways are defined.

Multiple Uses for Classroom Furniture.   Furniture obviously designed for student use consists primarily of desks or tables and chairs, computer booths, and, frequently, in the lower primary grades, a rug or two. To this basic student furniture, we can add new furniture in order to break up classroom space and at the same time create new space. It is best to use furniture that can be easily rearranged and that can serve a variety of purposes (Clayton, 2001). Another feature to consider in acquiring new furniture is whether it can help define learning activity space. For example, low tables can be used to define an area out from a corner or along the wall by providing one- or two-side protection. If we place the low table within a small area designed for three or four students, they can use it for written work while they sit on cushions (Nations & Boyett, 2002). On other occasions, students can use the same low table for teamwork on math problems, art construction, and bookmaking.

Other furniture pieces that can serve a variety of purposes and define learning space as well are large milk crates, bookshelves on wheels, revolving bookcases, bookracks, message boards, couches, chalkboards on wheels, throw rugs, and seat cushions. Low bookcases can be placed down the middle of the room, for example, to immediately divide the room into two halves. Add a message board at a right angle to the bookcase, and you create an additional space. A revolving bookcase placed on a small tiled area of the room can form part of a classroom library. A chalkboard on wheels can be moved around the room for teacher-led small-group work. Placed perpendicular to the wall, the chalkboard provides a relatively secluded learning space, the size of which can be adjusted by moving the chalkboard closer to or farther from any other piece of furniture that happens to be serving as the third side of the area. Large milk crates can be stacked to form a wall or be used to keep journals, magazines, and paper. Different-color rugs can be used to designate talk areas, quiet areas, be-alone areas. The possibilities are endless.

In addition to movable furniture, we can also learn to use the space in and around the permanent fixtures of our classrooms: the storage shelves, the storage closet, the coat room, the windows, and the bookcases. Once filled, storage shelves are rarely used throughout the year. So, instead of viewing them as teacher space (because they are filled with your junk!), look at them as walls to be covered or as the back side of a learning activity space. Try placing a table against them. If the shelves are low enough and strong enough, consider them as a kind of bench to use during singing and for watching a classroom play.

The storage closet and the coat room can also be made into excellent learning activity spaces. The storage closet can be converted into a special place for reading or studying individually. Loughlin and Suina (1982), for example, relate the story of a teacher whose lighted storage closet so attracted the attention of her students that she reorganized the higher levels for storage purposes and then added a small table and lots of books and pictures for students' use. Now the closet has become a special place for enjoying reading! On the door of the closet, you can tape a height chart to keep track of student growth or a long poem written by your students.

If the coat room is well-lighted and within your view, you may wish to consider adding a small table and chairs and equipping the space with tape recorders so that students can listen to taped versions of their favorite storybooks. Windows are also great learning spaces. You can maintain small gardens and observation charts near the windows. Students can record growth and weather information to share with the class throughout the week. As these examples illustrate, there are many ways to take advantage of permanent classroom furniture. The idea is to organize and arrange the room so that students have lots of activity spaces for talking, listening, reading, and writing about a variety of interesting topics (Clayton, 2001).

Movement In and Around the Classroom.   Every learning activity space in your classroom requires some empty surrounding space for movement (Nation & Boyett, 2002). Students need to be able to get to and from the learning space and be able to move around it without bumping into one another or interfering with activities occurring in adjoining space. Moreover, there must be clearly defined pathways that enable students to get from one learning activity site to another. To function effectively, a path should be visible at several different eye levels; students should be able to see it just as clearly from their chairs or floor-level angles as they do from their standing and walking heights.

In addition, the space arranged for paths should not be available for other uses. Paths should be vacant at all times. Students can interfere with the work of others if the pathways cross into learning activity space or vice versa. Thus, it is important to make sure that students are working within designated learning spaces and also that the paths to, from, and around the learning spaces remain empty to facilitate movement through the environment.

Paths are important not only because they can lead students to and from learning activities, but also because they provide access to valuable learning materials that support the activities. In classrooms with multiple contexts for learning, students will need to make use of raw materials (construction materials, fabrics, cords, papers), tools (for measuring, joining, computing, cutting, observing, viewing, recording, heating, expressing, and communicating), containers (flat and deep boxes, watertight pails, cages, racks, envelopes), and information sources (references, pictures, recordings, natural specimens, labels, books, magazines, models, charts, living things) at different times in the day for different purposes. (See Loughlin & Suina, 1982, pp. 78–101; and Loughlin & Martin, 1987, pp. 19–26 for additional examples.) To ensure that all students have access to the available support materials, we need to make certain that there are clear and visible pathways to the materials. However, it is equally important to consider the distribution of learning materials, because although some materials are best stored at centralized locations, other materials should be recentralized to minimize traffic problems and to get materials into students' hands when and where they need them (Loughlin & Suina, 1982).

The Distribution of Learning Materials and Resources.   There are essentially two ways to distribute learning materials. Each way regulates when and where students locate the learning materials and may also determine whether they are used at all (Loughlin & Martin, 1987). One way to distribute learning materials is to place them in *centralized* locations throughout the classroom (Loughlin & Suina, 1982). The most common way of distributing centralized materials is to store learning material by categories, such as art materials, reference books, writing and bookmaking materials, and recording tools. Each category of material is located and stored at a specific site. This means that when items from any of the categories are needed for a learning activity, students must travel to the site to gather the material.

Imagine the amount of traffic and the traffic jams that could easily result from students going after learning items located at a few centralized distribution sites in different parts of the room! Too often, the result is that students spend time doing things that are completely unrelated to the activity at hand. Moreover, once an activity has begun, there always seem to be students who realize they forgot to pick up a certain item or need more of something, so they get up to walk across the room while classmates are working and end up interrupting them. For example, on the way to and from the materials storage site(s), a student may stop and talk with friends or get caught up in events at other locations and eventually lose sight of the original reason for leaving his or her seat in the first place. The students who talk with their wandering classmate(s) may also veer from their work. In any event, there is a good chance that both parties will lose valuable time when materials are distributed only at centralized locations.

This is not to say, however, that getting up and moving around in the classroom is wholly undesirable. At times, moving about can be productive because it gives students a chance to see what their classmates are doing and to exchange ideas with them. They should have opportunities to consult with one another, to check out each other's projects, and to learn from one another, especially during small-group work, because it is through such genuine exchanges that students participate in share, fact, and thought discourse and have multiple opportunities for negotiating new identities as creators and users of language in the service of content learning.

A way to allow students to talk and collaborate freely without having to move about the room to fetch individual materials at different centralized locations is to divide commonly used materials into smaller quantities and *recentralize* them. (Loughlin & Suina, 1982, refer to recentralizing as *decentralizing*.) Recentralizing learning materials means that collections of learning tools and materials are placed at or near individual learning areas before the activity begins. The closer the combinations of tools and materials are to where the students will be using them, the better. Students are most likely to use the learning materials they can see and reach as they work (Loughlin & Suina, 1982; Nations & Boyett, 2002).

Recentralizing learning materials according to their role in the task at hand also reduces traffic and interruption problems. Because the key learning materials needed for the activities are within the students' reach, movement to and from centralized storage areas is reduced; hence, there are fewer instances of students potentially interfering with the work of their classmates. Ample opportunities remain, nonetheless, for students to talk and work together and to share ideas and materials, which is desirable in the promotion of collaboration and active participation (ACTIVE PARTICIPATION AND SOCIAL INTEGRATION TO FACILITATE THE CREATION OF NEW IDENTITIES AND SOCIOACADEMIC AFFILIATIONS).

Julia Shows Off Her Class to Jake

A week has gone by since Julia began redesigning her classroom to ensure movement, multiple work and fun places, and whole- and small-group teaching and learning. She invites Jake to come by to see her classroom and to touch base.

"Quite impressive!" Jake says, announcing his arrival. "Who did the artwork over there?" pointing to a large acrylic painting of pigs and flowers done in bright colors.

"Thanks. That's a painting I did last summer when I was experimenting with a genre called fantastic reality. Children love the painting because the pigs are flying and rolling around in fields of colorful flowers. I call it 'The Sweet Life of Pigs.' What's really cool is that I have embedded children's faces in the flowers and on several of the pigs. Can you see them?" she asks, as they approach the painting for a closer look.

"That's astonishing. You are so talented. And, I really like the way you have arranged your classroom, lots of spaces, and easy access to books, the computers and their tables." Jake utters as he moves away to survey the room.

"Yes, I paid lots of attention to pathways, and open spaces. I even got down on my knees to check out the view from where the kids might see it."

"Now, here's the thing, Julia," says Jake in a slightly serious tone. "Now that you have opened up the class to collaboration and having lots of movement available to your students, I think you need to be fairly explicit with your students about what is expected during whole-group and small-group activities. You need to have a serious discussion about sharing ideas and materials, and most of all, you will need to work with them on developing classroom rules for behaving and acting appropriately throughout the day."

"I understand what you are saying, Jake. I know that I have to be pretty strict during the first weeks of school to help the students learn how to talk, listen, and work together so they have rules for how to get along and learn at the same time."

"Part of the reason for talking with all of your students about how to be in class is also to ensure that the students who are adding English are given the best shot at seeing themselves as FULL classroom members, and as capable of participating AND contributing to learning in any number of ways. Let's face it, Julia, children who are adding English and children of color are too often degraded and positioned so that they are presumed to be less able, and consequently, they are blocked from access to rich learning activities. I know teachers who act that way toward kids who are learning English, and I detest it!"

"Me too," replied Julia, "and I WILL keep a watchful eye out to make sure that my English learners are not left out of learning activities; just because they are learning English while they are in my class does not mean that they can't learn or be active participants. I am going to pay attention to all the resources that children need and have available to them: language, readings, materials, ways of interacting, all of that stuff."

"I get it, Julia," Jake replies, meaning it. "Look, I have an errand to run. Thanks for inviting me to your classroom. I am excited for you, and I know that your class will be a magical place for children to be and to learn. You take care." Rudy takes leave with a smile, thinking to himself, *I think I misjudged you, Julia, and you certainly impress me.*

"You too, Jake," says Julia as she bids him good-bye, and returns the smile.

CONCLUSION

There are many social and physical adjustments to consider in organizing a joinfostering classroom. Julia's and Jake's concern over arranging the physical environment to support joinfostering principles is a real one that we will have to address many times over in our own classrooms. We know from having read this chapter that many (probably too many) classrooms in the United States are organized to suppress active participation, social integration, and opportunities for authentic language use and that many eschew a balance of rights, favoring instead a recitation mode where participation and interaction are controlled exclusively by the teacher. One of our first challenges, then, is to modify the existing social and physical organization patterns to include, in addition to teacher-led whole-class instruction, small-group work (both teacher-led and teacher-delegated), and individual learning. Each of the major social contexts for learning must allow second-language learners the opportunity to participate in lessons to the fullest extent possible (ACTIVE PARTICIPATION AND SOCIAL INTEGRATION TO FACILITATE THE CREATION OF NEW IDENTITIES AND SOCIOACADEMIC AFFILIATIONS). Moreover, we must be able to incorporate the conditions that are most favorable for second-language students to participate actively during content instruction (INTEGRATION OF ADDITIONAL LANGUAGE LEARNING INTO ACADEMIC LEARNING PRACTICES). In the next two chapters, therefore, we will examine the nature of classroom interaction to learn about ways to facilitate second-language participation within the major social contexts of content instruction, beginning with the whole-class setting.

ACTIVITIES

1. Interview two experienced elementary classroom teachers to find out how they differentiate access to classroom participation according to the balance of rights of participation model. Ask each teacher these questions:

   A. How do you handle turn-taking in your classroom? Are there certain times when you allow students to speak at the same time?

   B. How are the topics for learning selected in your classroom? Are there times when students choose topics?

C. Are there certain times during the day when students are allowed to talk among themselves to work on problems?

D. What kinds of opportunities are there for students to write to real audiences, such as children in other grades, peers, the teacher as a trusted adult, other adults?

Based on the answers you receive, try to determine whether participation is balanced in favor of the teacher or the students or whether the teacher attempts to share the rights of participation with students.

2. Write a set of classroom rules that you feel best reflect norms of participation that would require students to listen to their teacher and other students, to give others a chance to talk, to ask for others' ideas and opinions, and to make meaningful contributions during whole-class and small-group instruction. Share your ideas with classmates and discuss them.

3. Visit a local elementary school and draw the floor plan of a classroom that you feel best supports the variety and kinds of communication and social integration features you would like to incorporate into your classroom.

4. Interview two experienced elementary classroom teachers to find out (a) how they arrange and use furniture in their classroom; (b) where they collect learning materials and the kinds of things they look for; and (c) how they organize learning materials in their classroom. If there are animals in the class, tell where they are located and why.

5. Visit several elementary-level classrooms in which there are at least five students who are adding English to their home language. Observe over several days to look for opportunities students have for share discourse, thought discourse, and fun discourse.

REFERENCES

Au, K. H., & Mason, J. M. (1981). Social organizational factors in learning to read: The balance of rights hypothesis. *Reading Research Quarterly, 17*(1), 115–152.

Bakhtin, M. (1981). *The dialogic imagination.* Austin, TX: University of Texas Press.

Charney, R. (1992). *Teaching children to care: Management in the responsive classroom.* Washington, DC: Northeast Foundation for Children.

Clayton, M. (2001). *Classroom spaces that work.* Washington, DC: Northeast Foundation for Children.

Cohen, E. G. (1986). *Designing groupwork: Strategies for the heterogeneous classroom.* New York: Teachers College Press.

DeVillar, R. A., & Faltis, C. J. (1991). *Computers and cultural diversity: Restructuring for school success.* Albany, NY: SUNY Press.

Ellis, R. (1984). *Classroom second language development.* Oxford: Pergamon Press.

Enright, D. S. (1991). Tapping the peer interaction resource. In M. McGroarty & C. Faltis (Eds.), *Languages in school and society: Policy and pedagogy* (pp. 209–232). Berlin: Mouton de Gruyter.

Enright, D. S., & McCloskey, M. L. (1985). Yes talking!: Organizing the classroom environment to promote second language learning. *TESOL Quarterly, 19*(3), 431–453.

Enright, D. S., & McCloskey, M. L. (1988). *Integrating English: Developing English language and literacy in the multilingual classroom.* Reading, MA: Addison-Wesley.

Faltis, C., & Hudelson, S. (1998). Bilingual education in elementary and secondary schools: Toward understanding and caring. Boston, MA: Allyn & Bacon.

Fránquiz, M., & de la Luz Reyes, M. (1998). Creating inclusive learning communities through English language arts: From *chanclas* to *canicas. Language Arts, 75*(3), 211–220.

Freire, P. (1970). *Pedagogy of the oppressed.* New York: Herder and Herder.

Furst, N., & Amidon, E. (1962). Teacher-pupil interaction patterns in the elementary school. In E. Amidon & E. J. Hough (Eds.), *Interaction analysis: Theory, research and application* (pp. 167–175). Reading, MA: Addison-Wesley.

Goodlad, J. (1984). *A place called school: Prospects for the future.* New York: McGraw-Hill.

Heath, S. B. (1985). Literacy or literate skills? Considerations for ESL/EFL learners. In P. Larson, E. L. Judd, & D. S. Messerschmitt (Eds.), *One TESOL '84* (pp. 15–28). Washington, DC: TESOL.

Kliebard, H. M. (1989). Success and failure in educational reform: Are there historical lessons? *Occasional Papers,* The Holmes Group. East Lansing, MI: Michigan State University.

Kohn, A. (1986). *No contest.* Boston: Houghton Mifflin.

Lave, J., & Wenger, E. (1991). *Situated learning: Legitimate peripheral participation.* Cambridge: Cambridge University Press.

Loughlin, C. E., & Martin, M. (1987). *Supporting literacy: Developing effective learning environments.* New York: Teachers College Press.

Loughlin, C. E., & Suina, J. (1982). *The learning environment: An instructional strategy.* New York: Teachers College Press.

McGroarty, M. (1989). The benefits of cooperative learning arrangement in second language instruction. *NABE Journal, 13*(2), 127–142.

Nations, S., & Boyett, S. (2002). *So much space, so little room: Creating and managing the learner-centered classroom.* Gainesville, FL: Maupin House Publishing.

Ostrow, J. (1995). *A room with a different look: First through third graders build community and create curriculum.* Portland, ME: Stenhouse Publishers.

Paley, V. (1992). *You can't say you can't play.* Cambridge, MA: Harvard University Press.

Pease-Alvarez, L., & Vásquez, O. (1990). Sharing language and technical expertise around the computer. In C. Faltis & R. A. DeVillar (Eds.), *Language minority students and computers* (pp. 91–107). Binghamton, NY: Haworth Press.

Ramírez, J. D., & Merino, B. J. (1990). Classroom talk in English immersion, early-exit and late-exit transitional bilingual education programs. In R. Jacobson & C. Faltis (Eds.), *Language distribution issues in bilingual schooling* (pp. 61–103). Clevedon, England: Multilingual Matters.

Saville-Troike, M. (1984). What *really* matters in second language learning for academic achievement? *TESOL Quarterly 17*(2), 199–219.

Sirotnik, K. (1983). What you see is what you get—Consistency, persistency, and mediocrity in classrooms. *Harvard Educational Review, 53*(1), 16–31.

Trueba, H. T., & Delgado-Gaitán, C. (1983). Socialization of Mexican children for cooperation and competition: Sharing and copying. *Journal of Educational Equity and Leadership, 5*(3), 189–204.

Teaching for Active Participation in a Mixed-Language Whole-Class Context

4

OVERVIEW

The joinfostering framework is built on the premise that English learners need a variety of opportunities in the classroom for active participation (oral as well as written) about content and readings that combines authentic language and language uses with interesting topics that build upon prior experiences and knowledge. Furthermore, the topics at some point should inevitably enable students to question and discuss critically issues that surface in their lives. As was discussed in Chapter 3, there are three major social contexts in which these conditions take place and in which students can gain access to communities of practice. This chapter focuses primarily on the first social context for language and content learning: teacher-led whole-class teaching and how to engage students in this setting. There are a couple of good reasons for starting with this instructional context. First, whole-class teaching is thoroughly familiar to virtually all teachers (Cazden, 2001; Goodlad, 1984; Ramirez & Merino, 1990; Sirotnik, 1983; Toohey, 2000); that is, all teachers interact with their entire class many times throughout the day. This social context is so familiar that few teachers take notice of the extent to which they control student talk and writing opportunities, the topic of discussion, and turn-taking rights. One of our goals, therefore, is to make this familiar teaching context seem strange (Spindler, 1982) by consciously attending to the sociocultural dimensions of participation while planning for, guiding, and carrying out lessons and activities within this context.

A second reason for beginning with the social context of whole-classroom teaching is that it is in this setting that the teacher in a multilingual classroom has to attend to the widest range of language abilities. That is, when English learners and fully English proficient students are mixed in the same large group teaching setting, the teacher is constantly faced with the difficult challenge of tailoring instructional language to the needs of the English learners without losing the attention and interest of the fully English proficient students and vice versa.

Knowing how to tailor pedagogical language in the whole-class context requires a working knowledge of effective teaching strategies for facilitating second-language participation as students exchange information with the teacher and peers about subject matter content (INTEGRATION OF ADDITIONAL LANGUAGE LEARNING INTO ACADEMIC LEARNING PRACTICES). As we have already learned, small numbers of teachers nationwide possess this knowledge base. Put differently, few grade-level teachers belong to the community of practice that knows about and performs well when teaching English learners. What most all-English grade-level teachers do when faced with teaching to a mixed-language whole class is gear their language to the students who readily understand rather than consciously using language in ways that enable the greatest number of students to join in (Faltis & Merino, 1992; Wong Fillmore, 1982a). An unfortunate result of this tendency is that the second-language students participate considerably less than their fully English-proficient counterparts, because much of

what the teacher says may not make sense to them (Schinke-Llano, 1983). It is in this circumstance that English learners may become bored and inattentive at best and feel alienated and traumatized at worst (Trueba, 1998). In both cases, students are effectively denied the opportunity to participate in learning activities so that little, if any, language acquisition or academic learning takes place. Moreover, when access to whole-class interactions and activities is blocked, students are unlikely to claim identities as classroom members, and the teacher as well as classmates may ascribe identities to them, which position them as incompetent peers and learners. To counteract this possibility and its undesirable effects, it is essential to learn how to integrate language participation strategies with content teaching during whole-class instruction times so that English learners construct, negotiate, and transform their identities as capable and contributing participants and so that their classmates come to view them as such. This amounts to a commitment to go beyond the basics of what works for fully English-proficient students and incorporate a new understanding of teaching and learning for English learners.

As we learned in Episode One, Julia made a commitment to be the best teacher that she could be for all of her students, to help them see learning communities and opportunities everywhere, and to help them appreciate and get along with others. She made a commitment to learn about her students' prior schooling experiences and put a good deal of thought and effort into organizing her classroom so that her students would experience a variety of social settings and literacy experiences that would pique their curiosity. However, like many teachers, Julia has much to learn about how to help students navigate their way into social and academic communities of practice, learning to create new and varying identities of classroom members. Julia came into teaching with a solid communicative stance toward classroom learning and literacy, a stance she relies on heavily for planning and carrying out lessons. But she is often frustrated when she senses that her second-language students are not joining in and affiliating with the classroom practices as well as they could be. She is beginning to suspect that good content teaching is not necessarily the same as good language teaching and that good language learners need to see themselves as belonging to classroom communities of

practice (Norton & Toohey, 2001). Julia is beginning to understand the complexities of classroom life, especially for English learners who are struggling to appropriate new voices, not only in English, but as learners of academic content as well. Therefore, let's begin this chapter by stepping into Julia's classroom to see how she is faring as she learns to integrate language and content teaching in ways to help students appropriate multiple identities as learners. We will follow the episode with a general discussion on classroom communities of practice, the construction of multiple classroom identities, and the appropriation of new voices. Following this discussion are suggestions and examples of strategies for integrating second language acquisition principles with academic content learning.

Episode Four: Learning to Engage Students in Whole-Class Teaching

The first couple of months have passed by quickly and most of the students in Julia's class are showing signs that they have taken on the social norms for participating appropriately while still being curious, playful, and thoughtful in the variety of social contexts that Julia and the students have implemented. The classroom is arranged so that students work part of the day as a whole group (for routines, discussion, previews, inquiry, and storybook reading) and the rest of the day in small groups or individually. From garage sales and scrounging around the school, Julia has acquired some additional movable furniture to break up the classroom into learning centers, workspaces, and quiet reading and writing spaces. During whole-class teaching sessions, students are either seated at their tables, four students to a table, or cross-legged on the floor in the center of the classroom. Each student table has crayons, pencils, erasers, scissors, paper, a picture dictionary, and an appropriate bilingual dictionary. The walls of the classroom and several bulletin boards used as space dividers are decorated with students' artwork and writings that reflect their interests in current learning topics. Some students have begun to adorn the space around Julia's *Sweet Life of Pigs* painting with their own artwork. At the beginning of the school year, Julia decided to post the classroom rules for talking and listening near the water fountain. These are written in large letters and are accompanied by rebus symbols to support their meaning. Now she plans to replace them with student artwork. Julia wanted students to think about what they were doing, to do what works, and to not try to get out of being responsible in and out of class.

Virtually all of the furniture and provisions for learning are labeled with rebus pictures, words, or both. There is also a large map of the world with the birthplaces of all the students marked. Julia has placed individual photographs of the students around the map and used thick red yarn to connect the birthplace on the map to the corresponding student's photograph. In a number of special places around the room, Julia has organized literacy support materials, including puppets, tape recorders, wordless storybooks, comic books, picture books, and biographies of people from many different walks of life. She also has a special spot for Authors of the Week. These are children's book authors that she or the students select on a weekly basis. This week Julia is featuring books by authors who write about children who help older people. (See Hudelson & Rigg, 1994/95; and Rigg, Kazemek, & Hudelson, 1993, for references.) She uses an old magazine rack for this, and she includes student-authored books in the rack as well.

Julia's teaching units are organized so that most of the content-learning activities relate to a theme that unites concepts across the content areas and ties in the four language processes of speaking, listening, reading, and writing. She believes strongly that language is for constructing meaning, that written language is language, and that having students feel part of the classroom community is paramount for making sense of academic content and the language that supports it. Julia's long-term goals are to help students see learning communities everywhere; to enable students to think and take pleasure in using their thoughts and words to solve problems, to learn with and through text; and to help students get along with and appreciate others.

So far in the year, Julia has developed two thematic units and has just begun the third—on elephants, a theme suggested by the students as a result of an intriguing story about how much elephants weigh. Through brainstorming with the students and using some photographs and children's stories, she has established some of the students' areas of interest and knowledge about elephants, and she has a full set of questions about elephants that students would like to have answered. A very important goal of Julia's thematic units is to engage the students in sustained inquiry about some aspect of the major topics to be covered in the unit, and at the same time be sure to incorporate grade-level standards. In this manner, she uses themes as a way to get students to problematize issues associated with the theme, and she helps them inquire about the issues across content areas. As Ms. Constantino showed her during her student teaching, helping students problematize and study issues requires tapping into and building on prior knowledge to build a foundation upon which students can first ask what really happened, and then begin to question why events happened.

The students are excited about making elephant footprints, about finding out how much water an elephant's trunk can hold, about learning to do the elephant walk, about differences and similarities among kinds of elephants, about why elephants live in herds, about how elephants are trained for the circus, and about helping to stop elephant poaching. After spending some time researching their topics on the Internet, through reading, and interviewing family members, the students decide on a topic they want to inquire about over time. One group decides to develop a skit about elephants and their phenomenal memories; another wants to design posters that urge people not to buy ivory products; and several others are interested in learning about the role of elephants in several different cultures. One group of students even volunteered to find out if elephants are related to pigs! (What do YOU think?)

Although the level of active participation is generally high, Julia is still frustrated at times that inevitably, some of the English learners appear lost during whole-class teaching, especially when she is introducing and explaining new topics or when she is giving instructions about the learning activities. What bugs her the most is that some students choose not to talk in front of a group, except when the talk is embedded in some kind of choral presentation. One afternoon after the students have left for the day, while Julia is arranging some slides on elephant poaching for tomorrow's class, her colleague and friend Jake pops in to see how things are going. "Hey, Julia, what's happening? Everything cool?" *Wow, your room looks great.*

"Oh, hi, Jake, come in." *Perfect timing.* "Yeah, everything's going pretty well, in general. I'm glad you stopped by because maybe you can help me out." Julia describes what she has been doing in her class and shows Jake around the room to give him a sense of the kinds of activities that students have been involved in. "Here's my concern, Jake. It seems to me that, uh, sometimes my ESL students don't understand what I'm saying to them when I'm talking with the whole class." *It drives me crazy,* she didn't add. "And another thing: Sometimes they don't say anything!" *They just look at me with their beautiful eyes.* "Interestingly, they do try to write and stuff, and that's good, but I worry when they don't talk." *I so want them to participate.* "I want them to feel comfortable talking in this class, especially when I am presenting an idea in front of the whole class. Am I being too pushy? Is there something I can do that I'm not doing now to help them understand better and to help them join in and contribute more to the class?" *Come on, help me, Jake.*

"Well, Julia, I'll tell you, there are no easy answers to your questions, for sure." *Julia is asking the right questions. She's really smart.* "But, in my mind, the way you've organized your classroom to include the students' interests is bound to benefit the second-language students. You're giving them all kinds of opportunities to hear and use English while they're learning other stuff. What's fresh is that there are some things that you can learn to use that can help your students who are still learning English feel more comfortable making a contribution when you are addressing the whole group. You might want to start by noticing how you and the students use language when you're going through a lesson with them." *I need to be more specific here.* "You know, like, pay attention to the kinds of questions you and they use in writing and when you're talking with them. Your goal is for you and your students to find ways to use language in a variety of ways for making sense of what you're talking about, what you're studying. I mean, like, you have to adjust—consciously—how you interact with students, and you have to invite them, even nudge them into the interaction with you. Help them *see* and *touch* what you're talking about. In whole-group interaction, you should ask for students' comments, keep them brief, and spread interaction around. There is nothing worse than trying to get all students to talk in whole settings. The ones who are talking lose interest quickly. When you interact with the whole class, you should use lots of visuals, go for the big ideas, model for them, and talk about language and how you use it when you are doing school things."

"I think I try to do much of what you are saying, but can you tell me more?" says Julia with some heartfelt optimism.

In the following sections, let's pursue Julia's concerns and Jake's advice and consider ways to plan for and use language during whole-class content teaching, ways that will invite English learners to participate actively and in doing so, join in learning activities with their native English-speaking classmates. Jake is drawing on an understanding of teaching and learning that pays attention to how students participate in ways that lead them to identify and affiliate with classroom communities of practice. A critical aspect of this understanding is how learners are differentiated and positioned by the identities with respect to academic, language, social, and physical characteristics and abilities. In whole-class teaching, the goal is to ensure that students follow along and participate as needed so they are aware what to do next, what steps to take, what materials to use, and how to engage in supporting activities. From a joinfostering perspective, the goal is also to provide English learners with best opportunities for learning by participating in ways that integrate learners of diverse abilities, draw on learners' strengths, and facilitate the creation of positive identities with multiple academic communities of practice (SOCIAL INTEGRATION TO FACILITATE THE CREATION OF NEW IDENTITIES AND SOCIOACADEMIC AFFILIATIONS).

LANGUAGE-INVITING CONTENT TEACHING

Teaching that incorporates second-language acquisition and participation principles into whole-class discussion about procedures, inquiry, and content information can be called *language-inviting content teaching* (INTEGRATION OF ADDITIONAL LANGUAGE LEARNING INTO ACADEMIC LEARNING PRACTICES). This kind of teaching is necessary whenever you as the teacher are primarily responsible for the pedagogical language used in preparation for and within a learning activity designed to engage students in practices that lead to learning and identification with the particular practices. Three special abilities underlie language-inviting content teaching: (1) understanding the role of identity construction and positioning that occurs in whole-class teaching, (2) taking notice of content language and the kinds of discourse that organize the discussion and content during whole-class teaching, and (3) adapting that discourse so that students can comprehend the content and express knowledge about it both orally and in writing in ways that invite affiliation with the community of practice to which the content belongs.

Let's begin to address this challenge by considering the role of creating identities in classroom communities of practice, with an eye toward understanding the nature of communities of practice and how identity creation, negotiation, and transformation fits into the discussion. It bears repeating that students need to see themselves as affiliating with members of communities of practice. Now it is time to spend time learning about what this means for you as a teacher in a multilingual classroom.

Communities of Practice in a Whole-Class Context

Communities of practice focus attention on the idea that learning happens as people come together around specific tasks in specific situated practices over time (Lave, 1996). More specifically, learners construct what they learn through social practices that are situated within particular settings and activities. In this manner, learning takes place through active participation, and it is distributed among co-participants whose knowledge and ability to use resources associated with the community of practice varies. To learn, students enter into a set of relations with the teacher and other students, much in the same way they have already done and continue to do in their home cultures, as was presented in Chapter 1.

In school, where there are multiple communities of practice that overlap and contribute to one another in complex ways, students enter as newcomers and must be invited into communities of practice by engaging in the myriad processes (talking, thinking, writing, drawing, computing, critiquing, inquiring, feeling, analyzing, reciting, memorizing, playing, etc.) that community members who are familiar and knowledgeable of the practices use to get things done. However, in school, students are rarely true newcomers to the multiple academic communities of practice, especially if they have participated in activities involving literacy, content, and being students. They may be newcomers to new ways of talking about, thinking about, and getting things done as they are invited to participate in practices that already exist across space and time. So, for example, as students learn new ways of understanding and using arithmetic for measuring parts of an elephant, they engage in social practices that the teacher and perhaps some students are already familiar with and knowledgeable about. For any community of practice there are carriers and mediators of cultural knowledge and skills, which are both culturally situated and specific (i.e., done in certain ways with language and meaning systems that are particular to the community that fosters them). At home, parents and other family members socialize children in ways that ensure cultural continuity. In school, you as well as your students and their families and other adults who may participate are the carriers and mediators of academic knowledge.

A simple way to grasp the meaning of learning in communities of practice is to think of learning as constantly moving from the peripheral of a community knowledge base to its core or center. Along the way, newcomers begin to identify themselves as members of the community when they appropriate ways of talking about, understanding, and performing in ways that more centrally located members recognize and use for their continuing participation in the community of practice. In this manner, identity and affiliation with others who also engage in the same kinds of locally situated practice is paramount for continued participation and ultimately, learning. By identity, I mean how students understand their relationship to the class, how that relationship is constructed across time and space, and how the students understand possibilities for future membership in classroom life, moving from the periphery to the center of communities of practice (Hawkins, 2004; Norton, 2000).

But the concepts of communities of practice and identity construction with communities of practice are more complex than moving from the periphery identities to core identities, because as Lave and Wenger (1991, p. 36) point out, there are "multiple, varied, more-or-less engaged and inclusive ways of being located in the fields of participation defined by a community." Learners bring with them to any community of practice existing identities and knowledge that may or may not be recognized as important by others as useful for participation, making access to continued participation in certain communities of practice conflictual for certain learners (Kanno & Applebaum, 1995; Valdés, 2001). In a classroom setting where there are multiple sets of relations, identities, and practices, all members are not equal when they are participating in different learning contexts. Some students have struggles for position within certain communities of practice and have more easy access to others. Why is this so?

In all classrooms, learners are constantly being positioned and are positioning others through comparisons about how well they participate academically and socially with language and literacy. Predominately, learners are differentiated through assessment, which will be discussed in more detail in Chapter 7. Teachers assess everything from language proficiency to how well students participate in whole-group teaching. They judge how well students use English, how well they concentrate, how organized their thoughts seem to be, how they handle not knowing something, and how compliant they are with directives discussed and issued during whole-class teaching.

Classmates are also judging the abilities just mentioned, and their judgments also figure into how students are positioned and position themselves as classroom members. It is not uncommon for classmates to notice and comment on how well or poorly another student answers the teacher's questions, draws, prints, sits, and follows directions during whole-class teaching events. These assessments contribute to the identities that students assume as they move from one context to another.

Learners are also differentiated by physical presentation (Toohey, 2000). Children are identified by classmates and identify with classmates on the basis of clothing style, hairstyle, skin color, and physical adroitness. Students use physical features and abilities to form and re-form friendships both in and out of the classroom. Looking Mexican, Middle Eastern, or "American"; wearing certain clothes and clothes of certain brands; and having certain hairstyles all send powerful messages about who learners are and how others perceive them as competent members of the classroom community.

It is important to realize that how students in your class interact, behave, and present themselves reveals much about their identities and, consequently, their place in the hierarchies of the classroom community. If academic learning depends on the establishment of certain kinds of social relations that enable participants enough practice in community activities to become good at the practices, then it is imperative that we become aware of how children see themselves and how others identify them and that we take steps to enable those children who are blocked from academic learning to gain access and feel comfortable participating as who they are. When students are blocked from academic learning, they may join other nonacademic oriented communities of practices in concert with their developing identities or their participation in academic communities of practice may be truncated, feeding into identities associated with low status in the various classroom hierarchies.

Noticing the Language of Academic Communities of Practice

Academic content is at the core of school-related communities of practices. Teaching academic content in the elementary grades is ordinarily tied to a curriculum design that prescribes the scope and sequence of learning objectives for the subject-matter areas taught at each grade level. These objectives, in turn, are tied to statewide assessments (MULTIPLE WAYS OF ASSESSMENT TO OPTIMIZE ACADEMIC LEARNING PRACTICES, AFFILIATIONS AND CONNECTIONS TO WIDER ACADEMIC COMMUNITIES OF PRACTICE). Thus, for example, the learning objectives for language arts, science, social studies, and mathematics for the 2nd grade may differ in terms of both emphasis and order of presentation from those prescribed for and assessed at the 3rd grade and so on. Typically, the curriculum is organized so that topics presented in the primary grades are repeated in the upper elementary grades, this time with learning activities that incorporate more sophisticated concepts requiring different types of knowledge processing and deeper participation in and affiliation with various communities of practice. Moreover, as students progress through the grades, they are expected to show greater facility with the language of content learning by paying more attention to language cues and the meaning of text itself than to visual support for meaning in text (such as pictures, drawings, sidebars, and photographs). Moreover, the language of content learning becomes increasingly discourse-specific, reflecting a greater demand for participating with more stylized academic language abilities and an expanding reliance on participating in talk about written text for learning support.

The fact that academic content teaching, particularly in the whole-class context, depends almost exclusively on oral and written language means that content learning (developing an identity as a member of a community and becoming knowledgeably able to participate in it) is a formidable task for English learners who are also in the process of acquiring the language of that instruction. Bear in mind that language and literacy use becomes more aligned with written text and more associated with particular communities of practice (ways of talking, feeling, inquiring about and solving problems), as students move through the year and through grades. One of our challenges, then, is to learn ways to notice and use language during content teaching, not only to assist participation in content learning and facilitate second-language acquisition, but also to enable English learners to build identities that they and others recognize as valuable for classroom learning.

The Language of Teaching Academic Content

Whenever you present content orally or in written form to students in whole- or small-group contexts, how well students make sense of what you say or write depends greatly on their ability to use the cuing systems of language (phonology in spoken language, orthography in written language, morphology, syntax, semantics, and pragmatics) and to express their meaning so that students know what they need to know and what they need to do. In the teacher-led whole-class context, you typically use language to motivate students about topics of interest, to introduce advance organizers and other information about topics of interest (to discuss what they need to know and what they need to do), to elicit and evaluate student exchanges about their understanding of what they need to do and know about the topic, and to regulate student behavior during your interaction with them. Students use language to clarify word meanings, to ask about procedures and the topic at hand, and to add meaningful information to the topic at hand.

Taking notice of the language of content instruction requires an understanding of (1) the kinds of language (both oral and written) teachers use for teaching academic content, (2) the kinds of knowledge structures that underlie (spoken and written) academic content, and (3) the kinds of (spoken and written) language students use to make sense of academic content. In other words, teaching academic content involves using language to present knowledge structures that support the content of interest and understanding students' meanings of that content. For example, suppose you were introducing a lesson on elephant tusks to a whole class of third-graders, some of whom were second-language learners. The goal of the lesson is to work on description and analysis, using familiar language and topics. If you were to start out the lesson by having the class look at a number of slides on elephants and follow this by working together on describing the tusks and then on generating some hypotheses about the function of tusks, you would be engaging students in description and principle formation, two knowledge structures that require different ways of organizing and talking about information. Description involves the observation and identification of distinct features; principle formation, by contrast, invokes the use of explanation, prediction, cause and effect, means and ends, and general rules. While both may be challenging, depending on prior experiences with them, principle formation is an especially difficult way of talking about topics because it deals with more general, theoretical aspects of knowledge that account for phenomena across time and space (Mohan, 1986). Students may need to inquire about word and concept meaning in multiple ways to make sense of how to form principles and, therefore, might use lots of questions and guessing.

The discourse of academic content (especially academic text) used in academic communities of practice includes, but is not limited to, six major types of knowledge structures, which can be further classified into two groups: structures that deal primarily with specific aspects of knowledge and structures that deal with general, more theoretical features (Mohan, 1986). We can identify the knowledge structures underlying any academic content by asking about the kinds of specific and general information students need to know to understand the topic. The six major kinds of knowledge structures that cut across subject matter content are:

A. Particular aspects of knowledge about the topic
    1. *Description*—The who, what, and where of persons, objects, and events
    2. *Sequence*—The temporal process, cycle, and procedure of events, usually in narrative form
    3. *Choice*—The alternatives, choices, and decisions people make about people, objects, and events. Choice often entails recognizing and making comparisons and contrasts.

B. General concepts, principles, and values within the topic
    1. *Classification*—The definition and classification of words, people, concepts, and events
    2. *Principles*—The explanation, interpretation, and application of data (facts, details, characteristics) in order to develop generalizations and draw conclusions
    3. *Evaluation*—The judging, appreciation, and critique of objects, actions, and events using opinions and other evaluative criteria.

Knowledge structures underlie both what students need to learn and what they need to do as they learn. Academic communities of practice rely on these knowledge structures in various ways as learners progress toward greater participation. As learners gain practice with them, they simultaneously present themselves as increasingly capable community members.

A major idea here is that children need to be invited into the discourse of the various knowledge structures, because the knowledge structures are interconnected with content, which in turn is organized around recognizable practices. Knowledge structures are embedded in the discourse practices associated with multiple, often overlapping, academic communities of practice. The discourse practices enable learners to display through words, actions, values, and beliefs *membership in* and *affiliation with* communities of practice that have a common set of interests, goals, and activities (Gee, 1992; Pavlenko & Blackledge, 2004). Discourse practices are traditions of talking, writing, and being that are passed down from old-timers to newcomers through time. When we invite children into academic discourse practices, such as the classification of elephant types, we are reenacting a discourse performance that belongs to academic communities of practice. To be recognized as such, the performance must be similar to how those who do such work (for example, scientists) classify and talk about classification. But how the children classify and what they focus on as distinguishing features can be novel in the sense that their ways may differ from what more capable members of the discourse might use, and they are appropriating voice as school community members. Edelsky, Smith, and Wolfe (2002) refer to these kinds of practices as *hybrid activities,* practices in which some aspects of discourse are identical to those performed in actual communities of practice, while others are aligned with ways of doing things in school. The point is that children are entering an academic discourse and claiming identity as members of that school community of practice. It is in this sense that academic discourse acquires the learner, inviting him or her to claim an identity as a member of the community of practice.

As teachers, we are members of and claim identity with multiple and varying communities of practice (math, history, children's literature, art, science), all of which are organized around knowledge structures and particular oral and written language uses. But, as was mentioned above, we are not full members of these discourses; we are teachers of them with participation in them as mediators and carriers of their practices and language uses. When we invite or nudge children to participate in various knowledge structures, we are simultaneously engaging them in discourse practices and identity creation. Both processes necessarily entail getting children to use academic language and literacy in accordance with the knowledge structure and content area(s) practices involved (Solomon & Rhodes, 1995). Part of teaching mathematics, therefore, is to enable students to use comparisons (greater than/less than) and logical connectors (if . . . then, given that) in extended discourse in ways that members of the mathematics community of practice would recognize as appropriate and authentic (Haley & Austin, 2004; Spanos, Rhodes, Dale, & Crandell, 1988). Becoming a member of the discourse community of science entails learning to talk about the formulation of hypotheses, how to describe, classify, predict, and reveal findings using language in ways that are recognizable to members of the science discourse community (National Science Teachers Association, 1991). For example, science as well as math discourses require that members present information in the proper sequence, usually in the passive voice (Lemke, 1990). Thus, it is not uncommon to hear or read text such as, "Elephants, rhinoceroses, and hippopotami are classified as pachyderms." In the social studies, membership depends on the ability to explain, describe, define, give examples, sequence, compare, and evaluate social and historical events (Short, 1994). Historical discourse, in particular, relies a great deal on time-specific language, comparing and contrasting, and cause-and-effect relationships within a theme (Coelho, 1982).

Assuming that teaching academic content involves inviting and nudging children into knowledge that is organized around the above six categories and that these knowledge structures are critical for membership in and affiliation with academic discourses, what other kinds of language do English learners need to comprehend and participate in during whole-class teaching events? Up to this point, we have discussed academic content teaching as if it entailed only informative sequences in which teachers present grade-level subject-matter content to students. Clearly, however, instructional language in a classroom community must engage students in two-way interaction about content and within academic discourses. Not only do teachers exchange and negotiate meaning in discourse with students, but they also use language to regulate interaction with them, to sustain invitations to learning. Tables 4.1 and 4.2 illustrate the kinds of language uses students need to deal with during content instruction (Wong Fillmore, 1982b).

Table 4.1 shows the kinds of language that students need to comprehend in order to follow along and participate in the lesson. Table 4.2 indicates the kinds of regulatory language students need to comprehend during the lesson. From our perspective, the tables also present the kinds of language that teachers use routinely to exchange information via knowledge structures and to move students through the lesson.

You can see in Table 4.1 that the language used in exchanges of meaning includes all of the knowledge structures mentioned above, plus the kinds of language teachers use to set up and call attention to features within knowledge structures. While the informative sequences deal with information teachers present to students and therefore with the knowledge structures students have to understand, the elicitation-evaluation sequences have to do with requests for and evaluations of information from and by students. For example, during an explanation of how circus elephants are cared for when they are not in shows, students may also be asked for and helped to give examples of the kinds of food elephants eat or to provide an opinion

Table 4.1
Kinds of language that English learners need to understand during whole group interaction

Information sequences	Elicitation-evaluation sequences
Contextual support for activities	Specific information
Explanations of concepts, words, and procedure	Opinions and hypotheses
Descriptions and definitions of objects, events, and people	Examples with more information
Ties to prior study or knowledge	Word definitions
Calls for attention to specific information	Description of objects, events and people
Examples	Explanations of how you know
Summaries of events	Requests for clarification

Adapted from: Wong Fillmore, L. (1982). Language minority students and school participation: What kind of English is Needed? *Journal of Education, 164,* p. 150.

about the care the elephants receive. Thus students have to understand the explanation of the material, which may be organized around the discourse of sequential information and description, and that what the teacher has solicited is information concerning examples and evaluations.

The right side of Table 4.1 alludes to the interactional sequence that is especially common in whole-class teaching: The Initiation-Response-Evaluation (IRE) structure. This structure is so ubiquitous in whole-class and

Table 4.2
Regulatory language that English learners need to understand during whole group interaction

- Turn-taking rules and procedures
- Procedural information about what students need to do in small groups or individually as the lesson progresses
- Requests to pay attention during instruction
- Directives about appropriate behavior in whole class and small group work
- Statement about classroom norms of behaviors for whole class and small group work
- Reprimands for inappropriate behavior

Adapted from: Wong Fillmore, L. (1982). Language minority students and school participation: What kind of English is Needed? *Journal of Education, 164,* p. 150.

teacher-centered teaching that it has been referred to as the *default pattern of interaction* (Cazden, 2001). The structure works like this:

- Initiation
- Response
- Evaluation (sometimes referred to as *Feedback*)

The teacher initiates an exchange with a student or students. The structural purpose of the initiation is to elicit a response through a question or a request to continue the teacher's initiation (or a student's initiation). The student responds to the request by answering the question or offering additional information about the topic. This exchange forms the first half of the interactional sequence. The teacher or students may then close the sequence with some type of commentary on or continuation of the initial exchange. The second half is called the *evaluation slot* because in some cases, the teacher may wish to provide some sort of feedback about the student's response, such as whether or not it was adequate or on target. However, evaluation does *not* necessarily have to be an explicit judgment of the adequacy of students' elicited responses. In fact, evaluation may entail some reflection on the teacher's part about how well she has conveyed information or invited student participation in the initiation slot, and in most cases, it should be an extension of the student's contribution in the response slot, such as agreeing or disagreeing, asking for more information, and giving credit for thinking out loud (Edelsky, Smith, & Wolfe, 2002; Johnston, 2004). Here is an example of IRE sequences from Julia's class, when she is talking with the whole class after viewing a DVD on different types of elephants and how elephants work for humans:

Julia: Okay, who can tell me something about the elephants that you learned from the video we just saw? (Initiation)

Here Julia is asking for general information, aiming for responses from which she can then respond to or Teach Off (Edelsky, Smith, & Wolfe, 2002) in the third slot.

Several students raise their hands. Julia invites Lisa to comment:

Lisa: The ones we saw are from Africa. I saw some like that at the zoo. (Response)

Julia: I think I have seen those at the zoo too. (Smiles, and then moves closer to the students in a show of support) How do you know they are from Africa? Concepción? (Initiation embedded in Evaluation)

Here Julia is Teaching Off Lisa's response about being African as opposed to Indian elephants, a point that had been discussed in class over the last few days. Accordingly, the evaluation slot has the dual function of supporting Lisa's contribution and asking for additional information based on her contribution.

Concepción: I know *elefantes* have big ears and small ears. I see the *elefante* have BIG ears. So, I think is African. (Response)

Julia: Yes, the ears give us *clues.* Did anyone else notice the clues? There were lots of clues that we can look for to recognize, to identify the kind of elephant. Can someone else tell the class what they looked for? (Initiation embedded in Evaluation)

Julia gives a quick affirmation of Concepción's response and continues the exchanges, emphasizing the importance of noticing and naming various clues for distinguishing types of elephants.

There are many ways to respond to children's contributions. (See Johnston, 2004, for a cornucopia of ideas for interacting with children to enhance their classroom participation and build their identities as learners.) How you respond in the evaluation slot can offer children, even nudge them toward, productive classroom identities, making them feel invited and capable. For example, in response to students' contributions in the evaluation slot, you can say things like:

"As scientists, how do you know what to look for?" This question asserts that children are identified as scientists, and asks them for evidence, inviting and modeling science discourse practices.

"I know you are proud of yourself because this stuff is hard." This kind of evaluative response acknowledges the student for doing something that is difficult and helps create an identity of a persistent learner.

"Let's see if I understand what you are saying." This response might follow a student's contribution that you wish to summarize for the class. Not only does it show that you are interested, and that you validate the student's voice, it also allows students to hear their words rephrased in summary form.

"What are you sure about and what are you not sure about?" Suppose a student incorrectly spells the word *pachyderm,* but senses that he may be partially correct. The first part of the question directs the student to think about the successful parts; the second part invites the student to problem-solve about the word she thinks she may have gotten wrong. This kind of questioning focuses on what the student does well, and it encourages students to try out what they think they know.

So, as you can see, there are many ways to engage students in continued, sustained interaction using the IRE sequence. Below, you will be introduced to additional ways of enhancing student participation in whole-class interaction.

The last feature of language that you can notice in planning and conducting lessons is the vocabulary and grammatical structures of the content, including regulatory language, which you invite our students to appropriate and use as they participate in classroom communities of practice. Clearly, part of what English learners have to make sense of and appropriate within instructional language, be it informational or regulatory exchanges, has to do with surface language features. For example, suppose that Julia has her class watch a short DVD from Children's National Geographic about a small herd of elephants bathing in a pool of muddy water. The narrator of the film describes how the elephants cool down by spraying themselves with water and rolling in the mud. Julia writes the following sentence from the film on her whiteboard as a talking point to highlight and unpack some of the fun ways that English can be tricky:

> After filling his trunk with water from the pool, this elephant flips back his trunk and squirts the muddy water onto his back, cooling him down and protecting him from the blistering sun.

What do you think are some vocabulary items that English learners, especially beginners, might have difficulty understanding about this description? To begin, the sentence involves a cause-and-effect relationship signaled by the temporal conjunction *after*. So to follow the sequence, students will have to understand that first the elephant filled his trunk with water, and then he flipped it over his head. Julia points out that whenever you see a group of words that start with *after*, it is important to pay attention to what happens next in the sequence. Moreover, she has the students ask the question, "Who filled his trunk?" because the actor of the adverbial participial clause "After filling his trunk . . .," the elephant, is not identified until the main clause of the sentence. Julia gives several examples of similar sentences and then has students pair up and generate their own sentences using the following model: "After hitting the ball, the girl ran to first base." Next, there are the two meanings of *back,* as in "to the rear" and "the rear part of his body," the former being an adverb, the latter a noun. Julia explains to the children that many words in English have more than one meaning, pointing out that *front, back, side, over,* and *under* can all be used in several different ways. She reminds the children to think of words as Power Words, words that they might want to use in their own writing or for getting an idea across to classmates. She has a list of some of her own Power Words from discussions about elephants posted around the room. Whenever possible, she accompanies the words with drawings and pictures from magazines and old books.

In another exchange with a whole class of students, Julia has the students generate questions about elephant behavior that start with "I wonder . . ." (Allen, 2000). Her purpose is to help students build background knowledge that can be used later for in-depth study. She models several examples and asks students if they see a pattern, something that is the same or almost the same in every question:

> I wonder why the elephants always go to the same river?
>
> I wonder when the baby elephant grows tusks?
>
> I wonder how the elephants sleep at night?

Julia is attempting to get students to notice the interesting way people inquire by wondering about how things are or why things happen the way they do. She continues with a mini-lesson to distinguish asking information questions with *wh-* words (Why do elephants always go to the same river?) from musing (I wonder why the elephants always go to the same river?). This helps students see how language works for inquiring about what has just been viewed, read, or discussed, and wondering in general.

The point here is not that you need to consider *all* of the language that we use to exchange information and regulate student behavior, but rather that by paying attention to the vocabulary and grammatical structures that you expect students to understand and eventually appropriate as their own, you can anticipate some of the difficulties that students might have. The sentence above does not necessarily need to be simplified or otherwise changed to make it easier for English learners. Students make sense of language by attending to major propositions and vocabulary that is meaningful to them. They don't need to understand every word said to them to be able to understand messages! If you are aware of certain kinds of structures and vocabulary items that are likely to be conceptually difficult and unfamiliar to English learners, you can plan your lessons to highlight key vocabulary and adapt your discourse so that the ideas that are bound up in difficult grammatical structures are repeated, rephrased, and recycled throughout presentations, discussions of recalled highlights, previews and discussions of motion pictures, and procedural information about how to engage in academic practices.

Table 4.3 contains a general list of vocabulary items and grammatical structures that might be difficult for English learners, depending on the amount of visual and other contextual support provided along with them and the proficiency level of the students who may need to understand them. You can use this list for preparing learning activities, as a way to think about language objectives. For example, you can take existing content information that students will be experiencing during a lesson and look for core

Table 4.3
Selected list of potentially difficult vocabulary items and grammatical structures for English learners in all-English classrooms

Vocabulary items

- Collective nouns, quantifiers, and mass nouns
- Homonyms
- Idiomatic expressions and sayings
- Low-frequency and abstract words
- Prepositions of place
- Pronouns
- Slang
- Specialized vocabulary within each content area
- Unusual descriptors

Grammatical structures

- Comparatives and superlatives
- Indirect speech
- Passive sentences
- Sentences beginning with *There* and *It*
- Sentences containing cause-and-effect and sequential connectors
- Sentences containing temporal conjunctions: *before, after, until, while, when,* and *since*
- Sentences beginning with "They say that "

and specialized vocabulary items and marked grammatical structures that are critical for understanding the lesson. You can then plan your lessons to emphasize key vocabulary and to help students learn to understand and use the grammatical structures that underlie much of the content and academic language we want our students to acquire. The next section explores how you do this and adapt your lessons to facilitate the exchange of information and second-language acquisition. Within specific content areas, you can pay attention to technical language and terminology in math, science, and social studies. You can also be on the lookout for ordinary language that has different meanings in the particular content area. For example, in math, we have *square, carry,* and *take away;* in science, there are *table* and *mass;* and in social studies, *past* and *branches of government.* You can highlight patterns in language use that are especially germane to the kinds of things you want students to be able to do and identify with as they progress in school.

Adapting Teaching Discourse Practices

Once you have learned to notice the language of content instruction in terms of the dimensions and aspects presented above, you are ready to take on the third special ability involved in language-inviting content teaching: adapting your teaching discourse so that students can make meaning of the content by listening and reading and expressing knowledge about it by questioning, writing, and exchanging ideas in ways that enable them to claim identity as members of the academic communities of practice. Achieving this ability depends on how well you incorporate the following two practices into our teaching routines: (1) making teaching language meaningfully inviting for English learners of all levels, yet relevant and interesting for full English-proficient students, and (2) enabling students to express their knowledge in ways that are appropriate to their multiple abilities in English and the academic task at hand. Before presenting specific strategies to use with each practice, however, let's take a brief look at how learners gain proficiency in a second language. This will help us understand the significance of these two practices for facilitating second-language participation when students are learning academic content.

Facilitating Second-Language Acquisition

In the last 20 years, mainstream research in second-language acquisition has constructed for us the following scenario: In every case of successful second-language acquisition, learners had been exposed to regular and substantial amounts of *modified language input* and *modified verbal interaction* (Ellis, 1990; Faltis & Hudelson, 1998; Herrera & Murry, 2005; Long, 1996). Modified language input is more widely known as *comprehensible input,* oral and written language addressed to the learner that has in some way been adjusted to accommodate his or her needs (Krashen, 1982, 1985). According to Krashen (1982), comprehensible input is necessary for second-language acquisition because it supplies meaningful language to the learner. Krashen (1982) explains that learners move from one stage to the next higher stage by understanding the language of the next higher stage. If a learner is at stage i (the current level of competence), our job is to provide language that is at i plus 1, or slightly above the learner's current level of competence. Learners understand the i plus 1 by paying attention to context and by using what they already know about how language works in interaction. When learners understand language addressed to them, the language-acquisition device in their heads can operate on it, and if the device receives enough comprehensible input, it creates the rules that enable the learners to use language for communication.

Support for the role of comprehensible input in second-language acquisition stems from research on *caregiver speech,* simplified language used by Western caregivers to invite young children into culturally appropriate ways of being (Clark & Clark, 1977; Faltis, 1984; Hatch, 1983) and on *foreigner talk,* the modified language that proficient speakers use with language learners to summon or invite them into discourse exchanges (Ferguson, 1975; Long & Sato, 1983). Caregivers simplify their speech to young children, not to teach language explicitly, but rather to engage them in talk about situations that are in the "here and now," topics in full view of both participants. Many caregivers read dozens of storybooks to young children, pointing to pictures and modifying their speech as they move through the text (see Chapter 1). The combination of simplified speech with topics tied to the here and now provide linguistic as well as contextual support that engage the child to understand and participate in what is going on, even when it is clear that the child cannot participate at the level of the caregiver. Examples of the kinds of speech modifications that caregivers make in inviting participation include *pronunciation* (slower rate, clearer articulation, longer pauses), *vocabulary* (high-frequency words, fewer pronoun forms, marked definitions, gestures and visuals to accompany words), and *grammar* (shorter, simpler sentences, topic fronting, repetition and rephrasing) (Hatch, 1983; Cary, 1997).

Although caregiver speech is simplified in the sense that it relies less heavily on complex linguistic structures than does speech occurring between fully competent speakers, it is not finely tuned to the child's exact level of linguistic competence. Rather, caregiver speech is roughly tuned to the child's current level of competence. According to Krashen (1985), roughly tuned caregiver speech offers the following advantages in a child's first-language acquisition:

1. It ensures that language slightly beyond the child's level is provided.
2. It provides a built-in review, because with continued communication, the necessary input will occur and reoccur. (pp. 23–24)

I would also add that roughly tuned caregiver speech invites young children to participate in culturally specific identity-building activities. Thus, when a small child is invited into a storybook about a hungry caterpillar, the child is also being invited to learn colors, shapes, animal names, and many other items of culturally relevant information.

Adult speakers have also been found to modify their speech while conversing with second-language learners in a fashion remarkably similar to the adjustments caregivers make (Long, 1981). First, as in the case of caregiver speech, modifications are made for the purpose of communication, to invite the learner to understand the meaning of the conversation. Second, foreigner talk is roughly tuned to the learner's level, not to a finely tuned level. Accordingly, in attempting to communicate with a second-language learner, a helpful native speaker uses slower rates of speaking, clear articulation, simple vocabulary, and repetition and rephrasing, as in the following example:

English Speaker: Do you want the book?
English Learner: What?
English Speaker: Book. Book. BIG RED book. Do you want this book?
   (points to the book, picks it up, and hands it to the English learner)

Finally, in both caregiver speech and foreigner talk, native speakers use contextual support such as gestures, visuals, paraverbal expressions, and knowledge of the world to help support verbal language, especially when the child or learner is perceived not to understand the message (Krashen, 1982).

Attached to Krashen's theory of second-language acquisition is the idea that there are levels of language proficiency, ranging from pre-production to advanced abilities in listening, speaking, reading, and writing, and that language acquisition can be accelerated through the use of comprehensible input geared to the individual student's i plus 1, coupled with multiple, authentic opportunities for students to use language communicatively. Chapter 7 discusses the implications of relying on proficiency levels for entry and reclassification, as well as for assessing general language proficiency.

A Different Take on Second-Language Acquisition: Community Invitations

Another way to understand second-language acquisition in school context is what can be called *community invitations,* which, unlike second-language acquisition based primarily on comprehensible input, showcases how we use language practices to invite and nudge English learners to see themselves as actively participating members of the new knowledge system within academic communities of practice.

The use of the terms *invite* and *nudge* acknowledges that it is your responsibility to make academic learning communities enjoyable and challenging and not boring, frustrating, or divisive. However, no student enjoys or is challenged by everything that happens in a classroom, and some students may feel alienated from certain classmates or disinclined to participate in certain kinds of activities. From time to time, you will need to nudge students into participating as classroom members when your overt invitations fail. The following sections discuss strategies for inviting and nudging toward active participation and the creation of positive classroom identities.

Occasionally, the strategies are embedded in the examples presented; most of the strategies, however, are highlighted as sections.

The use of community invitations over comprehensible input as the *sine qua non* of second-language acquisition stems from a belief that language acquisition does not take place individually "inside the head of the learner" as Krashen believes, but as argued in several places in this chapter and elsewhere, learning is co-constructed and distributed across communities of practice, and it happens when learners claim membership and affiliation through active participation in the knowledge systems of these communities.

Inviting (and nudging) English learners into academic communities of practice necessarily requires you to use social and academic language that students may not understand initially or be able to use for immediate communication about academic content. Bear in mind, however, that students, even learners who are new to English using environments, can understand more language and communicate better with you and classmates if the language being used is inviting (Cary, 2000; Hawkins, 2004). For example, suppose Julia were talking with the whole class, which includes learners who are relatively new to using English in school about elephant tusks and how poachers kill elephants for their tusks. She shows them several photographs of elephants and ivory artifacts; she has several elephant replicas to pass around to the class; and she reads them a picture story about a baby elephant that loses its mother to poachers. Then, she asks students to say how it makes them feel about what happens to the elephants, using emotion words that she has put on an overhead. Each feeling word has a face next to it to capture the feeling. She also provides several models of what students might say. She encourages those English learners who share a home language other than English to exchange ideas in their home language; she tells those English learners who do not have someone to talk to in their home language to rely on buddies to understand the assignment. Julia's immediate goal is to enable English learners to experience language in both oral and written forms, and at the same time for them to use the language to express their feelings to build knowledge about elephants in ways that identify them as capable classroom community members. Her long-term goal is to help learners recognize and use language in ways that identify them as members of academic communities of practice.

Understanding second-language acquisition as community invitations is based on the proposition that learning is, first and foremost, social, and that it results from learners participating in goal-oriented social activities that are situated in physical locations (Lave & Wenger, 1991). As we have emphasized, the underlying purpose of all academic activities is to invite new learners to join into already established knowledge systems and practices and over time to identify themselves as members of those communities of practice. From this perspective, one of your primary roles as a teacher is inviting students to participate and create identities through participation in social practices that constitute appropriate activity within the community of practice (Miller, 2004; Wolfe, 1999).

From a community invitation perspective, second-language acquisition does not mean that English learners are not engaging their cognitive abilities when they participate in new communities of practice. Learners at all ability levels of English proficiency constantly try out language, using social and academic language together, coupled with actions (e.g., to hypothesize, overgeneralize, and predict rules and expressions) as they attempt to make sense of and identify with new communities of practice (Faltis & Hudelson, 1998). The point to emphasize here is that enabling students to try out language and actions in academic communities of practice is socially motivated and distributed among classroom members. It is the social environment of the classroom that encourages English learners to negotiate meanings of language and actions as they participate in and identify with academic and social practices.

Community Invitations and Negotiated Interaction

When English learners are invited and occasionally nudged to interact as members of new discourse communities, they need to have some way of knowing if the meaning they intended to utter or compose is clear, and if they understand what the teacher and other students say or write to them. This is one of the most intriguing parts of second-language acquisition. Here's why: When learners are invited and nudged to participate in new discourse communities of practice, they have to work to come up with meanings that are relatively precise, coherent, and appropriate to the particular community of practice. In other words, they have to negotiate meaning with the teacher or classmates as they grapple with language generally and specifically tied to academic knowledge systems they need to appropriate. Negotiation of meaning encourages learners to try out new language, and it may enable them to notice the gap between their existing language abilities (based on their prior knowledge systems) and the words and expressions they need to more clearly and precisely express how they know about concepts and practices that give concepts their meaning. Moreover, when you engage students in interaction that invites them to refine the meanings they bring with them, or when you teach off of their contributions, you also sustain discourse with them (ACTIVE PARTICIPATION). The continued exchanges re-supply them with relevant language experiences and practices

JOIN
FOSTERING

and, thus, lead to acquisition (INTEGRATION OF ADDITIONAL LANGUAGE LEARNING INTO ACADEMIC LEARNING PRACTICES).

Here is an example of Julia interacting with Do Thi about a movie the class has just seen. Do Thi is starting to feel more comfortable using English in a whole-class setting. Julia expands and clarifies what Do Thi says in order to be able to share her meaning, and thus, enable Do Thi to communicate her ideas:

Do Thi: Uh, how—how you feel 'bout elephants in movie Tarzan?
Julia: How did I like the elephants in the Tarzan movie?
Do Thi: Maybe, how you feel elephants like Tarzan?
Julia: Oh, I see. Did I feel Tarzan treated the elephants well?
Do Thi: Yeah, how did you feel about that? Was Tarzan a good man to them?

This type of negotiated exchange also "pushes" learners to use their developing language and discourse structures (Lemke, 1990; Swain, 1985). Through interaction with speakers who are highly proficient users of the language, English learners may be obliged to produce language that increasingly approximates English, especially if the more proficient speakers are asking for clarification, checking for understanding, and rephrasing learner language to confirm understanding. The learner's efforts to produce exacting language may force him or her to test hypotheses about or pay attention to word choice as well as the structure of the language, rather than relying primarily on semantic knowledge and inchoate language structures. Put differently, the learner is appropriating a new voice, which entails struggle at times. When you work to clarify or check for understanding, this eases the struggle of using someone else's words for communication of ideas.

Teaching for Community Invitations. Now that you have a good idea about the community invitations and negotiated interaction for facilitating second-language participation, you are ready for the nitty-gritty of language-inviting content teaching: using language and contextual support to invite and nudge students to participate in understanding and expressing knowledge about the range of academic content you are entrusted to invite students into at your grade level(s). In the whole-class teaching setting, participation ordinarily involves the presentation of academic content plus sequential interaction between you and the students with the goal of enabling students to participate in the appropriate community of practice. When you present academic content, your goal is to make language understandable and relevant on at least two levels: first, by adapting the way you invite students to understand content information, and second, by inviting them to interact with you and with their peers about the content under consideration. Recall that we are also striving for a balance of rights of participation so that you and the students will be sharing the three dimensions of participation (refer to Chapter 3).

Lesson Markers

An important goal in presenting information and ideas to students in a whole-class setting is to emphasize understanding what you will be covering and what they need to know and be able to do with the information and activities you present. Students understand the language of content best when they are focusing on content without having to figure out where they are in the lesson and when you provide multiple sources of context.

There are a number of features in how you organize and present content during whole-class teaching that you can focus on to ensure that students, especially English learners, are with you throughout the lesson. These features, which Wong Fillmore (1985) refers to as *lesson markers,* are signals that you provide to students to let them know where they are in the discussion or the event, what decisions you are asking them to make, and how you want them to continue at all times, regardless of the knowledge system being studied. For example, you can mark the beginning and ending of phases of an event with explicit cues, such as "Okay, let's begin by . . ." and "That's all for now; let's put our books away." You can also mark the signal movement through the phases of the lesson by telling students exactly what you are doing, how it relates to what you have done before, and what you will be doing. This is also a good time to refer to lesson and language objectives that you have written on the whiteboard. For English learners, lesson markers serve a very important purpose, as Wong Fillmore (1985) points out:

> Once [English learners] learn the sequence of subactivities for each subject, they can follow the lesson without having to figure afresh what is happening each day. They know what they are supposed to do and what they should be getting out of each phase of the lesson; thus they are ahead of the game in figuring out what they are supposed to be learning each day. (p. 29)

Discourse Markers

While lesson markers signal event boundaries, you can also work toward shaping and modeling the specific styles of language that you think are required of students during the academic task at hand. In this case, what is important is to help students participate in the discourse of the content area in ways that resemble the discourse of more capable members of the community of practice. For example, suppose you were working with the entire class on how to write a letter to various zoos throughout the United States. The purpose of the letter is to inquire about the kinds and numbers of elephants that are in the zoo and to ask some questions about their daily behaviors. As part of your language arts curriculum, you may wish to highlight different ways of organizing the letter using sample letters, before having students begin composing their own drafts. You can model how you write a letter by talking aloud how you might compose, edit, and rewrite ideas.

Another opportunity might occur when students are setting up science experiments; you can assist them in using terms that more experienced members of science discourse would use automatically, such as *steps, hypotheses,* and *conclusions* and point out to them the different meanings these terms have from the common meanings (e.g., step of stairs vs. step in a sequence). Again, it is worthwhile to talk out loud with students about how you pay attention to the power and diversity of word meanings in science and everyday language. This is an invaluable learning strategy for modeling how to think aloud about language and its connection to academic learning.

Contextualizing Whole-Class Discourse

In addition to helping students follow the instructional (declarative and procedural) presentations and exchanges by marking phases and boundaries, you can also contextualize your teaching by supporting it through paraverbal, nonverbal, and visual means. These three means of extralinguistic support not only facilitate the understanding of new information and knowledge structures to which the information is bound, but they also help to invite learners in the interaction with you and others in the class. There are three major ways to provide extralinguistic support to the language you use in soliciting information, teaching content, and responding to children in a whole-class setting:

1. *Paraverbal support.* Paraverbal support has to do with the ways you emphasize and use sounds and change the pace of your speech as you talk and invite students to participate in the lesson. There are many occasions, for instance, when you can illustrate the meaning of emotions, feelings, and senses through vocal sounds. As you say "A rose smells gooooooood," you can sniff and emphasize the word *good* by stretching it out with rising intonation. A story about a mean giant might call for a deeper voice with punctuated vocalization of key words in order to convey just how mean the giant really is! Turning the volume of your speech up and down also communicates meaning. Using whispers and howls to describe changes in the wind helps students understand vocabulary that might otherwise go unnoticed.

Another way to support instructional language through paraverbal means is to pay attention to the rate and clarity of your speech as you describe, explain, exemplify, elaborate, highlight, question, and evaluate. Speaking too quickly during the presentation of key concepts and vocabulary may cause you to lose second-language learners at a critical part of your interaction with them. Abnormally slow speech, on the other hand, can also lead to nonunderstanding, because students rely on the rhythm of your speech to make sense of what you are saying. Plus, by using really slow speech, you may be sending a message that English learners are somehow less capable than proficient English speakers. As a rule of thumb, the rate and clarity of your speech should resemble what you normally use in more casual conversation, with the proviso that you enunciate clearly. Last, humming and singing are wonderful ways of providing paraverbal support for learning words and phrases. There is an entire series of songs, known as *Jazz Chants* (Graham, 1978, 1988, 1992), built around catchy tunes and phrases that children can learn to sing along with and in the process learn fun and entertaining expressions.

2. *Nonverbal support.* Many teachers, particularly in the primary grades, routinely use their hands along with facial expression to illustrate meanings of concepts, notions, and actions. When there are English learners in the classroom, bodily and facial gestures are indispensable for making community invitations, such as soliciting student ideas, recalling highlighted ideas, and going over procedures. It is amazing how much meaning support can be generated from gestures such as pointing, waving, joining fingers, holding up fingers, and marking space with your hands. Some meanings can easily be portrayed through bodily movement. Can you, for example, think of ways to pantomime a baby elephant desperately searching for her mother or a cowgirl gracefully galloping on a horse? How about dressing up as Charlie Chaplin once a week to pass out Words of the Week—words that your students give you once a week to share with the class. You act them out and the children try to guess them.

As the need arises, you can also combine facial expressions with physical gesticulations to indicate surprise, anger, joy, sadness, disappointment, disgust, astonishment, and wonderment. While the facial expressions you use to convey emotions may not be entirely cross-cultural, with repetition and support from other contexts, students soon learn to interpret their meanings in ways that you have intended. Finally, facial expressions coupled with body gestures can show students that you are listening to them, that you are interested in what they have to say, and that you will stay with them in their efforts to express their knowledge (Enright and McCloskey, 1988; Johnston, 2004). In this manner, you convey to students that they are capable of actively participating and of offering insights that count.

3. *Visual and sensory support.* Visual aids are especially useful for organizing and displaying content information. For example, pictures, films, DVDs, and diagrams can be used to tie in and build background knowledge about a topic and then again later to synthesize new information gained from talking about the topic (Cary, 2000; Early, 1990). Many of the vocabulary words and academic concepts vital for following a story or participating in a discussion can be introduced via film and pictures, and then, reinforced in other ways. PBS shows such as *Nova, Nature, National Geographic,* and *Jeff Corwin's Animal Series* offer vivid images and a rich mixture of language and content cues. For students who are new to English, films offer multiple opportunities for participating that would otherwise be unavailable.

Visual aids can also be used to help students experience the different ways that knowledge is organized in structures. A sequence, for example, can be made visible by using a time line. A globe or a map provides visual evidence of the distance between Africa and Asia, two regions where elephants live in the wild. A web of ideas concerning elephant features can serve as a springboard to creative classification. Students can test hypotheses about whether concepts are similar or different by using a Venn diagram. All of these suggestions are examples of *graphic organizers,* ways of representing different kinds of thinking processes (Alvermann, 1986; Dunston, 1992; Gibbons, 2002; Haley & Austin, 2004). You can use graphic organizers to organize the lesson or theme with students. You can also teach students to construct their own graphic representations of the classroom content (Jones, Pierce, & Hunter, 1989). Some of the more common graphic organizers teachers find useful are Venn diagrams, time lines, story lines, semantic webs, fishbone maps, and causal change maps (Clark, 1991; Gibbons, 2002; Tang, 1992; Taylor, 1986). Other ways of providing support for information within knowledge structures include photographs, slides, CD-Roms, videocassettes, and DVDs.

In a classroom created to support joinfostering principles, you want students to experience a panoply of realia, or real-life objects, to feel and smell and to hear the sounds they might make. Realia are the ultimate visuals because they allow students to use all five senses to experience them. For example, suppose your classroom decided to "adopt" an elephant at the local zoo. As part of the project, your students would have to learn about the elephant's eating habits both in the wild and in the zoo. Visual aids could help them illustrate and classify foods that elephants eat. Students could also prepare a treat of roasted peanuts to send to their adopted elephant!

Print is also a form of visual support. You can fill the walls, ceilings, and doors with sayings, symbols, and announcements produced by students in your classroom: "An elephant never forgets"; "Slow down, elephants crossing"; "Don't buy ivory products"; and "There's an elephant in the room." Classroom furniture can be labeled for, as well by, the students. As students' literacy abilities improve, print can be used as visual support to teach songs and poems.

Inviting Student Participation

In addition to marking lesson boundaries and providing extralinguistic support to make lessons and activities understandable and inviting, we need to facilitate active student participation by providing opportunities for English learners to indicate and express understanding when they exchange and share information during the development of the lesson. The balance-of-rights perspective reminds us that we should constantly monitor our teaching discourse to ensure that we do not monopolize the topic, amount, or manner of talk during whole-class instruction. Thus, while we should be concerned with providing extralinguistic support to our discourse as we teach, we also need to encourage students to participate in multiple ways— verbally and physically and through drama, art, and in writing; in the case of some second-language learners, we may even need to "push" them gingerly to use their developing language to express meaning and show understanding (Swain, 1985).

Getting students to interact with you in a whole-class setting is a delicate task, requiring multiple strategies for both soliciting talk and responding to what students say. There are basically two ways to get students to talk: (1) ask them directly and (2) pique their curiosity. Asking them directly is the easier of the two. Here are five basic techniques for asking students to talk in a whole-class setting (Enright & McCloskey, 1988):

1. *Ask the question—call on a student.* In this technique, you simply pose a question and then immediately call on a student by name, without the student having to bid for a turn at talking. If you overuse or use this technique unwittingly with English learners, it can be ineffective because some students may be too embarrassed to express themselves in English while the whole class listens to them. It is important to remember not to draw undue public attention (often referred to as *spotlighting*) to students who are still struggling to communicate their ideas in English.

2. *Ask the question—students bid for the floor.* In this case, you ask a question and the students bid for an opportunity to talk by raising their hands. This technique works best when all students understand how to gain access to the floor. If only a handful of the same students raise their hands following a question, participation is not likely to be equitable. Also, in this technique, you need to keep a mental tally of which students have gained the floor and the kinds of questions to which these students have responded (Faltis, 1986).

3. *Ask a question—any student can answer.* There may be times when you pose an open-ended question to which anyone in the class might have an individual answer. To be effective, the students must understand that you want them to speak up without having to bid for the floor. Again, you will need to pay attention to who is responding, so certain students do not dominate the interaction.

4. *Ask a question—the entire class responds.* In this case, the entire class responds chorally to your directive or request to recite words, phrases, or long stretches of language, such as poems, songs, and important documents. Choral repetitions and responses allow second-language students to practice controlled language use safely within the group, and if you use them intermittently, students really enjoy them.

5. *Ask a question—students take turns responding.* There are certain times when you may want several students to answer the same question, one by one in a patterned sequence. For example, you may ask every fourth student what kind of food he or she would like to prepare for the elephant the class has adopted. Likewise, you can have students pair up, discuss an idea, and then talk about it or share information visually with the whole class.

   Each of these solicitation techniques has both advantages and disadvantages, but in order to maximize the advantages, it is essential to use all five techniques during whole-group teaching. Variety helps ensure that all of the students, regardless of their English proficiency, are given the opportunity to participate at least some of the time. Hence, they are likely to identify as classroom members.

Your classroom should be a place where students are constantly thinking and taking pleasure in using their intellect (Edelsky, 1991). While asking students questions can be helpful for some occasions, there are many times when you should provide only minimal help until the students first do some thinking. One way to get students to participate is to challenge them with thought-demanding projects. They will ask the questions about how to tackle the problem. You can also model that working hard is serious fun. When you pique their curiosity about amazing things, they will talk with you.

It should go without saying that when you pose a question to or solicit a response from an English learner, you should allow sufficient time for the student to answer. You can also give students an extra chance by repeating or rephrasing the question. If you feel that the student either does not understand the question or lacks the oral language proficiency to respond to it, you may also use alternate question forms. For example, in the following communicative exchange, the student, Aucencio, a beginning-level English learner in Julia's classroom, appears not to understand Julia's question. Julia rephrases the question, making reference to a specific idea. When this doesn't work, she uses a choice question to sustain the one-on-one interaction:

Julia: So, what do you think the elephant will do next? Aucencio, what do you think? (gives time to answer)
Aucencio: Next? Elephant?
Julia: Yes, what will the elephant do when he finds the water?
Aucencio: I think he's going there [pointing to a picture of a pond].
Julia: Yes, Aucencio, that's where the elephant is going. Do you think he will take a bath or look for trees?
Aucencio: I think he's . . . take a bath.
Julia: How did you figure that out?
Aucencio: I see the water pool and I see he wants to take a bath.
Julia: That's a great observation, Aucencio.

When Aucencio was unable to respond to the second, rephrased question, Julia could instead have used a yes/no question: "Will the elephant take a bath?" This question is a bit easier to respond to because it does not necessarily call for a verbal response; a nod of the head would also have indicated understanding. The point here is that you can vary your invites for student participation according to the student's communicative abilities. Accordingly, for beginning second-language learners, a nonverbal response such as a nod, a smile, or pointing to an object may be acceptable, while more advanced students should be nudged to use words and extended discourse. As students become more proficient in English and adjusted to the interaction patterns used during whole-class instruction, your goal is to help them improve the accuracy of their communicative abilities and to encourage language that reflects classroom discourse. One way to nudge your second-language learners to use language communicatively is to utilize discourse strategies in which you negotiate with students the meaning of responses to your questions, either to confirm that you have understood what you heard or to request additional information to clarify what you heard. Two well-known strategies for negotiating meaning with English learners are *confirmation checks* and *clarification checks* (Long, 1987; Schachter, 1984).

Confirmation checks are expressions by the teacher that confirm to the learner that his or her utterance has been correctly understood or correctly heard. Confirmation checks are invariably in the form of raising a question and always repeating part or all of the learner's preceding utterance (Schachter, 1984). Interestingly, confirmation checks not only help to confirm understanding, but they also may model in a nonthreatening manner the appropriate way to say an utterance. Here is an example of a confirmation check that also models vocabulary and conventional grammar usage:

Miguel: The feets of the elephant is the same on the hippo.
Julia: The elephant's feet are the same as the hippo's feet? (confirmation check)
Miguel: Yeah. The same as the feet of the hippo.
Julia: How are they the same as the hippo's feet?
Miguel: Well, the elephant gots toyes and the hippo gots toyes too.
Julia: They both have toes, huh? (confirmation check with model of conventional English)
Miguel: The toes are huge! Big, big toes.

Here the dialogue is continued because of Julia's initial effort to confirm Miguel's meaning. Accordingly, Miguel appropriates the conventional uses that Julia has modeled for him, and shows his ability to communicate effectively.

Sometimes learners, in response to a solicit for information, produce language that you may not understand or that needs clarification. When this happens, you can ask the English learner to furnish new information or to rephrase the information just given in order to clarify meaning. Ordinarily, clarification requests are in the form of information questions (what, where, who, how, when, why, etc.) or yes/no questions, but they can be expressed in other ways as well (Schachter, 1984). Clarification requests, such as the ones in the following exchange, enable Kyung to make his initially unclear messages meaningful:

Kyung: And they have tick skins.
Julia: Sorry. What do they have Kyung? (clarification request)
Kyung: Tick skins.
Julia: Tell me what you mean. (clarification request)
Kyung: Like, um, the skin is tick.

Julia: Yes?

Kyung: You know—the elephant skin is not skinny—it is lots and lots of skin.

Julia: Oh, thick skin—I see. You are absolutely right about that.

By negotiating meaning with the learner, Julia helps push Kyung to use additional language to clarify meaning, an effort that results in sustained interaction as well.

Clarification requests can also come from the English learner when the language used by the teacher is beyond the learner's understanding. In this case, the English learner may ask for a clarification, resulting in the teacher's adjusting his or her language to make it understandable to the learner and thus shared understanding through negotiation. Enright and McCloskey (1988) caution that teacher-initiated confirmation checks and clarification requests should be used with care because they "can make students feel that they have made some kind of mistake or that they are on the spot in front of class." However, if much of what you do in whole-class teaching involves genuine exchanges of meaning, there is little chance that these two strategies will produce negative results.

Peggy's Two Cents

Julia's classroom is abuzz with ideas about ways to study elephants, and Julia has asked the class to come up a list of sources for finding out more information from friends, family members, and other teachers. The class decides to put out a call for elephant stories, music, art, and artifacts (anything some person has made). Using a newsletter software program, the students develop a two-page information letter that explains what they are looking for. They distribute to all the school staff and take home a copy to their families.

After school, when Julia is planning her activities for the coming days, Peggy waltzes into Julia's classroom waving the Elephant Newsletter. Hearing footsteps, Julia looks up.

"This is a lovely idea about the elephants, Julia. Guess what? I just happen to have some wooden puppets of Ganesha, the most important deity in Hinduism. That's an East Indian religion. And I have a book for children about Ganesha, the Hindu elephant god, called *The Broken Tusk*.

"That's totally cool, Peggy. Do you think I can borrow them? Several students are looking into the role of elephants in Indian culture and religion. We will be very careful with them, I promise. We are doing all kinds of studies on elephants, and we are bringing in math, science, literature, and drama. You name it. My English learners are so involved in everything we do," says Julia, beaming with enthusiasm.

"I think I can find them for you. Yeah, I can do that. So, your ESL kids are doing okay?" Peggy says with a hint of surprise. "Well, mine aren't. Those little buggers keep speaking their foreign language in my class, and it burns me up. I tell them to *speak English,* and they just ignore me. I think they are just lazy most of the time. Plus, all they do when they go home is talk foreign, and their parents don't want to learn English either."

"Wait a minute, Peg. You are dead wrong about the children and their families not wanting to learn English. My English learners try really hard to talk and write in English. They are far from lazy. Maybe you aren't doing certain things in your class so that the English learners *can* participate." Julia comes out from behind her desk to face Peggy.

Peggy lifts her chin in the air and replies curtly to her, "Uh, I beg your pardon, young lady. I took those SDAIE workshops, and I know about comprehensible input and feedback and all that stuff. What those kids really need is lots of structure, and tons of practice. Lord knows they don't get it at home. I spend my *own* money on worksheets and ESL drills especially for them. I have one kid from Mexico who can't even say my name right! He calls me 'Meez Dimwill' or something like that. I try to get them ready for the district test, and how do they show their appreciation? They talk foreign." Peg then takes two steps toward Julia, looking her directly in the eye, and says in a serious tone, "And another thing: You can't trust them when they work in groups. They copy and don't do their own work. I tell you; some days can be so frustrating."

"Look, Peg. I am sorry you feel that way, and that things have not been going so well for you. But, my students are nothing like what you are saying about them." Julia places her hands on her hips in a show of determination. "My English learners are creative, thoughtful, and hungry to learn, as are all the children in my classroom. I may not have taken those workshops you mentioned, but I have done lots of reading and studying about ways to improve my teaching with English learners, and I talk a lot with other teachers who give me suggestions." Julia is almost shaking, but keeps her composure.

"Anyhow, let's change the subject, okay, Peg?" *You say one more negative thing about my kids and I am going to blow up, and you don't want that, Miss Dimwitty.* "How about this?" says Julia, offering a proposition. "When my kids are ready to report on their inquiry projects about elephants, I would like to invite you to class to see what they come up with. I know they will amaze you. Do you think you might be able to get a substitute to fill in for you for a few hours over a couple of days?"

"Hmmm, my time is pretty valuable, and Mrs. Turner rarely assigns a substitute for this kind of thing, but I will consult with her about it." Peggy makes a move toward the door. "Very well, then, I am going to track down those Ganesha elephant puppets and that book. I will drop them by your class in the next couple of days, either before or after school. I have to go work out. See you around." Peggy turns and walks out the door, taking all of her prejudices with her.

Julia returns to the work at her desk. Her determination to show Peggy what children can do is matched by her outrage over what just transpired. "Worksheets! My God, no wonder her ESL students aren't engaged," she utters to herself, and decides to let it go for now. *Good riddance.*

CONCLUSION

The major focus of this chapter has been on the development of language-inviting content teaching and interaction strategies for whole-class settings. An important goal for you is to facilitate second-language acquisition in your classroom and invite participation during academic content activities so that students can try out and use academic discourse in ways that are recognized and valued in particular communities of practice. Accomplishing this twofold goal depends a great deal on learning to notice the language of content teaching and interaction and on knowing the conditions under which second-language acquisition and participation are most likely to occur. We have learned about several strategies for meaningful interaction with second-language learners, language that assists active participation in oral as well as written communicative exchanges, and language to link prior knowledge to new classroom identities, two important joinfostering principles of practice. The next chapter turns to the social contexts of teacher-led and teacher-delegated small-group work. Much of what has been covered in this chapter will also apply to small-group learning, but we will be looking at ways to socially integrate English learners with native speakers to facilitate active participation in small-group work and to foster cooperative learning during group work.

ACTIVITIES

1. Using a large posterboard, write out your understanding of communities of practice, identity formation, and community invitations. Below the definitions, present the strategies you have gleaned from this chapter that you can use to enable English learners to make sense of and participate in whole-class teaching activities.

2. Select one science and one social studies textbook used for elementary-school children. Next, for both books, choose a chapter toward the middle and the end to analyze for the kinds of knowledge structures (using Mohan's six knowledge structures) that the author uses to present information. Compare and contrast the knowledge structures used in the

two books and discuss the kinds of difficulties a second-language learner might face in having to comprehend the material in each of the textbooks.

3. Using one chapter from each of the above textbooks, select what you would consider difficult vocabulary and grammatical structures for second-language learners. Justify your choices and suggest how you might present the vocabulary either before or during the lesson to make sure that the second-language learners understood the meaning.

4. Observe and, if possible, tape an all-English classroom containing second-language learners during whole-class instruction time. The observation should be for at least 20 minutes. During the observation, jot down the kinds of informative and elicitation-evaluation exchange sequences the teacher uses in talking to the students, as well as the kinds of regulatory language used. After completing the observation, tally the results and write up a snapshot description of the kinds of language exchanges and regulatory language that second-language students would need to understand to follow the lesson. Remember that any time you set foot on school grounds, you need to check in at the main office before going to the classroom in which you plan to observe.

5. Arrange to interview a 3rd-, 4th-, or 5th-grade second-language learner for about 15 minutes. Introduce yourself and tell the student you are interested in learning about what he or she does every day in school. Then, using the adaptation and negotiation strategies presented in this chapter, try to elicit as much conversation from the student as you can. Immediately after the interview, once the student is no longer present, write down what you think worked best and what you think you could have done better.

REFERENCES

Allen, J. (2000). *Yellow brick roads: Shared and guided paths to independent reading, 4–12.* Portland, ME: Stenhouse Publishing.

Alvermann, D. (1986). Graphic organizers: Cuing devices for comprehending and remembering main ideas. In J. Baumann (Ed.), *Teaching main idea comprehension* (pp. 210–226). Newark, DE: International Reading Association.

Brown, G., & Yule, G. (1983). *Teaching the spoken language.* Cambridge: Cambridge University Press.

Cary, S. (1997). *Second language learners.* York, ME: Stenhouse Publishers.

Cazden, C. (2001). *Classroom discourse: The language of teaching and learning (2nd ed.)* Portsmouth, NH: Heinemann.

Clark, H., & Clark, E. (1977). *Psychology and language: An introduction to psycholinguistics.* New York: Harcourt Brace Jovanovich.

Clarke, J. (1991). Using visual organizers to focus on thinking. *Journal of Reading, 34,* 526–534.

Coelho, E. (1982). Language across the curriculum. *TESL Talk, 13,* 56–70.

Dunston, P. J. (1992). A critique of graphic organizer research. *Reading Research and Instruction, 31*(2), 57–65.

Early, M. (1990). Enabling first and second language learners in the classroom. *Language Arts, 67,* 567–575.

Edelsky, C. (1991). *With literacy and justice for all: Rethinking the social in language and education.* New York: The Falmer Press.

Edelsky, C., Smith, K., & Wolfe, P. (2002). A discourse on academic discourse. *Linguistics and Education, 13*(1), 1–38.

Ellis, R. (1990). *Instructed second language acquisition.* Oxford: Basil Blackwell.

Enright, D. S., & McCloskey, M. L. (1988). *Integrating English: Developing English language and literacy in the multilingual classroom.* Reading, MA: Addison-Wesley.

Faltis, C. (1984). A commentary on Krashen's input hypothesis. *TESOL Quarterly, 18,* 352–357.

Faltis, C. (1986). Sway students in the foreign language classroom. *Foreign Language Annals, 19*(3), 195–202.

Faltis, C. & Hudelson, S. (1998). *Bilingual education in elementary and secondary school communities: Toward understanding and caring.* Needham Heights, MA: Allyn & Bacon.

Faltis, C., & Merino, B. (1992). Toward a definition of exemplary teachers in bilingual multicultural school settings. In R. Padilla & A. Benavides (Eds.), *Critical perspectives on bilingual education research.* Tempe, AZ: Bilingual Review Press.

Ferguson, C. (1975). Toward a characterization of English foreigner talk. *Anthropological Linguistics, 17,* 1–14.

Gee, J. P. (1992). *The social mind: Language, ideology and social practice.* New York: Bergin & Garvey.

Gibbons, P. (2002). *Scaffolding language, scaffolding learning: Teaching second language learners in the mainstream classroom.* Portsmouth, NH: Heinemann.

Goodlad, J. (1984). *A place called school: Prospects for the future.* New York: McGraw-Hill.

Graham, C. (1978). *Jazz chants for children.* New York: Oxford University Press.

Graham, C. (1988). *Jazz chant fairy tales.* New York: Oxford University Press.

Graham, C. (1992). *Singing, chanting, telling tales.* Englewood Cliffs, NJ: Regents/Prentice Hall.

Haley, M. H., & Austin, T. (2004). *Content-based second language teaching and learning: An interactive approach.* Boston, MA: Allyn & Bacon.

Hatch, E. (1983). *Psycholinguistics: A second language perspective.* Rowley, MA: Newbury House.

Hawkins, M. (2004). Researching English language and literacy development in schools. *Educational Researcher, 33*(3), 14–25.

Herrera, S., & Murry, K. (2005). *Mastering ESL and bilingual methods: Differentiated instruction for culturally and linguistically diverse (CLD) students.* Boston: Allyn & Bacon.

Hudelson, S., & Rigg, P. (1994/95). My *abuela* can fly: Children's books about old people in English and Spanish. *TESOL Journal, 4*(2), 5–10.

Jones, B. F., Pierce, J., & Hunter, B. (1989). Teaching students to construct graphic representations. *Educational Leadership, 46*(4), 21–25.

Johnston, P. (2004). *Choice words: How our language affects children's learning.* Portland, ME: Stenhouse Publishers.

Kanno, Y., & Applebaum, S. (1995). ESL students speak up: Their stories of how we are doing. *TESL Canada Journal, 12*(2), 32–49.

Krashen, S. (1982). *Principles and practice in second language acquisition.* New York: Pergamon Press.

Krashen, S. (1985). *The input hypothesis: Issues and implications*. New York: Longman.

Lave, J. (1996). Teaching, as learning, in practice. *Mind, Culture, and Activity, 3*(3), 149–164.

Lave, J., & Wenger, E. (1991). *Situated learning: Legitimate peripheral participation*. Cambridge, England: Cambridge University Press.

Lemke, J. (1990). *Talking science: Language, learning, and values*. New York: Ablex.

Long, M. (1981). Input, interaction, and second language acquisition. In H. Wintz (Ed.), *Native language and foreign language acquisition* (Annals of the New York Academy of Sciences No. 379, pp. 259–278). New York: Academy of Sciences.

Long, M. (1996). The role of the linguistic environments in second language acquisition. In W. Ritchie & T. Bhatia (Eds.), *Handbook of second language acquisition* (pp. 413–455). New York: Academic Press.

Long, M., & Sato, C. (1983). Classroom foreigner talk discourse: Forms and functions of teacher questions. In H. Seliger & M. Long (Eds.), *Classroom oriented research in second language acquisition* (pp. 268–285). Rowley, MA: Newbury House.

Miller, J. (2004). Identity and language use: The politics of speaking ESL in schools. In A. Pavlenko & A. Blackledge (Eds.), *Negotiation of identities in multilingual contexts* (pp. 290–315). Clevedon, England: Multilingual Matters.

Mohan, B. (1986). *Language and content*. Reading, MA: Addison-Wesley.

National Science Teachers Association. (1991). *Scope, sequence, and coordination of secondary school science*. Washington, DC: Author.

Norton, B. (2000). *Identity and language learning: Gender, ethnicity and educational change*. Essex, England: Pearson Education.

Norton, B., & Toohey, K. (2001). Changing perspectives on good language learners. *TESOL Quarterly, 29*(1), 307–322.

Pavlenko, A., & Blackledge, A.(Eds.). (2004). *Negotiation of identities in multilingual contexts*. Clevedon, England: Multilingual Matters.

Pica, T. (1987). Second-language acquisition, social interaction, and the classroom. *Applied Linguistics, 8*(1), 3–21.

Ramírez, D., & Merino, B. (1990). Classroom talk in English immersion, early-exit and late-exit transitional bilingual education programs. In R. Jacobson & C. Faltis (Eds.), *Language distribution issues in bilingual schooling* (pp. 61–103). Clevedon, England: Multilingual Matters.

Rigg, P., Kazemek, F., and Hudelson, S. (1993). A bibliography of books with non-stereotypical views of the elderly. *Rethinking Schools, 7,* 28–29.

Schachter, J. (1984). A universal input condition. In W. Rutherford (Ed.), *Language universals and second language acquisition* (pp. 167–181). Philadelphia: John Benjamins Publishing.

Schinke-Llano, L. (1983). Foreigner talk in content classrooms. In H. Seliger & M. Long (Eds.), *Classroom oriented research in language acquisition* (pp. 146–168). Rowley, MA: Newbury House.

Short, D. (1994). Expanding middle school horizons: Integrating language, culture, and social studies. *TESOL Quarterly, 28,* 581–608.

Sirotnik, K. (1983). What you see is what you get—Consistency, persistency, and mediocrity in classrooms. *Harvard Educational Review, 53*(1), 16–31.

Solomon, J., & Rhodes, N. (1995). *Conceptualizing academic language*. Santa Cruz, CA: The National Center for Research on Cultural Diversity and Second Language Learning.

Spanos, G., Rhodes, N., Dale, T., & Crandell, J. (1988). Linguistic features of mathematical problem solving: Insights and applications. In R. R. Cocking & J. P. Mestre (Eds.), *Linguistic and cultural influences on mathematics learning.* Hillsdale, NJ: Lawrence Erlbaum.

Spindler, G. (Ed.). (1982). *Doing the ethnography of schooling: Educational anthropology in action.* Prospect Heights, IL: Waveland Press.

Swain, M. (1985). Communicative competence: Some roles of comprehensible input and comprehensible output in its development. In S. Gass & C. Madden (Eds.), *Input in second language acquisition* (pp. 235–253). Rowley, MA: Newbury House.

Tang, G. (1992). The effect of graphic representation of knowledge structures on ESL reading comprehension. *Studies in Second Language Acquisition, 14,* 177–195.

Taylor, B. (1986). Teaching middle grade students to summarize content textbook material. In J. Baumann (Ed.), *Teaching main idea comprehension* (pp. 195–209). Newark, DE: International Reading Association.

Toohey, K. (2000). *Learning English at School: Identity, social relations and classroom practice.* Clevedon, England: Multilingual Matters.

Trueba, E. (1998). The education of Mexican immigrant children. In M. Suárez-Orozco (Ed.), *Crossings: Mexican immigration in interdisciplinary perspectives* (pp. 251–275). Cambridge, MA: Harvard University Press.

Valdés, G. (2001). *Learning and not learning English: Latino students in American schools.* New York: Teachers College Press.

Wolfe, P. (1999). *Situated learning in a transactional, secondary, English-as-a-second-language classroom.* Unpublished doctoral dissertation. Tempe, AZ: Arizona State University.

Wong Fillmore, L. (1982a). Instructional language as linguistic input: Implications of research on individual differences for the ESL teacher. In L. Cherry Wilkenson (Ed.), *Communicating in the classroom* (pp. 283–296). New York: Academic Press.

Wong Fillmore, L. (1982b). Language minority students and school participation: What kind of English is needed? *Journal of Education, 164,* 143–156.

Wong Fillmore, L. (1985). When does teacher talk work as input? In S. Gass & C. Madden (Eds.), *Input in second language acquisition* (pp. 17–50). Rowley, MA: Newbury House.

5
Facilitating Active Participation During Small-Group Work

OVERVIEW

In previous chapters, we learned that in addition to whole-class teaching, participation in language, literacy, and content learning activities in grade-level classrooms can also occur through (a) teacher-managed small-group interaction and (b) teacher-delegated small-group work in which students work together on their own in pairs or in groups of three to five students. Each of these two social contexts can supply English learners with myriad opportunities for authentic oral and written communication within academic communities of practice. However, because of their complexity and the fact that both social contexts favor a balance of rights in which students often control not only the opportunities for discussion but the topic of discussion as well, many teachers are reluctant to incorporate them as an integral part of their students' daily learning experiences. In other words, for many teachers, small-group work represents a yielding of power to students, and that can be threatening. When students work together in small groups, it is tempting to fall back on rules for participation that hinder rather than help English learners engage in activities, and thus, they have a more difficult time acquiring the language they need to successfully identify with and participate in academic communities of practice. Absolute rules such as the following can hamper English learners because they disallow important means of participation and identity negotiation on which these students rely for gaining access to academic discourse practices modeled and appropriated through small-group work (Toohey, 2001):

> No talking
>
> Use your own words and ideas
>
> Use your own materials

Small-group work requires learners to talk, share, and interact. Accordingly, you may need to remind yourself and your students that small-group work works best under the following rules:

> Yes talking
>
> Share words and ideas
>
> Share materials

Why these components are beneficial to English learners will become clear as you progress through this chapter.

A major goal of this chapter is to present ways of integrating the two kinds of small-group work into your classroom as a way to promote talking, literacy, sharing, and interaction, and to do so without compromising your need to have a well-organized and smoothly run classroom. Small-group work is an ideal place and manner for students to build knowledge and express their feelings about serious social and academic topics. It is also a time when students can learn about topics that bring enjoyment and new understanding. In both cases, small-group work is a social context in which English learners contribute to and transform their identities as classroom learners and participants of local academic practices used in and out of school communities.

In grade-level classrooms containing English learners as well as in dual-language classrooms, the incorporation of small-group teaching and learning requires that the second-language learners be socially integrated with fully language-proficient students and must actively participate in ways that necessarily enable them to use and understand authentic oral and written discourse as they work. Your ability to accomplish this depends partly on how well students are and have been prepared for and invited into the kinds of language uses, knowledge structures, and social requirements involved in small-group activities designed to engage students in academic communities of practice. To no small measure, successful small-group work depends on the ability to guide and assist student participation so that as students move through literacy- and talk-based activities, they eventually assume total responsibility for carrying out activities on their own, regardless of their language proficiency. This enables them to assume multiple identities as knowledge brokers, knowledge carriers, and capable participants who belong to various communities of practice.

Most teachers incorporate small-group *teaching* as a means to engage in literacy-related activities while the rest of the class works on assignments individually, but a significantly small number of teachers delegate authority to students for their own *learning* in small groups. Assigning students of mixed English-language abilities and/or social skills to collaborate and cooperate in small groups makes many teachers uncomfortable. One of the real concerns is that the students who are fully proficient speakers of a particular language, particularly the higher-status students, will end up doing most of the talking as well as most of the work and will consequently receive the greatest benefit from the learning experience (Cohen, Kepner, & Swanson, 1995). To address this concern, you need to prepare students for small-group learning to make it a beneficial experience for all students. Students are concerned about issues of fairness, and small-group interaction is a good time for exchanging ideas about fairness and justice.

Teaching effectively to students in a small-group context means that you are relying on teaching strategies that enable every student in the group to participate from the outset of our interaction with them. The strategies you choose should at the very least provide temporary assistance that is adjusted to the students' language and learning needs (Cazden, 2001). Beyond assistance, students also need acknowledgement of their efforts and acknowledgment that their voices count. Likewise, when you delegate authority to students to participate in small groups, you need to make sure that they know how to work in groups, that they have the social abilities that promote continuous interaction and collaboration, and that they see themselves linked together positively as members of a group.

Teaching and learning in small groups is highly complex compared to whole-class teaching, because in small-group work, students teach and are taught by peers of diverse language, social, and academic abilities. The knowledge that they construct through interaction stems not only from their own experiences, but also from the experiences of others who, like them, are learning the discourse of the task at hand. This is one of the best reasons to

place students into pairs and small groups (Calderón, 1994). No other classroom context intentionally or unintentionally offers this degree of interactional complexity or authenticity (Cazden, 2001; Fránquiz & de la Luz Reyes, 1998; Pérez, 2004). That small-group learning is complex and provides a relatively safe and authentic context for language use and that small-group learning benefits all students, and most especially English learners, are realities that Julia has come to appreciate as a result of using small-group teaching and small-group learning on a daily basis since the beginning of the school year.

Incorporating small-group learning wasn't easy for Julia when she first began trying it out. She experimented with different group compositions, different group assignments, and different lengths of time that students would stay in one or more groups. Some of the students engaged in disruptive behaviors, while others appeared lost and unfocused, both of which are typical as students negotiate identities as learners. Over time, she noticed that certain students participated more engagingly in small-group settings than others, depending on the type and duration of the activities. By observing students as they interacted, she also became aware of which students needed additional assistance before being ready to assume greater responsibility for unassisted participation. And most importantly, Julia became convinced that small-group work is an ideal setting for English learners to hear and use a variety of authentic discourse, especially when literacy engagement is involved.

Let us now look briefly into Julia's classroom as she works with a group of five students while the rest of the class is working in groups on a social studies project. Following this episode, you will learn about the kinds of specific interaction strategies to use for small-group teaching when one or more of the students in the group is an English learner. This discussion will be succeeded by a detailed discussion on small-group learning—specifically, ways to plan, organize, and manage small-group work in which students of varying English-language proficiencies interact and work together without the presence of the teacher.

Episode Five: Teaching Gets Better for Julia

By this time in the year, Julia realizes totally that English learners benefit from all social contexts for participating in academic communities of practice—whole class, small group, and individually. She has become much more aware of the extent to which language, literacy, and the formation of multiple identities play a role in classroom participation and learning. She habitually takes notice of her own language use, so that much of what she says to students throughout the day is adapted in one way or another to ensure that they understand her and are given the opportunity to talk with her and fellow students when necessary. She has also begun assessing their language and learning in small groups using observation records and student self-assessment. She reviews her scoring procedures for group participation and group projects, making sure that every student understands how they will be assessed. All 10 of the English learners are by now well adjusted to classroom life and attuned to the social and regulatory language of the classroom. Although several still receive extra help in English as a second language, the amount of time they spend out of class with an ESL teacher has decreased considerably. Their English-language progress is variable, but all have noticeably improved their oral and written abilities from the beginning of the school year. Julia meets regularly with each one to go over their progress and to discuss ways of improving their English and their participation as classroom members. As you have read, there are several reasons for their success, not the least of which is that Julia expects all of her students to do well and has made changes in her teaching and assessment strategies and the classroom organization to realize this expectation. The fact that a student is an English learner is *not* a problem in Julia's class. Her students are provided with many opportunities to be curious, to show ownership of knowledge systems, to inquire about social injustices, to be aware of their progress as learners, and to take on identities as capable members of the classroom communities of practice. One of the contexts in which Julia enables students to interact and make inquiries about topics of interest is having students collaborate in groups while she works with a small group of students, as in the following scenario.

Most students are chattering away, conversing with classmates who are working with them at their tables. Today, Julia has reggae music playing softly on a CD player in the background. Only a few children are up and about; one is heading to the paper shelves, another is conversing with a friend near the pencil sharpener, and another is at the world map looking for a particular country. At this time of the day, for approximately 35 minutes, five groups of students collaborate on assignments that involve various amounts of reading, writing, drawing, and coloring and lots of social interaction. Like an early morning fog, the students' voices mix across groups to produce an undeniable, but nonetheless pleasant, din. The groups, each of which contains an English learner, are spread throughout the classroom in areas with clearly marked physical boundaries. Today two of the groups are putting the finishing touches on their skits about ways to preserve elephants in the wild. Each group has created and written a short skit about some aspect of elephant preservation. The skits contain a short poem, some facts and figures, and a two-way dialogue using reported speech. Several of the skits are modeled after the Dr. Seuss storybook in which Horton the Elephant saves the day. Julia and the students have read the Horton story and other Dr. Seuss books, and she has encouraged students to incorporate some aspect of Horton and his outlook into their skits. Julia has also gone over how their skits will be graded using performance rubrics she developed.

Julia also invited the school librarian into the class to read two other children's books that feature elephant stories. Each group has also designed a 2-x-3-foot poster and has written a summary of their skit, which will be presented to the class and to parents on Back to School Night. One of the books that the librarian read was *Babar,* the story about a young elephant who becomes civilized by a rich lady who adopts him after a hunter has shot and killed his mother. Julia was disturbed by the messages in the *Babar* stories. The rich lady is portrayed as good in the story because she has money and the power to transform Babar into a human, teaching him human ways of eating, dressing, bathing, and counting. To become "good," Babar has to give up his old ways of being unclothed and uneducated. Once he becomes civilized, he returns to his elephant jungle abode and is eventually named the king because he has "learned so much living among men" (Kohl, 1995). The elephants themselves are portrayed as legitimizing the value of wealth and power that Babar has come to symbolize.

After the librarian leaves, Julia shares her concerns about the *Babar* story with the whole class, reading and musing aloud about several passages in the story. Several students immediately see how the story pits rich people against poor people (represented by the elephants) and how it glorifies the hunter who kills elephants as sport. The students decide to conduct a literature study on the *Babar* stories to learn more about how the author, Jean de Brunhoff, develops the idea through her writings that Western civilization is superior to ways of living in Africa. They want to learn how children's books might promote racism in subtle and often undetected ways. To help them get started, Julia does some extra reading about *Babar,* relying on Herbert Kohl's book, *Should We Burn* Babar*?* (Kohl, 1995) and a book entitled *Learning to Teach for Social Justice* (Darling-Hammond, French & García-López, 2002). The children have decided to study how Babar becomes distinguished from other elephants. Each group poses a list of questions they have about the story using "I wonder why" statements and then comes up with ways to find and present answers to the whole class.

While the groups are at work on their *Babar* and skit projects, Julia is attending to a group of students in a reading circle. Three of the students in this group are English learners; the other two are fully proficient speakers of English. For today's activity, the students are discussing and reading a book that one of the students chose about a small fish named Swimmy (Lionni, 1963). In this story, Swimmy joins a school of fish who are also small; together they form the outline of a large fish, which enables them to swim about safely, without being bothered by bigger fish.

Julia follows a relatively set procedure of first drawing out what students might already know about the topic of the text, modeling for them how to talk about literature, highlighting various parts of the book she really likes without giving away the theme. She wants the students to think about all stories she and they read as "deliberately crafted constructions" and to gain a sense of solidarity as co-participants in learning (Edelsky, Smith, & Wolfe, 2002). She consciously incorporates paraverbal, nonverbal, and visual support and varies her requests for student contributions to literate discourse practices according to their language abilities. At the outset of the interaction, Julia invites the students to converse and negotiate with both her and with peers. In this manner, she and the students listen to and use one another's comments for discussion. Julia wants the children to begin the conversation about *Swimmy* by thinking of ways to approach the text and how their personal experiences with and general knowledge about fish figure into the story, and then move the discussion to the theme of how working together enables individuals to accomplish tasks that would be impossible alone. Julia keeps a literature response scoring rubric at hand to keep track of students' contributions (MULTIPLE WAYS OF ASSESSMENT TO OPTIMIZE LEARNING PRACTICES).

Following a lively discussion on how big fish eat little fish and how sometimes the bigger kids pick on the smaller ones during recess and in the cafeteria, Julia rereads the story to the children and talks about the text in terms of the author's and the readers' stances, the possible theme of the story, and how the characters in the story bring it to life. Next, the students read parts of the story, looking for big ideas that tie the story together and commenting how the story makes them feel. Students are encouraged to help each other with unfamiliar words and with any difficult passages. When all of the students finish the story, Julia begins posing questions to help students think and talk about the story, at times bringing up questions posed prior to the reading, but mostly focusing on the story's theme. Julia varies her invitations not only to ensure participation, but also to lift the level of discussion, extending students' contributions and reshaping them, using their words, into more literate discourse. She continues to encourage students to interact with each other and to draw on their own experiences and understandings as they address aspects of the story that connect to their own lives. Throughout her interaction with the students, she models and encourages talk about the story in ways that reflect the ways members of literature discourse practices relate to, think about, and discuss stories. At the end of the session, she asks students to complete a self-assessment form on their participation in today's discussion group.

While Julia is teaching with her group, she is also monitoring what the rest of the class is doing in their small groups. Occasionally, when the noise level becomes too high, she raises her hand, which immediately triggers a few and then eventually all students to do likewise. This is the signal that is used to indicate that everyone needs to work at a much quieter level. It works! If one or two of the students start to dance to the beat of the reggae music, that's okay too, as long as it doesn't disturb others or get way out of hand.

Julia plans most of her small-group learning activities so that each member of the group has a particular role and a set of responsibilities that she has introduced to the whole class as team-building activities to help students see the value of different perspectives and to feel comfortable working together in a team for the longer, more complicated group activities. In addition, she frequently models, and has students practice, ways of asking questions, ways of talking about the assignment, ways of inviting others to talk, ways of responding to ideas, and ways of being polite about disagreeing with someone. This is about all of the planning Julia does for her groups to work together well. Much of what goes on in small-group work is spontaneous and creative, and along with the fact that students are engaged in activities that reflect academic communities of practice, that is what makes it so valuable for learning.

By this time in the year, Julia is feeling much better about how the class is progressing. She has arranged with fellow teachers to have the three students who receive ESL support each day work on activities from her class while they are in their ESL class, and vice versa. Also, she has invited Jake to work with students on the *Babar* critical consciousness project and to help her develop different ways to assess their learning, an invitation Jake was more than happy to accept. Through constantly watching how the students are participating in whole-class and small-group work settings, Julia senses that she is improving her teaching in the areas that concerned her most at the beginning of the year.

To expand upon what Julia has done to make her work with groups work, let's spend some time thinking about (1) small-group management strategies for engaging students in conversations about ideas and themes related to written text, and (2) ways to plan and carry out teacher-delegated small-group learning.

TEACHING AND CONVERSING IN SMALL GROUPS

Teaching to a small group of students while the rest of the class works with another adult (a teacher aide or a parent or grandparent volunteer), an older peer, with peers in small groups, or individually enables you to interact with students in ways that no other social context can provide. When you are working with a small group of students, not only can you contextualize your academic discourse through paraverbal, nonverbal, and visual as well as sensory support (see Chapter 4), you can also incorporate dialogue strategies to jointly construct conversations about knowledge and experiences that relate to knowledge in ways that reflect the practices of the desired community. The dialogue strategies discussed here rely partly on a way of understanding social interaction and learning in school settings based on the work of L. S. Vygotsky and partly on what was discussed earlier about community invitations to participation and identity formation in academic domains. You might consider the Vygotskian perspective as an added dimension to your own participation in a wider academic discourse about how children appropriate voice and identity affiliations with school and out-of-school communities, as presented in Chapter 3.

A Brief Introduction to Vygotskian Ideas for Small-Group Teaching and Learning

Lev Semenovich Vygotsky (1896–1934), a Soviet sociohistorical psychologist, was interested in the role of social interaction between children and more knowledgeable conversants for transforming children's understanding and abilities into higher levels of participation in communities of practice. He proposed that learning transformations depend on the presence of four interrelated preliminary components, which are as follows:

1. A teacher who identifies with and participates in a community of practice (the teacher can also be a more capable peer [MCP])
2. Dialogue between the learner(s) and the teacher or MCP

3. That the dialogue be carried out in language that is meaningful and that enables the learner(s) to identify with and participate in the community of practice

4. That the teacher or MCP provide participatory assistance within the learner's zone of proximal development.

Small-group teaching necessarily invokes only the first component; the remaining three require a desire and ability to implement them. You can minimally satisfy the second component by inviting English learners to converse and by building on their contributions to align them with practices in particular academic domains. Likewise, we can meet the third condition by actively providing meaningful invite through extralinguistic support, using negotiation strategies to get second-language students to talk, and by responding to and extending their initiations into the desired discourse practices. In other words, you invite students into discourse practices and the identities linked to them, and they draw on their own experiences as appropriate new ways of seeing, feeling, relating to, and doing academic practices. Before we can satisfy the fourth condition, however, it is worthwhile to gain an understanding of how, from a Vygotskian perspective, students, through the experience of joint interaction and practice with others (orally or through text), come to appropriate desired practices and participate in academic discourse communities.

Learning as the Social Appropriation of Voice and Identity.   In Vygotskian theory, learning entails a two-phase process that first requires learners to engage in assisted social interaction with others who already belong to particular communities of practice. By talking about a topic of interest with someone who understands it more fully, the way members of the community of practice understand and relate to it, and then practicing it within these new ways through talking, writing, and doing, the student ultimately becomes able to participate in and identify with the community of practice. However, learners do not merely take on the adult's or MCP's higher-level community knowledge and abilities, but rather co-construct ways of understanding and knowledge based upon prior (including the recent assistance) as well as present experiences. In other words, the student appropriates a new voice for responding to and solving problems within the community of practice that is aligned with but not necessarily identical to the teacher's voice (Hawkins, 2004). Vygotsky (1978) refers to this social appropriation of voice as moving from other-regulated to self-regulated learning (see Figure 5.1).

Other-regulated learning: social assistance

1. Adults or more capable peers assist learner's performance.
2. Adults or more capable peers negotiate meaning with the learner.
3. Adults or more capable peers model practices aligned with the desired academic domain.
4. Assistance provided is temporary and adjusted to learner's needs and abilities for appropriating new voice.

Self-regulated learning: appropriation of new voice

1. The learner practices and aligns understanding and ways of participating with desired community of practice.
2. The learner plans, guides, and monitors new tasks relying on practices and identities gained through assistance by members of the academic community of practice.

Figure 5.1
Other-regulated to self-regulated learning

The appropriation of voice and identity from other to self enables learners to converse about, identify with, and perform tasks that are beyond their individual capability at the time of their introduction. For example, with assistance from an adult or MCP, an English learner may be able to identify and discuss the motivation of the author and characters in a story or explain how and why a hot-air balloon rises, but the learner still requires experience doing so in ways that are recognized and used in the desired community of practice. Self-regulation is complete when the student is able to plan, guide, monitor, and identify with problem-solving activities similar to those once performed jointly, without adult or MCP assistance (Díaz, Neal, & Amaya-Williams, 1990). Using the same two examples, now the English learner would be able to discuss the author's and characters' motivations in ways that are aligned with literate discourse about books and be able to engage in discussions about problems involving the scientific principles underlying hot- and cold-air exchanges.

From a Vygotskian perspective, the teacher initially regulates the learning activity in order to create a level of *intersubjectivity*, which is the student's ability to redefine the problem situation in ways that make sense and that reflect how more experienced community members talk about and address the practice (Pérez, 2004). Once intersubjectivity becomes apparent, the goal of subsequent interaction between the teacher and the learner then becomes to gradually and increasingly shift the responsibility for appropriation of the practices to the learner.

Working in the Zone of Proximal Development. One of Vygotsky's most important social learning principles is that jointly constructed social interaction that begins with intersubjectivity and works toward the appropriation of voice must fall within the learner's *zone of proximal development.* Vygotsky (1978) proposes that collaboration with teachers and MCPs who are active members of academic communities of practice provides learners access to new areas of learning potential beyond what they can accomplish alone. He refers to these areas of potential as the "zone of proximal development," stating that each learner has an *actual* participatory level, which can be assessed by paying attention to what a learner can do without assistance, and an *immediate potential* for becoming recognized as a more capable member of a community of practice, which necessarily requires assistance through joint interaction and practice with activities and ways of talking that reflect the desired academic domain (Tudge, 1990). Thus, the zone of proximal development is the difference between actual and potential levels of learning. In Vygotsky's own words, the zone of proximal development is "the distance between the actual developmental level as determined by independent problem solving and the level of potential development as determined through problem solving under adult guidance or in collaboration with more capable peers" (Vygotsky, 1978, p. 86). (See Figure 5.2 for a schematic representation of the zone.)

Figure 5.2
The zone of proximal
development
Source: From "Spanish for Native
Speakers: Freirian and Vygotskian
Perspectives" by C. Faltis, 1990,
Foreign Language Annals, 23(2),
p. 122. Reproduced with permission
from the American Council on the
Teaching of Foreign Languages.

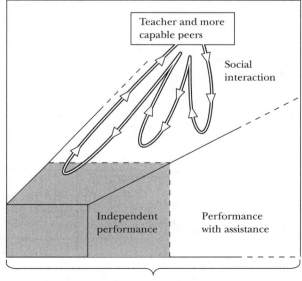

Zone of proximal development

The zone of proximal development is a function of both the learner's level of understanding and ability within a community of practice and the nature of the practices involved. To the extent that the teacher or MCP provides discourse assistance so that the learner can be an active participant in desired academic practices once the activity has begun, the teacher or MCP is working within the learner's zone of proximal development. For both English learners and fully English-proficient students to participate from the outset of an activity requires that the assistance given be presented through discourse that is suitably tuned to the learner's zone of proximal development and done for the purpose of inviting the learner into ways of thinking about, discussing, and relating to practice that are recognized and used in the academic domain of interest. Such discourse assistance must also be both *adjustable* and *temporary* (Cazden, 2001). As learners gain conceptual understanding through discourse and practice, the boundaries of the zone gradually expand into new areas of knowledge, in terms of both what can be done alone and what can be accomplished with assistance (Vacca, 2002). (See Figure 5.3 for a representation of the development of problem-solving ability in the zone of proximal development.)

Vygotsky's ideas about how learning takes place within academic communities of practice directly support three of the six joinfostering conditions: (1) ACTIVE PARTICIPATION OF ALL STUDENTS, (2) SOCIAL INTEGRATION TO FACILITATE THE CREATION OF NEW IDENTITIES AND SOCIOACADEMIC AFFILIATIONS, and (3) INTEGRATION OF AD-

JOINFOSTERING

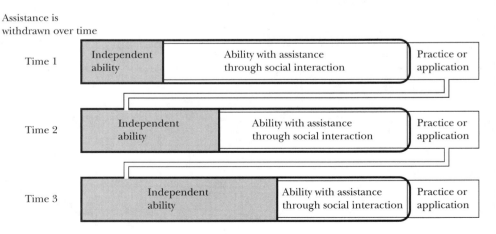

Assistance is
withdrawn over time

Figure 5.3
Problem solving in the zone of proximal development

DITIONAL LANGUAGE LEARNING INTO ACADEMIC LEARNING PRACTICES. Indirectly, social interaction within the zone of proximal development leading to learner appropriation of voice and identity also relates to assessment and the promotion of critical consciousness. You have to be able to assess the extent to which learners need additional assistance, and the kind of assistance they need to gain identity and membership within the community of practice. Moreover, you can bring up issues of justice and fairness in small groups, where status inequities can have a critical impact on who gets to talk and whose voices count when the discussion centers around issues of social inequality (Cohen, 1986; Darling-Hammond, French, & García-López, 2002).

Conversing with Scaffolds and Dialogue Strategies

Teaching to students in small groups is very much like conducting a grand conversation (Eeds & Wells, 1989), because it involves multiple channels of talk about topics that are tied together by the experiences of the immediate group, but that lead to new ways of experiencing academic discourse practices of a community that exists outside the group. You can learn to engage in and sustain small-group conversation within the zone of proximal development through the use of (1) scaffolding and (2) dialogue strategies for apprenticing students into desirable academic communities of practice.

Scaffolds and Scaffolding.   Scaffolding refers to visible and audible support that a teacher or MCP temporarily supplies to a learner, making it possible for the learner to participate in desired discourse practices from the very beginning that otherwise might be too difficult (Cazden, 2001; Gibbons, 2002). It might help to think of a scaffold in its ordinary sense, as a way for workers to reach higher levels when they need to. Furthermore, scaffolds used by workers come down when they are no longer needed. Scaffolds can be language-related, such as confirmation checks, requests for clarification, rephrasing, and extending student contributions, or they can foster academic understanding and participation, providing support through visual means (e.g., graphic organizers) and conversational dialogue aimed at getting students to talk and act in ways that are aligned with desirable discourse practices.

In the context of small-group teaching, scaffolding enables you to assist language and academic performance in the zone that is beyond the learner's individual ability. When you have English learners in the small group, for example, at times it may be necessary to verbally scaffold certain language expressions and constructions by spending time on special vocabulary and terminology so that students can participate in exchanges. At other times, you might find yourself talking with students about different ways of discussing ideas in particular academic domains, scaffolding instruction through mini-lessons and one-to-one reporting. For instance, you can make direct reference to how to say something in various ways and talk about how people say it when talking about it in certain academic domains. In this manner, the assistance you provide is aimed at helping students enter the academic discourse, where they can try out new identities and new practices that align them more closely with the community that regularly uses that discourse.

When you use language and instructional scaffolds to interact with English learners during small-group work, you should use them selectively to accomplish the following three goals:

1. As support, to remove the discourse responsibility that would normally be shouldered by the students

2. As a tool to guide learners who are on the scaffold to new ways of relating to, thinking about, discussing, and identifying with local and generalized knowledge systems

3. As an extension of your range as a teacher so that you can sustain a dialogue with English learners, a dialogue that would be unlikely without the assistance your scaffolds provide.

Dialogue Strategies that Scaffold Learner Participation and Identity Formation

Good dialogue in small-group teaching results from students contributing to scaffolded conversations with you that induct them into particular communities of practice in ways that are recognized by members who are already part of the generalized community. Students enter into a dialogue in one of two ways: (1) they can initiate talk through questions and comments, or (2) you invite them into the discourse using strategies that enable them to pursue ideas and identities that bring them into the community of practice. Either way, your role is to sustain the conversation so that as the dialogue progresses, you talk less and the students talk more and in ways that reflect membership practices in the community discourse. In the following section, you are introduced to three dialogue strategies for scaffolding teacher-managed small-group work, The Karen Smith Model (Edelsky, Smith, & Wolfe, 2002), Instructional Conversations (Goldenberg, 1991) and the Joan Tough Model (1985).

The Karen Smith Model for Apprenticeship and Solidarity Building

Smith's approach to small-group teaching is especially applicable for engaging English learners in literature study that is aligned with out-of-school literature study discourse practice. It is comprised of two types of strategies: *apprenticeship strategies* designed to invoke a generalized community of practice and *solidarity strategies* to position students as co-members in the local classroom community of practice. Solidarity strategies aim to create in students an identity affiliation with the community of practice.

Apprentice Strategies

1. *FYIs* (For Your Information) give students tips and general ideas about aspects of literature and writing, from the point of view of people who belong to this community of practice. In an FYI, you can identify the genre of writing (e.g., fantasy, mystery, scientific, biography, historical fiction) as a matter of fact. You can say things like "A lot of people say that . . ." or "People who write this way say that . . ." to talk about what people say about the various genres. FYIs provide general information about the desired discourse, and students are not expected to be held accountable for FYIs. You can use FYIs as a basis to show students how writers seek to bring readers into their world.

2. *Tourguiding.* With this strategy, the aim is to act as a tour guide by pointing out the parts of the story that interest you, by highlighting them, rereading them aloud, and commenting on them, using language identified with and used in literature study discourse. You model for students what people who love literature say and do when they share parts of the text of which they are particularly fond. For example, you can say, "The part I really like is . . ." and "When the author writes this way, I always get a good feeling. . . ." When you tourguide, your observations invite students to comment on aspects of the story that they also find appealing. With English learners, you can model expressions such as "I like how the author says. . . ," "When I tell my friends about this story, I talk about. . . ."

3. *Lifting the level.* This strategy builds on students' contributions by extending or reshaping them into broader issues that the literature piece addresses. From a Vygotskian perspective, you scaffold students' ideas to help them try out more abstract phrasing and to incorporate terminology that is part of the discourse domain. An example of lifting the level is *re-chaining* student ideas (Wolfe, 2004), in which you extend and link

students' experiential talk about stories to more domain-like ways, restating the student's comment using more general language, but assigning the content of the restatement to the student contributor. With English learners, you may have to fill in the gaps or request clarification using the community invitation strategies presented in Chapter 4.

4. *Spotlighting.* This particular apprenticeship strategy is useful when you are instructing students on what they need to do in literature study, focusing on key aspects of the assignment that make what they are doing part of a larger literary community. You can spotlight key aspects with FYIs or as specific information about how to proceed in the assignment, teaching off students' queries, or offering clarification about terminology.

5. *Setting it up.* This strategy orients students within the zone of proximal development to get ready for the main work of literature study. "Setting it up" means that the students are more or less ready to begin the difficult work of literature study. Your goal is to get students to talk about what is important to them, to decide on a focus for closer study, and to share individually with the groups what they think the focus might be.

6. *Unpacking and lowering the level.* In this strategy, you interact with students using terminology and desired discourse practices as if they understand and then lower the level to check and clarify students' understanding to scaffold interaction about ideas you have presented. This is a good time to use the IRE sequence mentioned in Chapter 4 to scaffold shared understanding of potentially difficult vocabulary and specific terminology. Use the IRE sequence sparingly, however, and use it only for those instances when you want to directly engage students in quick exchanges to ask about and explain troublesome words and ideas.

Solidarity Strategies

1. *Support/empathy before teaching.* This strategy focuses on offering explicit appreciation and acknowledgement of how difficult participating in academic discourse can be. You can tell students where you find the text to be difficult or confusing and encourage them to point out text that they consider to be problematic. Talking with students about how difficult literature study can be sends the message that as a member of the community of practice, you understand and at times share their frustration because it happens to all who enter the world of literate practices.

2. *One of the gang.* This strategy is to take up and add to a student's contribution without taking it over. You incorporate student talk word-for-word (or in conventional speech if needed) and extend it without necessarily lifting the level. The goal is to let students know that they are part of the discourse and that their ideas, regardless of their English proficiency, contribute in important ways to the ongoing discussion of the book. Accordingly, it is important to join in a student's contribution that you sense brings out an aspect of the story that might otherwise go unnoticed or that you might have mentioned yourself.

3. *Oh, you cute kids!* This strategy asks you to take on the role of a trusted, affective adult who cherishes the cute things that children say and affectionately acknowledges them with laughter and glee. There is joy in interacting with children about stories and literate practices. Oh, You Cute Kids! signals to students that learning can and should be fun, even if at times it is difficult and challenging.

Together, these apprentice-teaching and solidarity-building strategies enable English-learners and fully English-proficient students alike to experience and see themselves as participating members in an academic and out-of-school community of practice to which you may already belong. To begin, you should make a list of the strategies and then try out one or two at a time, until you feel comfortable using them and then add more.

Instructional Conversations for Academic Practices

Instructional Conversations (ICs) are ways of talking with students in small-group settings to explore academic ideas rather than having students answer your questions about what they are learning, making academic talk more like informal conversation (Goldenberg, 1991). Accordingly, ICs have both instructional and conversational features you need to plan for in order to use this model effectively with English learners. The features are as follows:

Instructional Features of IC

1. *Thematic focus.* You select an organizing idea or theme as a starting point to orient the conversation. You need to have a general plan for how the theme is to develop, including ways to enable the students to explore big ideas that relate to the theme, which should be meaningful and interesting to the students.

2. *Activation and use of background and relevant schemata.* You prepare students for the theme by engaging them in talk about their prior knowledge of the topic and by providing them with certain background

information relevant to the unfolding of the theme. You invite students to offer their feelings about an aspect of the theme and assist them in generating questions that interest them about topics that relate to the theme.

3. *Direct teaching.* There are times during an IC when you need to provide overt teaching of terminology and pertinent concepts that are directly related to participating in the development of the theme. You can use mini-lessons in the context of the activity to assist with language and content learning. Mini-lessons are short, FYI-kinds of information that are done quickly without disrupting the overall flow of the conversation.

4. *Promotion of more complex language and expression.* You lift the level of conversation within the students' zone of proximal development to engage them in academic discourse and practices aligned with how more proficient members recognize and use language to discuss academic content. This is a time to invite students to stretch their language use by asking them to comment on the discussion, to restate ideas using desired terminology, and to clarify meanings. You can also talk aloud with students about language expressions and terminology that may be difficult for some students.

5. *Promotion of bases for statements or position.* When students converse about academic ideas, they frequently express their opinions about what they are studying. Your goal is to invite students to base their opinions and arguments on evidence, reasoning, and consideration of alternative possibilities. You can invite (and nudge) students to state how they know something is this way or that way, asking them to explain their position. You can have them point to the text where it says something that they are claiming, using language such as, "Show us where it says that.", "Why do you think this is happening?", and "How do you know that happens?"

Conversational Features of IC

1. *Few "known-answer" questions.* Known-answer questions occur most often in recounts, when both the person asking the question and the person answering the question know what is coming. They are also used in traditional IRE sequences. In conversations where the goal is to generate a discussion about topics relating to the theme, you pose questions that enable students to carry on an academic conversation about their feelings, thoughts, and impressions of what they are studying.

2. *Responsiveness to student contributions.* Your interaction with students is geared to updating their understanding as well as to acknowledging unanticipated contributions. You can recast and expand students' contributions to extend and explore new, but relevant, topics that relate to the theme. For example, suppose you were having an IC with a group of English learners about why there are so many towns near rivers, and Xiancoung remarks that "The river next to my family house in Vietnam is very, very wide, and is much rain every day." You want to take up and acknowledge Xiancoung's contribution, perhaps by extending it as a possible new topic for discussion.

3. *Connected discourse.* Although a network of topics underlying a theme guides your discussion with students, you encourage students to speak without bidding for the floor and to build and extend what others have contributed. You talk with students about conversing directly with other students, rather than addressing all talk to you as the teacher.

4. *A challenging, but nonthreatening atmosphere.* Your conversation with students helps create a zone of proximal development in which students can converse in a nonthreatening manner about the topics at hand. You encourage students to take risks, to speculate about their understandings. You want students to practice academic discourse without the threat of being unduly evaluated on their attempts to try out language practices before they are fully acquired.

5. *General participation, including self-selected turns.* In ICs, you do not hold exclusive rights of participation, to determine who talks about which topic. Everyone talks. You ask students to volunteer or otherwise indicate who gets to speak next. You can teach students turn-taking gambits, such as "What do you think, Miguel?", "How about you, María?" and "Your turn, Kyung." Or you can use a talking chip (see below). The person who is holding the stick gets to talk, and then chooses the next person to talk, and so on.

Instructional conversations are well suited for teaching in small groups about topics that are thematically organized, and in which there is no set procedure that students must follow to achieve understanding or perform absolutely. In other words, ICs work well for language arts and social studies themes, which rely heavily on active participation and sustained conversations that lead students to try on and identify with practices aligned with these academic communities. To learn how to incorporate ICs into your teaching, it is best to start by becoming aware of which of the 10 strategies you already use, and then start adding new ones until you feel comfortable interacting with students through this approach.

The Joan Tough Model for Entering and Sustaining Academic Dialogue

Joan Tough (1985) offers a way to engage English learners in extended dialogue about academic topics in general. This model of academic dialogue is highly teacher-centered, relying on conversational scaffolds roughly resembling the IRE sequence for extended interaction within topics that might otherwise be difficult for English learners to discuss. Moreover, in this model, assisting students as they take work as part of their identity as members of a community of practice is implicit, as is the idea that teachers need to work in the student's zone of proximal development.

Academic Dialogue Strategies

Orienting Strategy.   Entering a dialogue with English learners requires you to establish the interpersonal and contextual foundation from which the dialogue will unfold. You can accomplish this by introducing a topic through statements and comments and then asking questions that invite students to think in a particular way about the topic. You have probably done this many, many times around storybooks. The statements and questions should be open-ended in the sense that they allow students a wide range of choices or options. You also want to let the students know from the outset that they can make a major contribution to the dialogue, so you should encourage and praise their efforts, letting them know how difficult and confusing some topics can be. Here is an example of Julia inviting Jaime to tell the group what he knows about circuses, before she begins reading a book on circuses:

Julia: [Holding up a picture of a circus act inside a tent] Jaime, what do you see happening here? Tell us about this [pointing to a circus elephant balancing on a ball].

Jaime: Elephant . . . The elephant is playing on ball.

Julia: [Looking around to members of the group] Yes, can you believe it? Have you ever been to a circus with elephants, and clowns, and all kinds of fun things to watch? [All of the students in the group nod their heads enthusiastically.] A lot of people work in the circus, and today we are going to read about what they do in their jobs. Jaime? [inviting him to comment]

Jaime: Oh yes, a circus. I know what is a circus. I going to a circus with my uncles. We see many funny things. I like-ed the clowns and I see the people swinging high in the air, in that circus. I like that.

Julia: Many wonderful and funny things happen in the circus. [She smiles at Jaime.] Today we are going to read and talk about circuses, and maybe we can find out how the animals learn to do tricks and how people learn to swing high in the air.

Julia follows this explicit reference to the main topic of discussion, and then asks other student about the kinds of jobs that people might have in the circus. Later on in the dialogue, Julia will introduce the issue of treatment of circus animals.

Enabling Strategies. On the basis of how students respond to orienting requests, you can decide how much and what kind of scaffolding assistance to provide in subsequent exchanges. When students respond with less expression of thought than you know they are capable of, you can pose new questions to guide them in the direction of the topic introduced in the orienting discussion, and hence, you can move the dialogue forward. Here are three enabling strategies for generating long as well as short exchanges from English learners:

Follow-through Questions. These are assisting questions that follow the student's response to an open-ended request for information. Follow-through questions aim to expand the student's ability to express ideas more fully and to lift the level of thinking about the topic. Typically, a follow-through question asks the student for more precise vocabulary, more explanation, or for a justification of an opinion or a statement. When you ask a follow-through question of an English learner, be sure to vary your requests for more information according to the student's language proficiency and social style. For example, for one English learner, the simple response "because I like it" might be appropriate to a follow-through question, whereas with another student you might feel a need to "push" for more information by requesting a fuller, more explicit explanation. Two useful rules of thumb to follow in varying your requests to English learners are (1) least proficient English learners may be more comfortable providing a description of a person, place, or thing, but they may need your assistance to give you a narrative of the events in a story, and (2) it is harder for students to justify a claim than it is to make one (Brown & Yule, 1983).

Focusing Questions. In responding to your questions or in initiating talk about the topic at hand, students inevitably say things that, with your assistance, could lead them to a deeper understanding and appreciation of academic content. Used carefully, focusing questions can direct a student's attention to a particular feature in something that was just said—for example, a fact or an event that was overlooked during the orienting and follow-through exchanges. Answers to focusing questions should be simple and short.

Checking Questions. These questions are identical to the clarification requests that you read about in Chapter 4, and they are assessing questions as well. Checking questions invite students to think again about what they have said and to clarify their meaning to you and others in the small group. Ordinarily, you ask checking questions in the form of a *wh-* question (what, where, when, who, why, etc.), but there are numerous other ways of requesting clarification. For example, you can use *yes/no* questions, choice questions, and directives. *Yes/no* questions are questions that can be answered with a simple *yes* or *no*. Choice questions are inquiries in which the answer is one of the choices you present, for example, "Do you mean that the man does not hurt the lions or that the man hurts the lions?" Choice questions are good to use because they usually enable the student to continue the dialogue. Directives are simple commands, such as "Tell me what you mean by 'the clowns have scary face'" and "Talk to me about what you mean when you say 'mens and womens sit on swings and go up and down'."

Informing Strategy. Informing strategies make up a large part of your contribution to dialogue with students. You are considered the expert and one of your charges is to help students buy into an activity, care about it, and come to believe that what they are learning matters to them. In this model, informing strategies are divided into ways of engaging students in new areas of academic content and ways of providing them with conventional and corrective language information. As teachers, you are constantly inviting students into new knowledge systems and the academic discourse practices aligned to them. For example, you present multiple descriptions of persons, places, and events; you invite students to consider certain facts and details; you suggest and make analogies to help students make connections between their lives and what they are studying; you read and participate in various kinds of narratives; you summarize events; you make guesses and wonder aloud why certain things happen the way they do; and you suggest and provide short and long explanations. You not only model these discourse structures for your students, you also want them to understand, use, and identify with them in ways that are recognized by more proficient members of the academic discourse.

The ways that you inform students depend both on the purpose of the information and the knowledge structure that underlies it (see Chapter 4), although most information can be presented through a variety of knowledge structures. English learners need to hear a wide range of ways for organizing and expressing information because you want them to be able to discuss and use the information in ways that are valued in both school and out-of-school communities of practice. Moreover, it is important at times to name for the students what you are doing as you inform. For example, you can let students know when you are summarizing the main steps in an experiment or comparing types of clouds with common household objects. This not only furnishes them with information, but it also models for them a way of talking about information that is valued in academic discourses.

Using informing strategies when you manage small-group activities requires sensitivity, not only to how information is organized, but also to how you are presenting it. Take care to support the language you use with extralinguistic cues so that students can understand the information you present and so that they can express their understanding through their own questions and comments.

English learners also need your assistance and guidance in the appropriate use of English. Thus, included in informing strategies are ways to extend vocabulary use and to bring attention to errors that may affect understanding and communication. Strategies for extending vocabulary use include checking on the meaning of a word, for example, "*belly* is another word for *stomach*" or giving several definitions of a word that students are having trouble understanding. For example, suppose that an English learner in your group of students has confused the meaning of *crosswalk* with *sidewalk* and that the distinction is critical for understanding a particular passage. One informing strategy would be for you to stop the discussion immediately and ask students for one or two definitions of each concept, allowing them to use extralinguistic support such as drawings and pictures. Even better is to encourage other students in the group to talk about the meanings they have of the concepts; then you can add a drawing or a picture as needed.

Attending to student language errors as an informing strategy should be done very carefully when students are engaged in authentic dialogue, and when it is done, its focus should be mainly on nonconventional uses of grammatical rules that govern the organization of connected speech. This type of nonconventional use has been referred to as a *global error* (Burt & Kiparsky, 1972). Nonconventional language use is considered global when it affects the overall understanding of an idea at either the sentence or discourse level. Thus, global nonconventional language use can range from improper word order within one sentence to the illogical sequencing of ideas across sentences.

Considerably less attention should be given to *local nonconventional language use,* minor mistakes, usually at the word or phrase level, that have little affect on comprehension or communication (Burt & Kiparsky, 1972). You may want to bring attention to a local error when it could potentially cause embarrassment or shame—for example, if a student were to write "My brother have fisteen years" or say "The elephant has big toyes" or use a taboo-like word such as "pee-pee" inappropriately.

Let's consider a sentence that contains a global nonconventional use and two local errors and see how correcting the global error clarifies the meaning: "They started to learn English as childrens, because they speak very good." In English *because,* a causal conjunction, is always attached to the event that happened first. However, in this sentence, *because* is incorrectly attached to the second event, making the overall meaning of the sentence unclear. By addressing the global error, the sentence becomes clear at once, even though the sentence still contains the two local errors, *childrens* and *good:* "Because they started to learn English as childrens, they speak very good." You should leave the local errors alone because they occurred during authentic conversation, and they do not interfere with the meaning of the sentence.

An effective way of informing students about global errors and nonconventional language is to first alert them to the usage by telling them that you don't understand something that they have just said. Next, tell them how the language works in this particular case, using clear language, and follow this with a concrete, here-and-now example to illustrate the rule. Then quickly return to the dialogue in progress. You might wish to follow Stevick's (1986) "5-second rule," which says that if it takes more than 5 seconds to explain a rule to a learner during a meaningful dialogue, it is probably not worth the effort.

Remember that all students make errors and use nonconventional language at times, that errors are essential to learning, and that correcting them doesn't mean learning has occurred. You may have to call attention to something several times before the student begins to reconstruct his or her developing language.

Sustaining Strategies.   When students have initiated talk or are contributing to the conversation, you can encourage them to continue talking and at the same time let them know that you are interested in what they are saying. Nonverbal expressions of agreement, such as smiling and nodding your head, looks of amazement, and vocal expressions of appreciation signal to the student that you are listening and you want the talk to keep going. Sustaining implies that you are using minimal scaffolding support. However, you should be listening for opportunities for re-employing scaffolds and enabling strategies according to the new language and learning needs that students display.

Concluding Strategies.   While continued talk is important for developing students' language and reasoning abilities, at some point you will need to draw the conversation to a close or move on to a new topic. Concluding strategies are statements to students that you are about to end the conversation or to change the topic. Marking the end of a dialogue is important because it prepares the students for what comes next.

As you use these dialogue strategies coupled with negotiated interaction, you should always remember that your assistance should be adjustable and temporary. If you feel that a student is capable of contributing more, raise the scaffold and propel the student to a new zone of proximal development. Likewise, if students are using language creatively and independently, remove the scaffolds until you are ready to draw the conversation to a close. Learning to use these strategies takes effort, lots of practice, and continued self-assessment. You can develop your own personal rubrics for the three models and monitor where you are and how well you are progressing as you try them out.

DELEGATING STUDENTS TO LEARN IN SMALL GROUPS

Small-group work can also be planned and implemented so that students of generally equal abilities but with differing language and skill preparation join together to talk and work among themselves in small groups of two to five students per group. In this section, we will discuss ways to delegate authority for learning to students as they collaborate in pairs and small groups, ways that incorporate Vygotskian ideas about the role of social interaction in learning and promoting second-language acquisition as well. To these ends, you will learn how to develop in students the social skills needed for continuous interaction and cooperative collaboration. But before embarking on the "how" of small-group work, let's examine briefly why peer interaction is well suited to your classroom.

Benefits of Peer Interaction

Small-group learning is advantageous to English learners because it provides access to practices that lead to successful second-language acquisition (Gibbons, 2002; Johnson, 1994; McGroarty, 1993). To begin, peer learning provides English learners with an acquisition-rich environment, an environment in which meaning is accessed through language that has been adjusted consciously or unconsciously to accommodate the learner's needs for active participation. Talk that occurs in small-group work gives English learners extensive exposure to contextualized language and thus multiple opportunities to build understanding and to practice the new discourse. Conversations generated from peer interaction also provide an authentic context for greater redundancy in communication as students share and build upon ideas (McGroarty, 1993). Hearing terminology and key expressions being repeated, rephrased, and recast helps English learners understand new language.

Another benefit for English learners stemming from peer interaction in small groups is the increased practice opportunities it provides for learning to talk and care about topics in the educational domain (Johnson, 1994). When students collaborate in small groups, there are substantially more, and more varied, opportunities for using language to express, generate, and build on ideas, opportunities that are absent in both whole-class teaching and individual seatwork. Peer interaction is an ideal "practice field" where students can try out expressions and negotiate meaning with a familiar audience without having to worry about getting everything right or adhering to external and conventional norms of correctness. These opportunities to practice language also help students develop interactional knowhow: knowledge about when, where, and how to communicate to get things done, as well as knowing what to say (Enright, 1991). Such practice prepares students for the other social contexts of learning in the classroom.

Last, small-group learning benefits English learners in another way, one that is often overlooked in the literature. Learning in small groups is intrinsically enjoyable! When students talk with one another, they are using language for authentic purposes. In other words, they are engaged in language use that is genuinely meaningful and that serves a functional purpose in completing the task at hand.

While the above benefits may occur as a result of peer interaction, you would be wrong to assume that second-language acquisition and academic language practices will occur naturally just because students of mixed language proficiency are physically grouped. There are plenty of instances of English learners being *physically grouped* with fully English-speaking students, but with little or no meaningful interaction taking place among them (Edelsky & Hudelson, 1982; Milk, 1980). Good small-group learning, then, may need to be complemented by features that ensure that all students are contributing through talk and action to the group effort. If you feel the need for structural support to help ensure equitable participation in small-group work, there are four actions that you can plan for. These four actions, which are interconnected and mutually supportive, are:

1. You can talk directly with students about interpersonal and small-group courtesy, teaching them polite ways of turn-taking, interrupting, and challenging other's contributions.
2. You can make sure that your students are face-to-face when they are in small groups.

3. You can organize the activity so that they depend on each other to complete the tasks at hand.

4. You can set up the learning activity so that each student is accountable for completing some aspect of the activity.

A Word About Group Size and Group Composition

Before we discuss small-group work further, it is worthwhile to consider the size of your small groups and the compatibility and language ability of students you wish to place together to carry out the various activities and roles that you intend to assign to them.

There are a number of factors that you should consider in deciding how many students to place in a group (Gibbons, 2002; Johnson, Johnson, & Holubec, 1986):

1. As the size of the group increases, so does the range of abilities and experiences of the members. The larger you make the group, the greater the number of "more capable peers" with knowledge and discourse practices that may be helpful to the group.

2. The larger the group, however, the more important social interaction abilities become. In groups of more than three students, students must have social abilities for enabling everyone a chance to interact and to remain on task as the activity unfolds.

3. The nature of the activities and the materials required for the task may also play a role in determining the size of the group.

4. The less time available for group work, the smaller the group should be. Smaller groups are more effective for accomplishing shorter tasks because less time is needed for getting organized, and there is more participation time for each member.

An equally important consideration in forming groups has to do with the compatibility and language proficiency of the students you place together. In your classroom, you want English learners to interact socially with fully proficient English-speaking students, and small-group work provides you with an ideal setting for this to take place. But you need to keep in mind that students have different interaction preferences and interests, and that these vary greatly according to the topic and the activities you have planned. Moreover, students have all sorts of social relationships with other students in the class, and these can enhance or diminish interaction and learning within an activity if you do not remain vigilant to ensure English learners are not being blocked from participation. For example, it may be unwise to place students who intensely dislike one another together for doing an assignment that is critical for achieving a class grade, but it may be helpful to assign them to work together on a project that is intrinsically interesting. Likewise, placing best friends together may lead to imbalanced interaction during some activities but well-rounded interaction during others.

Home- and second-language proficiency also affect student interaction and productivity. Every time you place an English learner into a group of fully English-proficient speakers, in addition to social styles and student interests, you should also consider the language and literacy abilities of the student. A general rule of thumb is that the lower a student's home language literacy and English-language proficiency, the more important it is to place him or her with peers who are most likely to work together cooperatively. If you place more than one English learner in a group, you should also think about whether you want students of the same home language background together in the group, or whether you want students of different home language backgrounds in a single group. If your goal is primarily language practice in a peer-managed group, it may be best to select two students with different language backgrounds and different proficiency levels in English. If you are more concerned about academic content understanding and discourse practices, having two students of the same language background may be beneficial because they can explain ideas to each other in their home language, if necessary.

Preparing for Small-Group Work

Most students need at least some preparation in interpersonal and small-group relations to be able to collaborate effectively with their peers when you are not directly supervising or managing them. The social interaction required for small-group work operates on the principle that everybody needs to talk and listen, but not necessarily all at the same time. Some of your students may not have had the experience of working effectively in small groups, where task completion and, ultimately, learning depend on cooperation and collaboration among group members. In other words, when you assign students to work in groups, they need to be responsible not only for their own behavior in the group, but for group behavior as well (Cohen, 1986). This is one reason why it is essential to engage students in multiple discussions about how to participate in academic communities of practice when you teach them in small-group settings.

One of the most important interpersonal and small-group abilities that you need to stress in your small-group teaching and that students need to develop is how to share in the exchange of ideas so that all students contribute more or less equally. Students can learn to distribute talk fairly among themselves by following three basic rules of behavior:

1. Everyone in the group must have an equal chance to talk.
2. Everyone needs to listen when a member is talking to the group.
3. Everyone must contribute ideas, even when they are potentially in conflict with those of others.

The first rule speaks to the need for equitable access to participation; the second, to a key requirement and component of all communicative exchanges; the third, to the need for participation from all.

There are a number of ways to help students internalize and apply these cooperative behavioral rules. One way is to teach them the rules directly and then have them practice applying the rules during group work. Following group work, you can also have students evaluate the group process by having each group member respond to the statements about how well they carried out the rules.

Here is an example of how this might be done. At the end of a small-group activity, pass out and read the following statements to all students. They are to respond by circling YES or NO on the sheet. (As a variation, you could use a happy face and a sad face with each statement and have the students circle the face that best represents their opinion.) Once completed, the members of each group can share responses. Finally, the group decides which social skill they will work on the next time they meet.

Working and Sharing in My Group

1. I shared with my group today.	YES	NO
2. I encouraged others in my group.	YES	NO
3. Others shared with me.	YES	NO
4. I listened when others were talking.	YES	NO
5. Others listened while I talked.	YES	NO

As always, you can and should talk these over with students, using extralinguistic support as needed to make sure that English learners understand the instructions and the purpose of the evaluation. There is no need to conduct this type of evaluation more than three or four times per year.

In addition to explicitly teaching these general rules, you can also model and reinforce them throughout the day as students work in small groups with you and among themselves. Students appreciate hearing that they are behaving appropriately during group work. For example, to reinforce rule number 1, you might draw the class's attention to a group and publicly announce, "Class, I am really happy about how nicely everyone in Group Three is working together. It is great to see that everyone is getting a chance to talk." On other occasions, to reinforce active listening, you might point out to the class how pleased you are to see that students in a particular group are visibly listening to one another.

Small-group abilities can also be learned by adding a particular structure to the group assignment. The idea is to structure the interaction so that everyone in the group gets to practice carrying out the rules that underlie successful small-group behavior. Here are some examples of structures that you can use to prepare students for small-group learning (these suggestions may sound pretty controlling to some of you, but at least try them to see how they work with different groups of students):

Talking Chips   This structure distributes talk more or less equally among members of a group. At the beginning of the activity, each student in the group is given some kind of marker, which serves as a talking chip. Every time a student wishes to talk, he or she must place a chip in a central place, usually the center of the table. No one in the group can talk again until everyone has placed a chip in the pile, at which time all the chips are retrieved, and the process begins again (Kagan, 1989). Adding this structure to group work ensures that everyone talks, and that no one student will do all of the talking.

Paraphrase Passport   The purpose of this structure is to encourage students to contribute to the discussion and to listen as others in the group speak. Access to talking comes from correctly paraphrasing the student who has just spoken. After a member of the group has contributed an idea, the next person to speak must accurately rephrase that idea before contributing a new idea. This structure reinforces group listening and at the same time enables second-language students to hear other ways of saying the same thing. Moreover, when their turn comes, second-language students are compelled to create a new way of saying something without repeating it word for word. Paraphrase passport encourages children to appropriate others' words.

Finally, here are two highly structured small-group activities that allow students to practice all three rules for effective group behavior. Both of these activities are designed for maximum student involvement, and neither should last less than 10 minutes.

The Three-Step Interview   This activity consists of three steps and is best suited for groups of four (Kagan, 1989). In step one, students are assigned to work in pairs, with one student serving as an interviewer and the other as an interviewee. The interviewer's responsibility is to gain as much information from the interviewee by asking as few questions as possible. In step two, the students reverse roles: the interviewee now becomes the interviewer, and vice versa. In step three, each student shares with the group what was learned from his or her interview partner, moving in a round-robin sequence. The content of the interview can cover a wide range of topics, but a good way to begin is to have students exchange personal experiences related to the topic at hand. For example, after viewing a short movie on the lumber elephants of India, you could have students engage in a three-step interview on their feelings about aspects of the movie and why they feel that way. You could also ask students to come up with questions about the work done by the elephants.

Think-Pair-Share   A variation of the three-step interview, think-pair-share is also conducted in three steps, preferably in groups composed of four students (Lyman, 1987). In step one, you pose a relatively open-ended question to all groups, usually about a topic all students are currently studying and then allow them a minute or so to contemplate how they would answer it. In step two, pairs of students orally exchange their answers with one another. In step three, students share their partner's answer with the members of the group, again in a round-robin fashion. This third step of sharing responses within the group encourages students to actively participate through talk and to listen for meaning in step two. You can vary step three by asking one member of each group to summarize to the entire class his or her group's response.

Face-to-Face Interaction

One of the simplest yet often overlooked features of small-group learning has to do with how students are physically arranged for small-group work. They need to be within personal talking distance (within 2 feet) and be physically facing each other. For example, if students are seated at a small rectangular or circular table, they need to be positioned so that at least the pairs of students are face-to-face (see Figure 5.4).

Face-to-face interaction ensures that students can hear each other speak and actually see any paraverbal and nonverbal support that may accompany what is being said. Under these circumstances, students are more apt than not to comprehend and actively engage in dialogue generated by members of their group. You may find that some students will need to be physically moved so that they face their partners or team members. If you do have to move students a bit closer to one another, be sure to explain to them that being face-to-face improves interaction because now, not only can they see each other better, they can hear each other better as well.

Figure 5.4
Face-to-face interaction in small-group work

Positive Interdependence

Positive interdependence is the heart and soul of small-group learning, especially when English learners are in peer-managed small groups. Students are positively interdependent when they see themselves as linked with their group members in such a way that no one can succeed unless everyone in the group does and when they realize that the contributions each member makes benefit everyone in the group (Johnson, Johnson, & Holubec, 1986). Positive interdependence is a type of solidarity among students in which sharing words, ideas, and materials is valued. Without positive interdependence, students placed together to work in groups see little value in helping their fellow students learn, even though they may have had some preparation in social skills development.

When students are not linked together through positive interdependence, an inevitable result is that only certain students benefit from the experience. What typically happens in small-group work sans positive interdependence is that the students with identities as readers, as being smart, and as being popular benefit most while the condition of other students either worsens or, at best, stays the same. The reason for this is fairly straightforward: In small-group work, learning and identification formation are directly tied to the extent to which students converse, share ideas, and use materials as they work on an assignment. Students who participate by interacting and sharing with others benefit more because they use language and materials as tools to mediate their learning. But the relationship between active participation and learning is not merely a quantitative one. By talking and sharing more, students are likely to practice a wide range of discourse functions, such as expressing and finding out about agreement and disagreement, about emotional attitudes (likes and dislikes, surprise, hope, satisfaction), about appreciation, about regret, and about getting others in the group to do things (inviting, advising, warning, and instructing), in addition to describing, narrating, and offering opinions and justifying them. Consequently, you need to promote solidarity and positive interdependence to ensure that all students participate optimally during small-group learning. Sometimes students of different English language proficiencies are positively interdependent on their own; they just connect with one another because of the kinds of activities and assignments you guide them through. At other times you may need to help students who may be blocked from participation to get connected. Here are five simple ways to organize small-group work in ways that promote positive interdependence and reinforce your efforts to build solidarity identities in your students (Johnson, Johnson, & Holubec, 1986; Kagan, 1989; McGroarty, 1989):

1. *Goal interdependence.* When you assign a student-managed group project as an extension of your thematic work, such as the development of inquiry questions, a mural, a fact-finding report, or a mathematics problem set, you can have students sign their names at the bottom of the product to indicate that they all contributed, and could, if asked, describe and justify their participation.

2. *Reward interdependence.* You can assign the same reward to each member of a peer-managed group for completing the assignment. You can also give bonus points when everyone in the group achieves a certain predetermined score. Or you can calculate the average of individual scores and give a reward when the average reaches a predetermined criterion. A rule of thumb in giving rewards for group work is that the more intrinsically interesting the assignment is, the less need there is for a group reward. Once the motivation for learning becomes apparent, you should probably dispense with the reward.

3. *Labor interdependence.* You can divide the assignment into subcomponents that must be completed sequentially in order to

accomplish the overall goals. In other words, you might divide the labor involved in the assignment so that one student has to complete a part of it before anyone else in the group can move ahead. Labor interdependence is especially useful as members of a small group learn how to conduct research on the Internet and compose on a classroom computer. It can also be incorporated in science projects and other assignments that are organized to follow a linear, step-by-step set of procedures.

4. *Resource interdependence.* You can assign activities in which each member of the group possesses only a portion of the information, resources, or materials needed to complete the task. Jigsaw (Aronson, Blaney, Stephan, Sikes, & Snapp, 1978; Gibbons, 2002) is one of the best illustrations of resource interdependence. For jigsaw activities, students are responsible for reading and being able to talk with some authority about a text that you have divided into three to five subtopics. Each student in a group becomes an "expert" on one subtopic by working with members from other groups assigned the corresponding subtopic. When the students return to their home group, which now contains experts on all of the subtopics, each expert student in turn "teaches" the group, and then all students are assessed on all areas of the general topic. Other ways to promote resource interdependence include limiting the resources given to a group so that members must share them and assigning brainstorming and writing activities in which students share in the composition of stories, reports, or poems.

5. *Role interdependence.* You can assign complementary and interconnected roles that give each student a responsibility that the group needs in order to function successfully. Examples of roles that give everyone a part to play are (a) a *group leader* to answer any questions about the task and to see that everyone gets the help they need to complete the task; (b) a *recorder* to write down the group's ideas and answers; (c) a *checker/encourager* to make sure that everyone in the group is participating and has completed all of the work and that everyone understands what is being agreed upon; (d) a *setup/cleanup* person who is responsible for setting up all of the required materials, and/or also for putting away materials properly and cleaning off the table; and (e) an *evaluator* to keep track of how well the group members are working together.

In addition, you can boost the strength of positive interdependence by playing cooperative games during recess and physical education time and by exposing your students to children's literature in which characters solve problems through positive interdependence and demonstrate their concern for helping one another (Barone & Faltis, 1990; Faltis, 1989b). Some excellent sources for cooperative games are Gregson (1982), Orlick (1978, 1982), and Sobel (1983). *Swimmy* by Lionni (1963) is a good example of a storybook that reinforces the value of positive interdependence (Barone & Faltis, 1990). Other examples are *Squares Are Not Bad* (Salazar, 1967) and *The Case of the Dumb Bells* (Bonsall, 1966). See the Resource List (page 195) for an annotated bibliography of children's storybooks that promote the value of cooperation among characters. The more opportunities students have to see the value of positive interdependence in other contexts, the more likely they are to make sure that their peers are participating optimally during small-group work.

Student Accountability

A primary purpose of peer-managed small-group learning is to ensure that group members have the opportunity to engage in academic practices that support learning and help learners build strong identities as classroom members. Occasionally, when you assign peer-managed, small-group learning activities, you will find that some students are not participating to their fullest potential. Unequal participation in small-group work may be the result of multiple factors, making it difficult to know for sure why it is happening. As has been pointed out elsewhere, there are many ways that students can block the learning of their peers, and if the assignment is not set up well, there can be unequal effort. And sometimes, the assignment is simply not interesting to students. Whatever the case, you may still need to remind students that they are each accountable for their work in small groups.

Creating individual accountability for work completed as a group is especially critical when you place English learners with fully English-proficient speakers. Suppose that each group in your class will receive a team grade for completing certain assignments, but that there is no individual accountability. Some fully English-proficient students may decide to take control of the assignments to decrease the involvement of the English learners, believing that they will slow down the process and even lower the quality of the work to be completed. Moreover, the English learners may defer to the fully English-proficient students, letting them do the lion's share of the work. However, if the group grade is based on the participation of every student in the group, it is less likely that any one student will do more or less than others and more likely that students will help one another to ensure that all are participating equally.

You can encourage student accountability by randomly selecting members to explain what they are doing, by having members edit and review each others' work, and by randomly picking from the group the completed task of one student and using that as the grade for the group (Johnson, Johnson, & Holubec, 1986). One cool way to practice individual accountability when students are in either whole-group or small-group settings is to use *Numbered Heads Together* (Kagan, 1989). In this activity, which also promotes teamwork and positive interdependence, students who are in close proximity to one another form groups of four, and count off from 1 to 4. At an opportune time during your presentation, ask the students a question, usually a convergent one, and then say, "Okay, everyone, let's do Numbered Heads Together. I'll give you a couple of minutes to talk about your thoughts." At this point, the students physically huddle together to talk about the answer, and when they have agreed, they consult to make sure everyone understands and is able to express the group contribution. When time is up, you choose a number from 1 to 4, and then call on the students who correspond to the number you selected.

Other ways of practicing individual accountability are the Three-step Interview and Paraphrase Passport. Both of these activities encourage students to be accountable for listening to others in their group.

Julia the Mediator

Julia's students have been working on their Elephant Inquiry assignments for the past 2 weeks at various times in the day. Today, students are managing their own group work, while Julia circulates the room observing students, answering their questions, and guiding their ideas, much as she normally does. All of a sudden, a commotion on the other side of the room ensues. Concepción and Frank, who are assigned to the same group and have been working together, begin arguing loudly. Frank accuses Concepción of using one of his colored pencils. "I told you not to use my stuff! That pencil is mine, and nobody gets to use it but me," he says, red-faced.

"Is not fair, Frank. I need that color for this picture," replies Concepción, almost in tears. They continue back-and-forth, their voices getting even louder.

Julia steps in between them to mediate, asking somewhat sternly what is going on. Each student gives his or her side, but neither one is willing to budge.

"He never shares, only Gina and Amy share with me," says Concepción with conviction.

"But Miss Felix, Concepción never asks to borrow, she just takes it," counters Frank, "and these are *my* pencils."

"Frank and Concepción, this is not a good way to treat each other. You are classroom and team members. Frank, are you saying that you are not willing to share your pencils with the group, *even* when it enables the group to do the assignment, which also helps you? Don't the other students share with you? And

Concepción, it is always best to ask someone before you use something. There are lots of ways to ask politely. You can say 'Can I use your pencil?', 'May I use your pencil?', or even something like 'How about letting me use your pencil?' That's the right way to share materials, don't you think? There are good ways to work together and ways that end up like this. Children, let's try this again, and see if we can solve this by being polite, and learning to share."

Julia stays with the group a while longer, changing the subject to what they are doing, and how the work is coming along. Within minutes, Frank and Concepción are busily working on their projects, smiling and giggling among themselves. Julia hopes her talk with the students helps them become better friends and classmates.

CONCLUSION

This has been a long and rather detailed chapter about teaching and learning in teacher- and peer-managed small groups. And there is much more to learn about these exciting contexts and effective ways of integrating English learners into the all-English classroom. Much of what you are learning in your methods courses on teaching language arts and literacy, mathematics, social studies, and science to children can be combined with the perspectives and strategies presented in this book. By this point, if you have understood the assistance you can provide in small-group work to make language and content meaningful so that English learners can participate actively and fully, you are well on your way to becoming a teacher who is better prepared to work in multilingual classroom and school settings. Also, if you understand the merits of small-group learning for promoting communication and critical awareness among students of diverse language and cultural backgrounds, and you feel ready to try it out in your

classroom, you will be helping all of your students learn how to use discourse in ways that shepherd them to identify as members of academic communities of practice. It is important to keep in mind that it takes some time to develop a classroom community of practices and to develop solidarity and interdependence among students of diverse backgrounds. However, you can be certain that if you prepare students for small-group learning and engage them consistently, and you monitor, talk aloud about, and reinforce acceptable group behavior, the quality of their interaction and learning will improve and their ability to work well cooperatively and by themselves will become self-regulated over time.

Small-group work helps create a classroom community where students rely on one another for help and learning (Gibbons, 2002; Johnson, 1994). But a classroom community that views the students as separate from their home communities is sorely lacking. You need to extend into the home communities of the students themselves so that the classroom community ties into the students' home communities, giving multiple voice opportunities to parents and other significant caregivers.

In the following chapter, we will learn about ways to improve and expand parental engagement and participation in the home, the classroom, and the school.

ACTIVITIES

1. Arrange to have a 15- to 20-minute interaction with an English learner at a local public school or at the English Language Center at your college or university. For this activity, look for a student who has at least some communicative proficiency. You should audiotape the dialogue, using an MP3 or some other small recording device. To scaffold the interaction, select and use one of the dialogue models presented in this chapter. Your goal is to assist the student so that as the dialogue progresses, he or she is doing most of the talking. An hour or so after the dialogue, listen to the recording and identify the various strategies of the dialogue model you used and note any places where you think you could have done something differently to engage the student and further the dialogue.

2. In a group of four or five students, elect one person to guide the others through a problem using scaffolds and dialogue strategies. The student who serves as a guide reads the following instructions to the group:

   > Here is the problem that I want you to try to solve: You have 23 coins of exactly the same size, weight, and value, and one coin that is identical to the other 23 in every way *except* that it weighs more. Your task is to determine which coin weighs more than the others by using a balance scale. No other method can be used. And you must be able to pick out the heavier coin in just *three* weighings.

   The student teacher's task is to assist the group members by using assessment and assisting questions. (You'll find the solution to this problem and ways to scaffold the dialogue following the Activities section.)

3. Here is a fun small-group team-building activity presented in Kagan (1989). Organize groups of four. Use a random group assignment procedure: Divide the total number of the class by 4, and then have students count off by the resulting number. For example, in a class of 25, students will count off by sixes, making five groups of 4 and one group of 5. Once in the group, your goal is to come up with at least one *uncommon commonality*. That is, try to find out something that all of you have in common that is truly uncommon. For example, you may learn that you have all been hit by a car when riding a bicycle or that you all have

twins in your family and that they all drive Volkswagens!

Once you have generated your uncommon commonality, the next step is to come up with a group name based on your uncommon commonality. How about the Volksy Twins or the Banged-Up Bikers?

If you want to continue, you can invent a handshake to go with the group name. The only rule on the handshake is that everyone in the group has to be connected at one point in the shake.

4. In groups of three, read the children's story by Ellen Levine (1989) called *I Hate English!* and discuss what you think about the author's views on the acculturation process. Look for evidence in the book that gives clues about the author's view. Discuss the main character in the book to trace her identity formation and transformation as she begins using English. What messages about bilingualism does the story convey? What, if any, do you consider to be the hidden agenda of this story? You may also wish to consult Lessow-Hurley's review of the book (Lessow-Hurley, 1991).

5. Visit the children's section at your local public library or in your campus library and look for storybooks in which the characters are able to accomplish feats that they would otherwise be incapable of doing alone. Also, seek out children's storybooks in which the characters show a social concern for the welfare of others. As a class, put together an annotated bibliography and share it with classmates and teacher acquaintances.

6. Interview several classroom teachers to learn about the kinds of small-group work that they use in class. Ask about pair work as well. Do they use dialogue journals? Do they do team-building activities? How do they organize peer-managed small groups? What do they have to say about making sure that English learners are not blocked from participation in small group activities?

ANSWER TO THE SCAFFOLDING ACTIVITY

The solution to this problem rests in the ways you divide the coins for each weighing. You can expect most group members to begin by dividing the 24 coins into two piles of 12 coins and weighing them to reduce the number of coins to 12. This typical first step makes it impossible to solve the problem in three weighings. Allow the students to proceed in the process anyway. In the next weighing they will again probably divide the coins into two groups of 6, and then into two groups of 3. This uses up the three weighings and it is still not possible to pick out the heavier coin.

So what do group members do next? Here is where you can provide some valuable scaffolded assistance through questions. For example, suppose you say something like:

> Let's start again with the 24 coins. The first time you divided them into two equal parts, didn't you? Now, is there another way of dividing them?

If they need further assistance, you can continue with:

> Is there another way to divide the coins so that you have an equal number of coins on each side of the scale and the same number of coins off the scale?

What you want them to understand here is that they can also divide 24 by 3, giving them three piles of 8 coins, two piles for the scale and one off the scale. If the heavier coin is in either of the piles on the scale, the scale will tip and reveal its location. If it doesn't tip, we know immediately that it is in the pile off the scale.

Next question:

> So how do you wish to divide up the remaining 8 coins?

The goal is to guide the students to divide the 8 coins into 3, 3, and 2: 3 coins on each side of the scale and 2 off the scale. The reason: No matter which pile contains the coin, we can pick it out in the next and final weighing. If the coin is in one of the piles of 3, then in the third weighing we place one coin on each side of the scale and one off. A tipped scale gives us the answer, as does a balanced one. If the coin in the pile of 2 is off the scale, then simply place the 2 coins on the scale, and select the heavier one according to which side of the scale tips.

REFERENCES

Aronson, E., Blaney, N., Stephan, D., Sikes, J., & Snapp, M. (1978). *The jigsaw classroom.* Beverly Hills, CA: Sage Publications.

Barone, D., & Faltis, C. (1990). *Cooperation-fostering beginning literacy events in the linguistically diverse classroom.* Unpublished manuscript, Center for Language and Literacy, University of Nevada, Reno.

Bonsall, C. (1966). *The case of the dumb bells.* New York: Harper & Row.

Brown, G., & Yule, G. (1983). *Teaching the spoken language.* New York: Cambridge University Press.

Burt, M., & Kiparsky, C. (1972). *The gooficon: A repair manual for English.* Rowley, MA: Newbury House.

Calderón, M. (1994). Cooperative learning for bilingual settings. In R. Rodríguez, N. Ramos, & J. Agustín Ruíz-Escalante (Eds.), *Compendium of readings in bilingual education: Issues and practices* (pp. 95–110). San Antonio, TX: Texas Association for Bilingual Education.

Cazden, C. (2001). *Classroom discourse: The language of teaching and learning.* Portsmouth, NH: Heinemann.

Cohen, E. (1986). *Designing groupwork: Strategies for the heterogeneous classroom.* New York: Teachers College Press.

Cohen, E., Kepner, D., & Swanson, P. (1995). Dismantling status hierarchies in heterogeneous classrooms. In J. Oakes & H. Quartz (Eds.), *Creating new educational communities* (pp. 16–31). Chicago: University of Chicago Press.

Damon, W. (1984). Peer education: The untapped potential. *Journal of Applied Developmental Psychology, 5,* 331–343.

Darling-Hammond, L., French, J., & García-López, S. (Eds.). (2002). *Learning to teach for social justice.* New York: Teachers College Press.

DeVillar, R. A. (1990). Second language use within the non-traditional classroom: Computers, cooperative learning, and bilingualism. In R. Jacobson & C. Faltis (Eds.), *Language distribution issues in bilingual schooling* (pp. 133–159). Clevedon, England: Multilingual Matters.

DeVillar, R. A., & Faltis, C. (1991). *Computers and cultural diversity.* Albany: State University of New York Press.

Díaz, R., Neal, C., & Amaya-Willams, M. (1990). The social origins of self-regulation. In L. Moll (Ed.), *Vygotsky and education: Implications and application of sociohistorical psychology* (pp. 127–154). New York: Cambridge University Press.

Edelsky, C., & Hudelson, S. (1982). Reversing the roles of Chicano and Anglo children in a bilingual classroom: On the communicative competence of the helper. In J. A. Fishman & G. D. Keller (Eds.), *Bilingual education for Hispanics in the United States* (pp. 303–325). New York: Teachers College Press.

Edelsky, C., Smith, K., & Wolfe, P. (2002). A discourse on academic discourse. *Linguistics and Education, 13*(1), 1–38.

Eeds, M., & Wells, D. (1989). Grand conversations: An exploration of meaning construction in literature study groups. *Research in the Teaching of English, 23,* 4–29.

Enright, D. S. (1991). Tapping the peer interaction resource. In M. McGroarty & C. Faltis (Eds.), *Languages in school and society: Policy and pedagogy* (pp. 209–232). Berlin: Mouton de Gruyter.

Enright, D. S., & McCloskey, M. (1988). *Integrating English: Developing English language and literacy in the multilingual classroom.* Reading, MA: Addison-Wesley.

Faltis, C. (1989a). Classroom language use and educational equity: Toward interactive pedagogy. In B. P. Baptiste, H. C. Waxman, J. Walker de Felix, & J. Anderson (Eds.), *Leadership, equity, and school effectiveness* (pp. 109–124). Newbury Park, CA: Sage.

Faltis, C. (1989b). Spanish language cooperation-fostering storybooks for language minority children in bilingual programs. *Journal of Educational Issues for Language Minority Students, 5*(1), 41–50.

Faltis, C. (1990). Spanish for native speakers: Freirian and Vygotskian perspectives. *Foreign Language Annals, 23*(2), 117–126.

Fránquiz, M., & de La Luz Reyes, M. (1998). Creating inclusive learning communities through English language arts: From "chanclas" to "canicas." *Language Arts, 75,* 211–220.

Gibbons, P. (2002). *Scaffolding language, scaffolding learning: Teaching second language learners in the mainstream classroom.* Portsmouth, NH: Heinemann.

Gregson, B. (1982). *The incredible indoor games book.* Belmont, CA: Pitman Learning.

Goldenberg, C. (1991). *Instructional conversations and their classroom application.* Santa Cruz., CA: National Center on Cultural Diversity and Second Language Learning.

Hawkins, M. (2004). Researching English language and literacy development in schools. *Educational Researcher, 33*(3), 14–25.

Johnson, D. (1994). Grouping strategies for second language learners. In F. Genesee (Ed.), *Educating second language children* (pp. 183–211). New York: Cambridge University Press.

Johnson, D. W., Johnson, R. T., & Holubec, E. J. (1986). *Revised circles of learning: Cooperation in the classroom.* Edina, MN: Interaction Book Company.

Kagan, S. (1989). *Cooperative learning resources for teachers.* San Juan Capistrano, CA: Resources for Teachers.

Kohl, H. (1995). *Should we burn* Babar? *Essays on children's literature and the power of stories.* New York: New York Press.

Lessow-Hurley, J. (1991). Review of *I hate English!. TESOL Journal, 1*(1), 35–36.

Levine, E. (1989). *I hate English!* New York: Scholastic.

Linfors, J. W. (1989). The classroom: A good environment for language learning. In P. Rigg & V. G. Allen (Eds.), *When they don't all speak English: Integrating the ESL student into the regular classroom* (pp. 39–54). Urbana, IL: National Council of Teachers of English.

Lionni, L. (1963). *Swimmy.* New York: Alfred A. Knopf.

Lyman, F. (1987). Think-pair-share: An expanding teaching technique. *MAA-CIE Cooperative News, 1*(1), 1–2.

McGroarty, M. (1989). The benefits of cooperative learning arrangements in second language instruction. *NABE Journal, 12*(2), 127–143.

McGroarty, M. (1993). Cooperative learning and second language acquisition. In D. Holt (Ed.), *Cooperative learning: A response to cultural diversity* (pp. 13–27). Sacramento, CA: Delta Systems.

Milk, R. (1980). *Variations in language use patterns across different settings in two bilingual second grade classrooms.* Unpublished doctoral dissertation, Stanford University, Stanford, CA.

Orlick, T. (1978). *The cooperative sports and games book: Challenge without competition.* New York: Pantheon.

Orlick, T. (1982). *The second cooperative sports and games book.* New York: Pantheon.

Penfield, J. (1987). ESL: The regular classroom teacher's perspective. *TESOL Quarterly, 21*(1), 21–39.

Pérez, B. (2004). Creating a classroom community for literacy. In B. Pérez (Ed.), *Sociocultural contexts of language and literacy* (pp. 309–338). Mahwah, NJ: Lawrence Erlbaum Associates.

Salazar, V. (1967). *Squares are not bad.* New York: Golden Press.

Sobel, J. (1983). *Everybody wins: 393 non-competitive games for young children.* New York: Walker.

Solomon, J., & Rhodes, N. (1995). *Conceptualizing academic language.* Santa Cruz, CA: The National Center for Research on Cultural Diversity and Second Language Learning.

Stevick, E. (1986). *Images and options in the language classroom.* Cambridge: Cambridge University Press.

Tharp, R., & Gallimore, R. (1988). *Rousing minds to life: Teaching, learning, and schooling in social context.* New York: Cambridge University Press.

Toohey, K. (2001). Disputes in child L2 learning. *TESOL Quarterly, 35*(2), 257–258.

Tough, J. (1985). *Talk two: Children using English as a second language.* London: Onyx Press.

Tudge, J. (1990). Vygotsky, the zone of proximal development and peer collaboration: Implications for classroom practice. In L. Moll (Ed.). *Vygotsky and education: Instructional implication and application of sociohistorical psychology* (pp. 155–172). New York: Cambridge University Press.

Vacca, R. (2002). From efficient decoders to strategic readers. *Educational Leadership. 60*(3), 6–11.

Vygotsky, L. S. (1978). *Mind in society.* Cambridge, MA: Harvard University Press.

Wertsch, J. V. (1984). The zone of proximal development: Some conceptual issues. In B. Rogoff & J. V. Wertsch (Eds.), *Children's learning in the "zone of proximal development"* (pp. 7–18). San Francisco: Jossey-Bass.

Wolfe, P. (2004). "The owl cried": Reading abstract literacy concepts with adolescent ESL students. *Journal of Adolescent & Adult Literacy, 47*(5), 402–413.

RESOURCE LIST

Groups Working Together

Balian, L. (1972). *The Aminal.* Nashville, TN: Abingdon Press. Patrick finds an animal, which he calls an *aminal.* He tells a friend about his new pet without saying exactly what it is. His friend tells another and so on. Eventually, all of the friends decide that the pet might hurt Patrick. So they all arrive at Patrick's house to protect him only to find that his pet is really a turtle.

Bonsall, C. (1965). *The case of the cat's meow.* New York: Harper & Row. Snitch is worried that someone will steal his cat, Mildred. His friends assure him that no one will take his cat. However, Mildred soon disappears. The boys work together to find the cat. Eventually, they locate Mildred in the basement with three new kittens. The story concludes with each child taking home a kitten.

Bonsall, C. (1966). *The case of the dumb bells.* New York: Harper & Row. Skinny, Wizard, Snitch, and Tubby are private eyes. They earn money to buy two telephones and they install them themselves. Unfortunately, they hook up the phone wires to the doorbell. The boys attempt to solve the case of who is ringing the doorbell. When they discover the answer, they are angry at first, but then declare that they "stick together through thick and thin."

Bonsall, C. (1971). *The case of the scaredy cats.* New York: Harper & Row. The boys' detective club excludes girls. When the girls decide that they also want to be members of the club, a fight ensues, which results in the boys running away. Then the girls discover that Annie is missing. The boys and girls put their differences behind them to join together and find Annie.

Ginsbury, M. (1974). *Mushrooms in the rain.* New York: Macmillan. Various animals hide under a mushroom for protection from the rain. But one day a fox comes by looking for a rabbit who is hiding under the mushroom. The animals band together to protect the rabbit and divert the fox to another location.

Peet, B. (1972). *The ant and the elephant.* Boston: Houghton Mifflin. A turtle accidently falls over on his back. He asks various animals for help, but all refuse. After refusing, each animal finds itself in a disastrous predicament. The only animal that does not follow this pattern is an elephant who helps an ant across the river. The elephant then continues to help all of the other animals. At the conclusion of the story, the elephant falls into a ravine. An entire colony of ants, working together, carry the elephant out of the ravine and save him from danger.

Salazar, V. (1967). *Squares are not bad*. New York: Golden Press. The various shapes—squares, circles, triangles, and rectangles—each live alone and do not like each other. One day the shapes are playing together and they accidently bump into each other. They discover that they are able to form wonderful new shapes and figures by working together.

Pairs Working Together

Cohen, M. (1971). *Best friends*. New York: Collier Books. Paul and Jim are usually best friends, but they have some difficulties in this story. When the light goes out in the incubator, the boys work together to fix it and save the baby chicks.

Delton, J. (1974). *Two good friends*. New York: Crown Publishers. Duck and Bear are friends who have opposite skills. Bear likes to cook and Duck likes to clean. They surprise each other one day by doing their favorite activity for each other.

Johnston, T. (1972). *The adventures of Mole and Troll*. New York: G. P. Putnam's Sons. Mole and Troll work together to accomplish various goals, as when Mole models for Troll so that he can make a dress for his grandmother.

Lobel, A. (1979). *Days with Frog and Toad*. New York: Harper & Row. Frog and Toad help each other through many interesting episodes. One example is when Frog offers Toad encouragement as he tries to fly his kite.

6

Inviting and Engaging Families and Communities in Schooling Activities

OVERVIEW

Up to this point, we have concentrated exclusively on providing for learning inside your classroom. However, for learning as participation in academic domains to enable students to enjoy multiple identities as learners, it is important to learn about and find ways to invite the students' caregivers and home communities into the world of schooling. Once again, your role is critical for building bridges between the community and the school by extending what you do in your classroom and school into students' homes and enabling family members to reciprocate by becoming involved on many different levels of engagement.

Involving the community—especially non-English-speaking parents and other family members—in educational activities at home and in the school is no simple matter. There are language barriers to consider in addition to various ways that adult caregivers in different cultures and communities view their role and the school's role in educating their children (Coelho, 1994; Delpit, 1998; Schecter & Bayley, 2002; Tse, 2001; Valdés, 1996). Within the Asian immigrant community, for example, many parents feel that they are solely responsible for their children's learning—particularly how the children approach learning—both at home and in school (Chang, 2004; Constantino, Cui, & Faltis, 1995). The school's job is to provide a workplace where children can be exposed to and practice basic skills of reading, writing, spelling, and arithmetic (Chang, 2004; Cheng, 1987). In contrast, many recently arrived Mexican families see

197

the school as the sole authority on what needs to be learned and how it should be done (Scarcella, 1990; Schecter & Bayley, 2002; Valdés, 1996; Valdés, 2000). At home, although parents constantly teach their children to be respectful to elders, to care for family members, and to be accountable for their own actions, they rarely work with their children on school-related activities (Delgado-Gaitán, 1987). For many of these parents, school, not home, is the appropriate place for learning about content and basic skills. Within both cultural groups, parents are deeply concerned about the education of their children (Chang, 2004; Delgado-Gaitán, 1994; Olsen, 1997; Ramos & Santos, 1994; Trueba, 1998; Yao, 1988). However, in both cases, the ways that parents and other adult caregivers see their role in schooling often differ considerably from the way that mainstream, middle-class English-speaking communities view their relationship with schools (Leitch & Tangri, 1988; Olsen, 1997; Tse, 2001; Valdés, 1996).

Parents from mainstream communities, partly because they speak the language used in school and partly because the majority of school personnel are members of their communities, tend to share with schools the view that parental involvement at home and in schools is positively related to school achievement (Epstein, 1991). Consequently, most mainstream, middle-class parents agree that they are responsible for helping schools do their job and that they can do so by engaging in the following kinds of behaviors:

1. Tutoring their children at home
2. Helping them with homework
3. Helping their children sell raffle tickets or candy to neighbors and friends
4. Attending class plays
5. Accompanying children on field trips
6. Attending parent–teacher conferences
7. Helping out with PTA (Parent–Teacher Association) or PTO (Parent–Teacher Organization) activities

In addition to these standard (middle-class oriented) parental involvement activities, many mainstream, middle-class parents also function as advocates for change by attending school board meetings, as co-learners by attending workshops with teachers in which participants learn more about children and schooling, and as decision makers by becoming members of advisory boards or school committees (Chavkin & Williams, 1989; Epstein, 1995).

The fact that great numbers of mainstream parents or other adult caregivers engage in these activities demonstrates the tremendous degree of familiarity that these adults have with the way schools expect communities to be involved in supporting the education of their children. However, the fact that non-English-speaking parents and adult caregivers do not engage in many of these activities does not mean that they are any less concerned about their children's education or about how they are prepared to enter the adult world of work and families. In all likelihood, the reason that many of them are less involved or uninvolved in school-related activities than their English-speaking counterparts has as much to do with the schools' unfamiliarity with what non-English-speaking families and communities value as it does with these families' and communities' unfamiliarity with the schools.

This chapter discusses ways to help parents and other significant caregivers become increasingly familiar with how they can be more involved in schooling matters if they so desire. It also presents suggestions about how teachers can become engaged in students' communities and become aware of the kinds of activities parents and others feel comfortable doing in school and at home. A few words of caution are in order, however, before we continue.

It is important to understand that parental involvement as a joinfostering principle necessarily moves you out of the classroom and into the communities you serve. This may come relatively easily in some cases, but it may cause feelings of anxiety and insecurity in others. Moreover, building home–school relationships may move you into school-level politics, due to the fact that some of the strategies advocated in this chapter may require support from the principal and other school-level authorities. Thus, you can expect many different kinds of resistance from both the school and some immigrant parents. For example, many school people are against using a language other than English to invite parents to school functions and making sure that information about bus schedules is available in the parents' home language. Likewise, some immigrant parents hold views of education that may

run counter to your own. Garnering support for action may require you to get into some potentially bitter battles with colleagues and non-school people who do not share your perspective. Choose your battles wisely, and don't expect to win every one. Instead, look for ways to advocate for actions that you believe are clearly needed to improve education for all students and that you know parents also accept. Work with other teachers and with parents who share your views about teaching and learning and culturally relevant involvement of parents in the school and of the school in the community. Finally, constantly revisit your personal stance about what you are doing to help your students and their communities join in the educational process at home as well as in school to ensure that you are empowering parents in ways that make sense to them.

With these caveats in mind, let us now proceed to Julia's classroom to learn how she is going to inform parents about the upcoming presentations her students have prepared on ways to study and preserve elephants in the wild. Surprises await her on Back-to-School night. Following this episode in Julia's classroom, we will examine a structured two-way approach to parental involvement that divides the process of parental involvement and participation into four levels. At each level the engagement of some parents in the school increases proportionately to the school's involvement in the communities it serves. For each level of involvement, we will discuss specific strategies and activities for teachers and parents alike.

Episode Six: Almost All The Parents Showed Up

Back-to-School night is scheduled for next Wednesday from 7:00 to 9:30 P.M. This gives Julia and her students less than 1 week to finish rehearsing their skits before presenting them to an audience of parents, family, and friends. The school's principal selected Wednesday night after learning from a majority of both non-English-speaking and English-speaking parents across the grades that it was the best night for them to come to school. With the support of the principal's office, Julia and several other teachers made sure that the general invitations to Back-to-School night were written and sent out in the language of the home at least 1 week before the event, with a short reminder going home with students on Monday. Peggy Dimwitty was the only teacher adamantly opposed to using the parents' home language, arguing that it is up to parents to learn and use the language of the school and not the other way around.

Julia's students also sent out a personal invitation to their parents and other family members to come to the auditorium on the evening of Back-to-School night to watch the students in her class present their skits and supporting materials to the entire school. Along with the invitation, Julia sent an accompanying letter written by her students explaining the purpose of Back-to-School night and the kinds of activities they could expect. Because the letters were composed in English, Julia hoped that the students would be able to translate them for their parents and other family members as needed. Julia knew that all of her non-English-language parents spoke and understood very little English, but she was not sure about their English-reading abilities. She took some class time to talk with students about how to describe and explain their assignments and the way the class functioned on a daily basis.

With the help of her fellow teacher and friend Jake and one of the teacher aides, Julia also located and talked with community workers who spoke the four non-English languages represented in her class: Spanish, Korean, Chinese, and Vietnamese. She explained to them about the presentations her students would be making and about other events that were planned for Back-to-School night. Julia also inquired about the appropriateness of having someone besides the teacher contact parents by telephone and invite them to Back-to-School night. All of the community workers felt certain that the parents would understand and would most likely welcome the invitation.

Julia asked the community workers to make one other request of the parents. On the general invitations, each household was also invited to bring one item of food (but it was okay if they could not). One of the English-speaking mothers had already volunteered to help Julia call the English-speaking families and find out what they would be bringing. Julia wanted the community workers to let parents know that she hoped they would bring foods typical of their countries. She also asked the community workers to share the telephone numbers of bilingual compatriot parents in other grades who they knew were bringing food, with the hope that the parents would talk among themselves about the meaning and purpose of Back-to-School night.

On Wednesday afternoon, Jake enlists three 6th-grade students to help Julia finish setting up the posters and the cardboard backgrounds for the evening skits. "Jules," cries Jake as he enters the cafeteria, "I brought some re-inforcements for last-minute touches."

"Gracias, Jake," says Julia. "I'm going to need some help setting up the stage." The students go to work while Julia and Jake carefully pin the cardboard scenery to the walls.

That evening, Julia's and her helpers' efforts pay off. Virtually all of the parents of Julia's students show up for the performance, and most stay afterward to visit her classroom to learn about the kinds of activities their children are doing. Needless to say, Julia is elated with both the turnout and the children's performance.

As the evening progresses, Peggy shows up in Julia's room, obviously perturbed about something. Catching Julia's eye, she motions her over.

"Julia, my, my, my. You have quite a show going on here tonight."

"I am so proud of my students, and have you tried some of the different foods that the parents brought in? You should have seen the PowerPoint[™] slide show that Emma and Do Thi put on. It was fabulous. The report on elephant measurements was so creative, and the puppet show by Gina, Emma, and Guadalupe about Ganesha was extraordinary. Their families were so happy."

"I think I will pass on the food; it looks sort of weird, and I don't how safe it is to eat, with my stomach and all."

Peggy goes on to tell Julia that only a few of the "minority" parents showed up to her classroom, offering an expected explanation: "They don't think much of education."

"You know what, Peg? That just isn't so. Look around. The families of my English learners are here, and they are walking around, talking with their children about their schoolwork, and they have approached me to ask about their children. As a matter of fact, here comes Mrs. Ochoa."

"Mrs. Ochoa, this is Miss Dimwitty," says Julia introducing the two.

"Oh, I know Miss Dimwitty. She the teecher of my son from las' year." Turning to face Peg, she continues in a serious tone, "You are a very bad teecher. You don't like Mexican children, and my son, Miguel, he tells me you no help him in class, and you make him feel bad. You only give him worksheet, and tell him no espeak Espanish with his friends. That's no right. My son is very esmart, and he is learning English and much more in Miss Felix class. Miguel is a very good boy. He take care of his baby sisters and little brother. I'n a good mother, and my family working hard every day. I say no more. Pardon me, please." Mrs. Ochoa walks away, visibly upset, leaving Peggy and Julia stunned at what had just transpired.

"I don't know what *that* was all about. That woman can't even speak English right. Where does she get off telling me that I am a bad teacher? As far as I remember, Miguel sat in the back of the room and talked with his Hispanic friends. The nerve of that woman," says Peg, obviously embarrassed.

Julia pauses a few seconds to gather her thoughts. *You got what you deserved, lady.* "Peg, I may be young and new to teaching, but I know this: Mrs. Ochoa loves her son and wants the best for him. I stretch my hands out to children and families, knowing that I know very little of their hardships, hopes, and desires. I don't care what language they speak at home or at school, or how well their parents speak it. What does concern me is what I can do to engage children in my classroom so that they feel safe to be themselves when I ask them to learn and question new ideas. I don't insist that parents sit around and read to their children every night, just because that is what middle-class parents might do. I assume that the parents of my English learners are concerned about their children's survival and health, about fostering their children's ability to make a living, and about developing in their children the will and abilities for maximizing the cultural values dear to them. If they want to become more involved with school literacy practices at home, I will be happy to help, but I do not and will not judge them as parents on whether or not they behave in ways that I might value. I think you would do well to take what Mrs. Ochoa said to you to heart, and start examining your own prejudices and practices. I have one more thing to say, and then I will stop. I would appreciate it if you would stop saying that English learners speak foreign languages. They speak the language of their mothers and fathers, brothers and sisters. Their language is central to who they are and how they become members of their communities and society. They speak Spanish, Vietnamese, Korean, Chinese, and they are learning English."

"Are you saying I am a racist? Well, I am not. I have Mexican friends I went to college with. I eat Chinese food. I just happen to believe that kids need to learn English. Hanging on to their old ways is not going to help them," Peggy avers. Julia knows that she is unknowingly clinging to a belief system that differentiates people on the basis of how well they conform to a system set up to reward mainstream, middle-class values and behaviors at the expense of children and families who come from working-class and, often, non-English-speaking homes.

"I disagree, Peggy. Your characterizations of English learners as lazy, as eating weird food, and as requiring worksheets while other students do fun things smacks of racism. These children deserve better than what you are giving them. Excuse me, but I too have other things to attend to." That said, Julia bids farewell and looks for a friendly face.

On the drive home, Julia thinks about the events of the evening. She realizes that for some of the non-English-speaking parents, this is the first time they have attended a school function. She wonders whether some of the parents might feel comfortable contributing to classroom as well as school-level activities and eventually to schoolwide decisions. She knows that she has to continue her involvement with her students' families and communities and to help those families who want to become involved in school in ways that are comfortable to them. She makes a note to ask Jake for suggestions. Her thoughts shift to Mrs. Ochoa and the courage she showed in standing up to Peggy Dimwitty. *Karma,* she smiled as she pulled into her driveway.

In the following sections, let's consider the kinds of things that you might do if you were in Julia's place, sharing her enthusiasm for building bridges between the home and the school and ultimately giving parents a voice in helping to improve education for their children.

A TWO-WAY PARENT–SCHOOL INVOLVEMENT MODEL

The lion's share of the research on the relationship between parental involvement and academic achievement reports that parents who participate in the schooling experiences of their children have a positive impact on attitudes toward schooling and ultimately on school success (Bermudez & Padrón, 1987; Epstein, 1991; Solomon, 1991). The relationship between parental involvement and school success is based on the assumption that children whose parents participate in school-related activities become more invested in school because their parents talk with them about the value of schooling for success in life (Hidalgo, Siu, & Epstein, 2004). The fact that parents are participating in school-related activities, however, presumes a mainstream, middle-class familiarity with schools and a belief that schools provide access to a variety of professions and occupations (Ogbu, 1983). Accordingly, parental involvement is perceived as a one-way venture, from the parents to the school. That is, the school does not need to reach out to parents, because parents implicitly understand the value of being involved in schooling matters. However, many immigrant parents of English learners and particularly working-class parents with sporadic and little formal schooling may possess little understanding about the way U.S. schools work (Olson, 1990; Valdés, 1996). Moreover, while these parents care about education, they may not make education their first priority as parents (Trueba, 1998; Valdés, 1996); instead, these parents are more concerned that their children come to identify with and learn to behave in ways that support the value of good manners, responsibility to the family, and the capacity to make a decent living as adults. Last, but not least, many immigrant parents share a distrust that schools prepare all children equally (Torres-Guzmán, 1991). The following statement by a Honduran mother captures the essence of this concern:

> My son needs an education here. That is the way for him to have a good life. I fear for him, though. Here the teachers don't keep an eye on the children. He misses school and the teacher doesn't discipline him. He says the teacher doesn't care if he does his work. I try to teach him respect for his teacher, but he says that is not how it is here. (Olsen, 1988, p. 82)

What can this parent do to allay her fear that her son is not getting a good education? And what could you do as a representative of this school to enable this parent to turn these concerns into action that will benefit not only her children, but other children as well? This is one question this chapter hopes to address.

A MULTILEVEL APPROACH TO HOME–SCHOOL RELATIONSHIPS

Building bridges between the home and the school inevitably depends on the cooperative efforts of the school, the teachers, and the parents. But you as a teacher have the primary responsibility for initially enabling parents to become involved in schooling matters. Reluctant and unknowing parents will not get involved in schooling simply because the principal wants them to. They may get involved, however, if you reach out to them and present them with multiple opportunities to become involved at home and in school. The key to involving parents within the joinfostering framework, therefore, is to strike a balance between your learning about the values parents hold about their children's safety, morality, and the capacity to live with the cultural boundaries they set for them, while your students' parents come to understand school-oriented activities and programs.

You can work toward this balance of involvement by dividing the process of building bridges between the home and the school into four levels. This multilevel approach to parental and teacher involvement is based on the works of Epstein, Sanders, Simon, Salinas, Jansorn, & Van Voorhis (2002); Petit (1989); and Rasinski & Fredericks (1989). The approach is especially well suited for working immigrant children of non-English-speaking families and communities because it begins with the teacher learning about

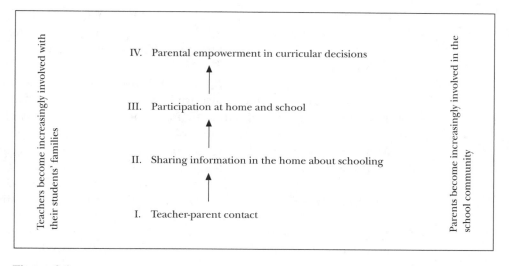

Figure 6.1
A multilevel approach to teacher and parental involvement
Source: From "Dimensions of Parent Involvement" by T. Rasinski and A. Fredericks, 1989, *The Reading Teacher,* November, 181. Copyright © 1989 by the International Reading Association.

the parents' community support systems and about stress factors related to living in a new environment, and it ends with the parents actively contributing to curricular decisions. It is based on a partnership between families and the school, which "*acknowledges that neither the family nor the school alone can socialize and educate children for success in school or in society*" (Hidalgo, Siu, and Epstein, 2004, p. 649, emphasis in original). Figure 6.1 presents a visual representation of the four levels of teacher and parental involvement.

Level I

Your goals in Level I are (a) to learn about your parents' daily experiences, family values about education, and the community in which they live; (b) to initiate individual contact with the parents and other adult caregivers through informal chats, get-togethers, and home visits; and (c) based on (a) and (b), to begin to work with parents and other caregivers to offer them ways to monitor their children's progress in school.

An effective way to develop and establish rapport with parents and learn about their community is through a home visit, which enables you to gain firsthand knowledge of some of the constraints that parents may face. For example, immigrant parents live in crowded conditions with little room for study in isolation (Olsen, 1997; Suárez-Orozco & Todorova, 2003). Children are often attended to by siblings and extended family members (Delgado-Gaitán, 1987); parents work long hours and sometimes have two or more jobs (Hidalgo, 1994; Valdés, 1998).

You should begin scheduling your home visits early in the year and continue them on a regular basis, not just when a problem arises. Every visit you make should have a specific purpose, and the parents, as well as the student, should be aware of that purpose before the visit (Gestwicki, 1987). In addition, before you visit immigrant parents, make inquiries about any special protocol or taboos that you should be aware of. You are likely to have a more successful encounter if you learn about greeting and leave-taking rituals and politeness formulae. (See Dien, 2004, for Vietnamese families; Scarcella & Chin, 1993, for Korean families; Chang, 2004, for Chinese families; Kang, Kuehn, & Herrell, 1994, for Hmong families; Yao, 1988, for Asian families; Delgado-Gaitán, 1987, and Valdés, 1996, for Mexican families; McCarty & Watabomigie, 2004, for Native American and Alaskan Native families; Wong Fillmore, 1990, and Suárez-Orozco & Todorova, 2003, for Latino families; Torres-Guzmán, 2004, and Hidalgo, 1994, for Puerto Rican families; and Delgado-Gaitán, 1994, for Russian families.) If there is no adult in the household who can serve as an interpreter, bring a trusted translator from school. Before your visit, talk with the translator about how you would like your interaction with the parents to be translated. Do you want paraphrased translations or word-for-word translations? It is important that the translator translate literal information as well as cultural nuances. The translator may also be able to provide you with valuable information about the community and answer questions about appropriate cultural behavior.

In addition to making contact with parents through home visits, you should be learning about the community-based organizations that provide information and support services for different ethnic and language communities. Make an appointment to talk with a worker or counselor at the local community-based organization. In the meeting, try to learn as much as possible about the services the organization provides and talk about the ways you want to involve parents over time. The organization's staff should be able to provide you with lots of information about the needs of the community. You should also ask about places in the community where families might shop for ethnic food and music and where they go for entertainment. You can inquire about home-language religious services and places of worship. You might even attend a church service or visit a marketplace to get a better feel for the community.

Learning about the community enables you to tap into the funds of knowledge that families rely upon in their daily experience. Greenberg

(1989) referred to funds of knowledge as an "operations manual of essential information and strategies households need to maintain their well-being" (p. 2). These funds of knowledge may be useful to you in getting information out to the community and in developing thematic units around topics that are community based (Moll & Gonzalez, 2004).

Your efforts to learn about the community and your students' parents at Level I should help you decide on the most appropriate kinds of schoolwork monitoring. For example, suppose you learn that many of your second-language parents work at jobs that require long hours and that they have relatively little time to monitor children's schoolwork at home. You also find out that a local neighborhood center offers after-school and weekend peer-tutoring services. What you might do is inform parents about the services and help them set up a ride-share program if needed. Next, you can suggest a plan whereby you or students from a higher grade check their child's homework 3 days a week and the parents or other caregivers check it 2 days a week. You might also ask parents to spend at least 3 minutes every evening talking with their children about schoolwork and any homework they might have. You can even suggest the kinds of questions they might ask. Obviously, if you do not speak the parents' language, you will need to work with a bilingual liaison to assist you in communicating with them.

In summary, your primary goals at this level are to establish contact with parents, begin learning about the community, and let parents know that you are there for them and that you will continue to support them throughout the school year. As you gain their trust, you can begin suggesting simple ways to monitor schoolwork assignments done at home. You will increase the likelihood of getting parents involved in their child's schoolwork to the extent that your suggestions take into account the constraints under which the family operates.

Level II

The second level of involvement broadens the kinds of communication you have with parents. From your perspective, Level II involves informing parents through written sources, telephone calls, and informal conferences about their child's progress, classroom activities that may involve their community, upcoming events, and basic school policies. From the parents' perspective, the communication might range from providing you with feedback on how the child is responding to schoolwork at home to inquiring about holidays and bus routes.

At this level, involvement is tantamount to information sharing, so that parents begin to feel comfortable relying on you for information about school policies and activities, while at the same time you increase your personal contact with them. Here is a list of some of the kinds of information that you might wish to share with parents in person, on video or DVD, through newsletters, and/or on your school/classroom Web site:

1. Important school dates (e.g., workshop days, half-days, holidays, registration days, report card days)

2. Information about school events and meetings that parents might attend

3. Information about the school board and the kinds of issues it is currently addressing

4. Summaries of the minutes of school board meetings with a schedule of the next meeting

5. Information about changes in bus or school-day schedules

6. Information about and telephone numbers of bilingual liaisons who work for the school and the community

7. Information about community-based organizations

8. Information about upcoming television programs on the parents' community and/or country of origin

9. Information about local community events (e.g., music festivals, plays, carnivals, art displays, or speakers)

10. Tips about the kinds of academic help that parents can provide at home

To the extent possible, you should provide all of this information in the parents' home language, preferably by enlisting the help of adults who are fully proficient speakers and writers of the language. You will probably need the help of bilingual liaisons working in the school or the district office. But as the year progresses, you may find that there are a number of parents who would be interested in helping with this kind of information sharing.

Another way to inform parents about classroom and school activities is to send home a weekly newsletter based primarily on ideas generated by your students. The easiest way to produce a newsletter is to set aside a few minutes one day a week and, in a group meeting format, solicit news items from students. You should immediately write down the items and then have students transfer the information to a computer using a newspaper software program. News items can range from students discussing what they are studying or what they liked about something they read or experienced in class to the kinds of issues they would like to tackle in the coming weeks. The newsletter should have a name (e.g., *Bruner Bobcat Weekly News*), a volume number, and a date at the top of the page. Most of the space on the paper should be reserved for student ideas. As the year progresses, you may need to add a second page from time to time. The computer software programs that generate newsletters provide numerous formatting options.

The newsletter can also serve as a means to briefly announce upcoming field trips and special events; other reminders to parents and adult caregivers can be placed in a small rectangle toward the bottom of the page, under the heading of "Community News." In addition, the newsletter can devote a small space to a special phrase written in the native language of one of the groups represented in your class. For example, in Julia's classroom, where there are four languages in addition to English, Julia asks students for a fun or interesting saying in one of the languages each week. She repeats the cycle at the end of every fourth edition. If your students can't or prefer not to come up with a saying, Gertrude Moskowitz's (1978) *Caring and Sharing in the Foreign Language Class: A Source Book on Humanistic Techniques* offers an extensive list of wonderful sayings in several different languages. And, with your school librarian's help, you can also make weekly suggestions about age-appropriate storybooks written in the home language.

Finally, you can appoint two students a week to use the computer to write a kind statement about their families or their community. You can label this special section something like "People in Our Community. " You can scan the students' work into a file and place it in the appropriate place in the newsletter. When the newsletter comes out, it should look something like the example shown in Figure 6.2.

A weekly newsletter is a good way to get parents and other family members and caregivers involved in schooling. Students enjoy reading about their classmates to just about anyone who will listen. Moreover, Hakuta (1990) has shown that bilingual children from the 3rd grade on up are very capable of translating from English to their home language and vice versa. Thus, your English learners should be delighted to translate the newsletter for their parents and other family members.

Another increasingly popular way of sharing classroom activities with the local and global communities is to have students help design a classroom Web page. You can download classroom photographs and upload student work. You can also attach the weekly newsletter in electronic format. Julia has developed a Web page for her class, and she has downloaded several photographs she took at the Back-to-School activities, all of which are available through the Bruner Elementary School Internet home page.

You can also strengthen your relationship with parents and adult caregivers by writing occasional personal notes and making telephone calls. In personal notes addressed to parents, you should share observations or anecdotes about how well the child is doing in class, especially in subjects that

5 BRUNER BOBCAT WEEKLY NEWS VOLUME 10, 2005

- Leon finished his elephant story.

- Concepcion and Ryan learned how to whistle.
  They love to whistle together!

- Fran wants to show the class how to make a lantern.
  His uncle will help.

- Xiancoung's grandmother is coming for a visit
  all the way from China.

OUR COMMUNITY	SPECIAL PARENTS
• We have two good bakeries in our neighborhood. • Nos gusta pan dulce.	• Field trip to zoo • Need help with art project. Call Miss Felix.

Figure 6.2
Newsletter example: *Bruner Bobcat Weekly News*

might be of concern to parents and adult caregivers. The notes should be brief and written in clear English or in the parents' or adult caregivers' home language. (You need to find out early on whether there are adult family members who can read English. This will save you from having to rely so much on a translator.) Personal notes take less than 5 minutes to write. If you send out approximately 10 notes a week, each student in your class will take one home at least every 3 weeks.

Telephone calls may be a bit more complicated, because if you need a translator, you will also need a special telephone system set up for conference calls. Telephone contact may be the only way for you to personally contact some parents and adult caregivers, however, so you may want to put forth the effort. Before you start making phone calls, you should find out about any special telephone protocol that might be required in the cultural groups represented in your classroom. For example, in Latin American culture, it is considered rude to telephone someone and immediately go to the reason for calling. The appropriate behavior is to exchange relatively lengthy greetings and to ask about the health and well-being of the family. Once you have completed this opening ritual, it is then acceptable to state the purpose of your call. The bilingual liaisons or community workers for the various language communities are probably aware of any special telephone protocol.

To summarize your goals in Level II, you work toward broadening the information you provide to the parents and adult caregivers about their child through several kinds of personal contact. At the same time, you can carefully encourage those parents and adult caregivers who inquire to communicate with their children about information and schoolwork that you send home. If you reach these goals, parents and adult caregivers will begin to sense that school is not as foreign a place as they might have thought.

Level III

You can begin to invite parents and adult caregivers to participate in your classroom and in school-related activities as soon as it becomes clear to you that they are responding favorably to your efforts to contact and inform them of schooling and community-related activities. Your primary goal in Level III is to invite parents and adult caregivers into the classroom to informally observe and eventually help with classroom activities and school events. At the same time, you want them (with your guidance) to take on increasing responsibility for monitoring their child's schoolwork habits at home. In essence, you want the parents' and adult caregivers' experiences in school to serve as a model for the kinds of support and monitoring that they can provide for their children at home. That is, as a result of working in your classroom environment, you may want to suggest to parents and adult caregivers that they try out some of the interactional strategies that they see occurring in the classroom when they assist their children with school tasks at home.

It is important to understand that while you may have contact with 100% of your parents and adult caregivers as a result of your efforts in Levels I and II, in all probability there will be some who prefer not to become involved at this third level for any number of reasons. For example, immigrant parents and adult caregivers who speak or understand little or no English may feel uneasy about coming into your classroom or participating in school activities. Others may have work schedules that simply prohibit them from participating during school hours. These reasons should not deter you from maintaining contact with them or from offering tips for improving their involvement in schoolwork at home. Another adult family member who is bilingual might be able to participate on the parents' behalf. Moreover, there are activities that do not require interactive English proficiency and school events that take place on weekends and evenings.

Let's consider the kinds of help that parents and adult caregivers might provide in Level III. First, you can invite parents and adult caregivers to come into your class to observe for a few minutes during the school day. For example, you can invite those who drop off their children to stay a few minutes in the morning and those who pick up their children to visit a few minutes before the school day ends. For families who live far from the school and have their children bused, you can still set aside special parent visit days. You can work with parents and adult caregivers who drive their children to organize ride-sharing programs so that parents or other family members who live far away can come in for a brief visit on key days.

You can also invite parents and adult caregivers to come to special events involving their children. At times during the year, you may put on a play, present a musical extravaganza, or have a storybook/poetry reading session. Before and after the presentation, you can have students show their parents and adult caregivers around the room and talk about the class's current art, writing, science, and social studies projects. These kinds of informal involvement can occur in any language! In fact, you should encourage parents and adult caregivers to speak with their children in their native language in your classroom just as you should encourage them to do so in their homes.

In addition to the sheer enjoyment that parents and adult caregivers experience from watching their children in your classroom, you can help them become more aware of how learning takes place there by giving them a few tips on the actions and events to look for. For example, you can have them pay attention to the different kinds of verbal and written interaction the students engage in. Have them watch you teach to the whole class or to a small group. Encourage them to notice the types of visual and nonverbal support you provide as you teach. Both before and after they observe your teaching, ask them to look for events and actions that you plan to emphasize in the lesson. If you know ahead of time that parents or adult caregivers who don't speak English are coming to visit your classroom, try to have another bilingual parent or a bilingual liaison there to help you communicate with them.

As you learn more about your students' families, you are bound to uncover the wealth of experiences parents and other family members have. In fact, you may even wish to engage your students as budding anthropologists to learn about the funds of knowledge that adults in their household rely on for any number of functions within their communities. For example, Heath (1983) tells how students learned from local gardeners about the best time to plant and harvest vegetables and then compared that with what the science books said. Moll and González (2004) have students discover what community members knew about banking and other important business concepts, which might then be incorporated into thematic units. Bausch (2003) suggests that teachers take students on a Neighborhood Walk in their schools and communities to learn about the multiple ways that people use literacy to share ideas, inform, persuade, and announce. Students take observation notebooks and write down examples of reading and writing. The teacher does the same and also uses a video camera to record examples for discussion and comparison. Neighborhood Walks not only help students learn more about literacy in their communities, but they also help teachers become more aware of the communities in which their children live, play, and construct their identities (Taylor & Dorsey-Gaines, 1988). Both kinds of information can be shared at home and in school domains.

One of the many benefits of talking with parents and other family members is that students learn about new sources of information in their own communities. Doing so elevates the status of community-based knowledge and makes it easier to invite family members into the classroom to share their personal knowledge about how things work and how things are done. For example, suppose your class is interested in finding out how people acquire sense about directionality (i.e., north, south, east, and west), and you collect lots of information from parents and family members. You can invite several parents and adult caregivers to share with the class how they tell about directions, and students can try out the various methods.

Parents and adult caregivers who speak a language other than English can also be invited to share their knowledge of directionality, or a particular practice, through a translator. It is the knowledge that is important, as well as the fact that the parent is participating in the class. There is an additional benefit to having non-English-speaking parents present a demonstration of a particular practice in their native language: Students get to hear different languages, and they find out that teaching and learning can occur in any language.

There is one possible drawback to using ethnographic techniques to bring community knowledge and, ultimately, parents and other family members into the classroom. There are some kinds of community knowledge that adult members do not want children to bring into the school. To illustrate this point, Lipka (1989) tells a poignant story of a group of well-meaning educators and curriculum developers who were bent on developing a school curriculum that was responsive to the needs of the Yup'ik Eskimo community of Bayup in rural Alaska. One of the teachers involved in the project guided a group of students in producing a questionnaire to find out how the community survived in the bitter winter months and how they gathered food. According to Lipka (1989), here's how the community responded:

> . . . as soon as students began interviewing parents throughout the village, concerned community members got on the C.B. [radio] and warned everybody not to fill out the questionnaire. (p. 223)

The parents later explained that they felt threatened by attempts to take certain kinds of cultural knowledge outside the community and place them in the school. Their objection was essentially that "if kass'at [white people] teach our culture to the students, then what is left for us? Our culture belongs to the community" (Lipka, 1989, p. 223).

What Lipka and his colleagues learned subsequently, however, was that the native community did respond to efforts to construct curricula that dealt with contemporary issues of concern to the community. For example, community members were eager to work with the school on issues of land use and land management. Lipka learned from this experience that the information you gather from the community has to be relevant and purposeful to that community. In other words, rather than the community just being a resource for the school, the school has to become a resource for the community. For our purposes, this means that when you invite parents and other adult caregivers in to speak about their knowledge and practices, you need to consider ways that you and the school can provide better resources to meet their needs as well.

Another way of involving parents in the classroom is to have certain parents or adult caregivers help with making bulletin boards and other kinds of decorations and building projects. For example, if you decorate your classroom around thematic units and festivities, parents and adult caregivers can help. You can set aside several locations in your classroom for non-English-language bulletin boards. If you use the ceiling for decorations, as was suggested in Chapter 3, you can have a crew of parents help you put up the students' work and then add their own creations around a particular theme.

Parents and adult caregivers can also help in the preparation of classroom materials. They can come to the classroom to work on assembling a stage for a play, or they can sew and cut materials for a cooperative game.

There are many activities they can help with regardless of their English-language proficiency.

Finally, at the school level, parents and adult caregivers can observe and help with many of the same kinds of activities that they did in your classroom. They can attend school functions, assemblies, and parties. They can be enlisted to help with food preparation and serving at these events. They can help set up and take down tables before and after functions, assemblies, and parties. You need to be there, however, to support them and make them feel comfortable as they are learning to get involved in the school.

In summary, your goals in Level III are to get parents and adult caregivers to participate in your classroom and in the school, engaging in many different kinds of activities, while you improve and increase your communication with them and show them how schools work. They will participate in your classroom and in the school when they start to feel that the school is a comfortable place to be and that it is a potential resource for them.

Level IV

In this fourth and highest level of parental, adult caregiver, and teacher involvement, the goal is to enable parents and adult caregivers to play a more decisive role in school decisions and policies and at the same time to increase the level of confidence and trust they have in you as the teacher. This level is what Rasinski and Fredericks (1989) referred to as the "empowerment" level. To achieve this highest level of involvement, you and the parents and adult caregivers must have experienced each of the first three levels. Accordingly, Level IV is clearly not for every parent or adult caregiver, and, in fact, few aspire to it. Reaching the level of empowerment depends in great part on the mutual trust and bond that form between you and certain parents and adult caregivers who want to invest extra time and effort in the schooling process (Rasinski & Fredericks, 1989). Those who do decide to participate in Level IV activities often become community spokespersons to whom you and the school can look for both advice and support. In other words, due to their intense involvement in the schools, they become your colleagues in matters of curriculum and education in general. As such, you can ask for their opinions on classroom ideas and, as their participation progresses, for their advice on curricular decisions at the school level.

Your involvement with parents and adult caregivers at this level is tailored primarily to providing suggestions to them with the confidence that they will implement the suggestions. So, for instance, let's say your school has plans to decrease the number of contact hours for art and music or to require all teachers to acquire advanced preparation in teaching English learners within a certain time period. If you suggest to Level IV parents or adult caregivers that they organize a get-together to discuss community opinions about these plans, you can be certain that they will do it. Moreover, because of your commitment to the various communities represented in your classroom, you may be asked to attend meetings and offer opinions at community-based organizations, or you may even be asked to give rides to parents who lack transportation.

An excellent example of what empowered parents and teachers can accomplish is the Pajaro Valley Experience (Ada, 1988), a family literacy program designed by Spanish-speaking parents with the help of teachers in the Pajaro Valley School District near Watsonville, California. Between 60 and 80 Spanish-speaking parents come together each month to discuss children's literature in Spanish and to read the stories that their children have written in Spanish. Over time, the parents join in to write stories and poems along with their children. Parents also learn how to talk about books with their children and eagerly share these discussions with fellow parents at the next monthly meeting. Ada points out that the program is successful because a few parents worked to get others involved and because a few teachers helped with invitations, transportation, and book selections.

The establishment of a family literacy program is one of many kinds of activities in which empowered parents and adult caregivers can engage (Valdés, 1996). They can also set up after-school tutoring programs. Padilla (1982) reports that parents in many communities throughout the Southwest have organized *escuelitas* ("little schools") to provide help with schoolwork, promote Spanish-language development, and reinforce Mexican culture. The *escuelitas* are run by parents and other students who volunteer to work with young children. Trueba, Moll, and Díaz (1982) discuss a similar effort by Mexican immigrant parents in California who organized *Cafés de Amistad* ("Friendship Coffees") for interested parents to come and share their concerns and knowledge about school. Whatever type of program for parents you support, it must be based on a solid understanding of and an appreciation for the internal dynamics of the families involved, and you must respect and give legitimacy to their cultural values and beliefs (Valdés, 1996).

Parents and adult caregivers can also organize parent advisory committees and work toward affecting change in school. Parent advisory committees represent the voice of the community on issues that concern their children. To be effective, parents who become involved in these committees must "be informed not only about the legal realities but also about the attitudes and activities of the local policy makers" (Curtis, 1988, p. 291). Moreover, the school district needs to be made aware, on a continuous basis, of the parents' position on certain issues, just as the parents and adult caregivers need to be apprised of their rights and of their power to impact school policy (Curtis, 1988).

Due to the intense nature and relatively narrow focus of efforts, only a few parents or adult caregivers participate in Level IV activities. The fact that some of these people may eventually become involved in curricular and other schoolwide decisions does not mean, however, that you can lessen your communication with and commitment to other parents and adult caregivers. You still need to maintain contact with all of them and continue to encourage their involvement in school-related activities both at home and in your classroom.

In summary, your main goal at Level IV is to involve parents and adult caregivers from the language groups represented in your class in advising, planning, and developing programs that they and you feel are needed for their children. Level IV parents and adult caregivers have traversed the first three levels of involvement and are committed to working with you on improving education for their children. At this level you and the parents and other adults work with many people, ranging from school board members and the school principal to fellow parents and local community leaders. Level IV involvement is intense and usually long term, but the benefits are also rewarding and long lasting.

Julia Makes a New Friend

For the next several days following the Back-to-School-night presentations, the din of classroom work is music to Julia's ears. The children have decided to tackle one more group activity that even has Julia's attention. They all want to make and paint papier-mâché elephants that can be displayed around the school and in their communities.

That weekend, Julia goes to the local art store to purchase the materials she needs, and on Saturday she decides to give Mrs. Ochoa a call. Seated at her kitchen table, she reaches for her phone.

"*Bueno, ¿quién habla?*" says Mrs. Ochoa as she turns down the radio.

"Hi, um *hola,* this is Julia Felix. I am Miguel's teacher. We met at the Back-to-School night last week. I hope this is not a bad time to call you."

"No, Miss Felix, I am happy you call. I am sorry about what happen the other night with Miss Dimwitty."

"That's no problem. Sometimes people have to hear the truth before they can change." Julia asks about Mrs. Ochoa's children and reiterates what a joy Miguel has been in class.

Mrs. Ochoa mentions how excited Miguel is about school. She asks about Julia's family and laments that her parents live so far away. "I have family in Oaxaca, and I miss them very much too."

"Oh, thank you, Mrs. Ochoa. I try to visit my family during the holidays. Speaking of visits, I would like to invite you to come visit our classroom to see how we do things during the day. This week the children and I are working on several fun and interesting projects." Julia explains how she organizes her day and what Miguel and his group are working on. She also describes what it might be like in class if Mrs. Ochoa were to visit and what procedures she needs to follow for obtaining a visitor's pass.

Mrs. Ochoa thanks her for the invitation. "Is very hard for me to get away from home. Sometimes my sister, she can babysit. But I also have much work at home every day. Maybe I can come on a Friday, 'cuz sontime my husband no work on Friday."

"That would be wonderful, Mrs. Ochoa. I will call you early next week to see if we can make a plan to have you visit class next Friday. Okay? I can have a school mother come to your house to give you a ride and take you home, too, if you don't have transportation."

Julia and Mrs. Ochoa talk a few more minutes before saying goodbye. Julia senses that this may be the beginning of a new and lasting friendship. Looking down at her daily planner, she sees that in 2 weeks there will be interviews and testing for the gifted. *I can't forget to remind Aucencio's and Do Thi's parents to think about my recommendation for getting their children tested for the Gifted Math and Computer programs. Maybe I should call them right now.*

Julia flips her planner back to her class phone directory and begins punching in numbers for Do Thi's house.

CONCLUSION

This chapter began by emphasizing how difficult it may be to involve parents and other adult caregivers from diverse language and cultural backgrounds in school-related activities. In addition to language barriers, the ways that parents and other adult caregivers from different cultures view their role and the school's role in educating their children may be quite different from the expected pattern of school involvement (Chang, 2004; Dien, 2004; Trueba, 1998; Valdés, 1996). Despite language and cultural differences, however, there are ways to involve parents and adult caregivers in school matters that minimize the barriers that language and cultural differences can create. The multilevel approach to home–school relationships is one way to minimize barriers and build bridges between the home and the school. The success of this approach rests on you working together with parents, caregivers, and community members to learn about each other's worlds and, as a result, build bridges that help children succeed in both. The reason for this is that teachers, students, and the community are inexorably connected in the process of education. Accordingly, no one should be left out of the education process due to a language or a cultural barrier. The multilevel approach to home–school relationships presented here provides you with a means to complete the joinfostering mission of providing all parents and adult caregivers variable access to and participation in schooling in ways that are culturally and personally comfortable to them.

ACTIVITIES

1. Contact a local elementary school and ask for a copy of the parent handbook. Review the handbook, determine which sections might be difficult for second-language parents, and rewrite them, using scaffolds, visuals, and other kinds of support. Work with an adult bilingual fully proficient speaker of one of the languages represented in the school, and translate the section you rewrite. Design a Web page for the school, and attach this information to it.

2. Using the parent handbook as a guide, prepare a DVD in English and in the other major languages represented in the school to explain registration day and school policies concerning absences, the school lunch program, bus services, and discipline.

3. Contact a local parent advisory committee and interview one of the members. Find out how the committee works and what some of the major issues have been in the last couple of years. Ask about committee membership of bilingual parents and what the school is doing to prepare teachers for teaching English learners.

4. Visit a community-based organization serving a language-minority community and interview one of the community workers. Find out about the history of the community; about major community events; and where the people in the community shop, worship, and go for entertainment. On the basis of what you learn about the community, attend an event or ceremony and notice (a) the roles that men and women play, (b) how and the extent to which children are involved, and (c) whether and under what conditions English is used for communication among members attending.

5. Interview two parents from the same non-English-speaking background to find out their perceptions of parental involvement, without imposing a standard definition of parental involvement. Try to find one parent who has minimal involvement in the school and one who is intensely involved in the school. Using the multilevel approach to guide the interview, ask each parent to comment on how parents and the school can build better bridges at each level of involvement. Compare and contrast the parents' responses.

REFERENCES

Ada, F. A. (1988). The Pajaro Valley experience: Working with Spanish-speaking parents to develop children's reading and writing skills through the use of children's literature. In T. Skutnabb-Kangas & J. Cummins (Eds.), *Minority education: From shame to struggle* (pp. 223–238). Clevedon, England: Multilingual Matters.

Bausch, L. (2003). Just words: Living and learning the literacies of our students' lives. *Language Arts, 80*(3), 215–222.

Bermudez, A., & Padrón, Y. (1987). Integrating parental education into teacher training programs: A workable model for minority parents. *Journal of Educational Equity and Leadership, 7,* 235–244.

Chang, J. (2004). Language and literacy in Chinese American communities. In B. Pérez (Ed.), *Sociocultural contexts of language and literacy* (pp. 179–206). Mahwah, NJ: Lawrence Erlbaum Associates.

Chavkin, N. F., & Williams, D. L., Jr. (1989). Community size and parent involvement in education. *The Clearing House, 63*(4), 159–162.

Cheng, L. R. (1987). *Assessing Asian language performance.* Rockville, MD: Aspen.

Coelho, E. (1994). Social integration of immigrant and refugee children. In F. Genesee (Ed.), *Educating second language children: The whole child, the whole curriculum, the whole community* (pp. 301–327). New York: Cambridge University Press.

Constantino, R., Cui, L., & Faltis, C. (1995). Chinese parental involvement: Reaching new levels. *Equity and Excellence in Education, 28*(2), 46–51.

Curtis, J. (1988). Parents, schools and racism: Bilingual education in a Northern California town. In T. Skutnabb-Kangas & J. Cummins (Eds.), *Minority education: From shame to struggle* (pp. 278–298). Clevedon, England: Multilingual Matters.

Delgado-Gaitán, C. (1987). Parent perceptions of school: Supportive environments for children. In H. T. Trueba (Ed.), *Success or failure? Learning and the language minority student* (pp. 131–155). New York: Newbury House.

Delgado-Gaitán, C. (1994). Russian refugee families: Accommodating aspirations through education. *Anthropology and Education, 25,* 137–155.

Delpit, L. (1998). The silenced dialogue: Power and pedagogy in educating other people's children. *Harvard Educational Review, 58,* 280–298.

Dien, T. (2004). Language and literacy in Vietnamese American communities. In B. Pérez (Ed.), *Sociocultural contexts of language and literacy* (pp. 137–178). Mahwah, NJ: Lawrence Erlbaum Associates.

Epstein, J. (1991). Paths to partnerships: what we can learn from federal, state, district, and school initiatives. *Phi Delta Kappan, 72,* 344–349.

Epstein, J. (1995). School/family partnerships: Caring for the children we share. *Phi Delta Kappan, 76,* 701–712.

Epstein, J., Sanders, M., Simon, B., Salinas, K., Jansorn, K., & Van Voorhis, F. (2002). *School, family, and community partnerships: Your handbook for action.* Thousand Oaks, CA: Corwin Press.

Gestwicki, C. (1987). *Home, school and community relations: A guide to working with parents.* Albany, NY: Delmar.

Greenberg, J. B. (1989). Funds of knowledge: Historical constitution, social distribution and transmission. Paper presented at the annual meeting of the Society for Applied Anthropology, Santa Fe, New Mexico.

Hakuta, K. (1990). Language and cognition in bilingual children. In A. M. Padilla, H. H. Fairchild, & C. M. Valadez (Eds.), *Bilingual education: Issues and strategies* (pp. 47–59). Newbury Park, CA: Sage.

Heath, S. B. (1983). *Ways with words: Language, life and work in communities and classrooms.* Cambridge, England: Cambridge University Press.

Hidalgo, N. (1994). Profiles of a Puerto Rican family's support for school achievement. *Equity and Choice, 10*(2), 14–22.

Hidalgo, N., Sui, S., & Epstein, J. (2004). Research on families, schools, and communities. In J. Banks & C. Banks (Eds.), *Handbook of research on multicultural education* (pp. 631–655). San Franciso: Jossey-Bass.

Hoskins, M. W. (1971). *Building rapport with the Vietnamese.* Washington, DC: U.S. Government Printing Office.

Kang, H-W., Kuehn, P., & Herrell, A. (1994). The Hmong literacy project: A study of Hmong classroom behavior. *Bilingual Research Journal, 18*(3/4), 63–84.

Leitch, M. L., & Tangri, S. S. (1988, Winter). Barriers to home-school collaboration. *Educational Horizons,* pp. 70–74.

Lipka, J. (1989). A cautionary tale of curriculum development in Yup'ik Eskimo communities. *Anthropology and Education Quarterly, 20,* 216–231.

McCarty, T., & Watabomigie, L. (2004). Language and literacy in American Indian and Alaska native communities. In B. Pérez (Ed.), *Sociocultural contexts of language and literacy* (pp. 79–110). Mahwah, NJ: Lawrence Erlbaum Associates.

Moll, L., & González, N. (2004). Engaging life: A funds-of-knowledge approach to multicultural education. In J. Banks & C. Banks (Eds.), *Handbook of research on multicultural education* (pp. 699–715). San Franciso: Jossey-Bass.

Moll, L., & Greenberg, J. (1990). Creating zones of possibilities: Coming social contexts for instruction. In L. Moll (Ed.), *Vygotsky and education: Instructional implications and applications of socio-historical psychology* (pp. 319–348). Cambridge, England: Cambridge University Press.

Moll, L., Vélez-Ibáñez, C., & Greenberg, J. (1989). Community knowledge and classroom practice: Combining resources for literacy instruction. *Year one progress report.* Tucson: University of Arizona, College of Education.

Moskowitz, G. (1978). *Caring and sharing in the foreign language class: A source book on humanistic techniques.* Rowley, MA: Newbury House.

Ogbu, J. (1983). Minority status and schooling in plural societies. *Comparative Education Review, 27,* 168–190.

Olsen, L. (1988). *Crossing the schoolhouse border: Immigrant students and California public schools.* San Francisco: California Tomorrow.

Olsen, L. (1997). *Made in America: Immigrant students in our public schools.* New York: The New Press.

Olson, L. (1990). Misreading said to hamper Hispanics' role in school. *Education Week, 9*(32), 4.

Padilla, A. (1982). Bilingual schools: Gateways to integration or roads to separation. In J. A. Fishman & G. D. Keller (Eds.), *Bilingual education for Hispanic students in the United States* (pp. 48–70). New York: Teachers College Press.

Petit, D. (1989). *Opening up schools.* Harmondsworth, England: Penguin.

Ramos, N., & Santos, R. (1994). Promoting community-school partnerships in bilingual education. In R. Rodríguez, N. Ramos, & J. A. Ruiz-Escalante (Eds.), *Compendium of readings in bilingual education* (pp. 267–273). San Antonio: Texas Association for Bilingual Education.

Rasinski, T., & Fredericks, A. (1989, November). Dimensions of parent involvement. *The Reading Teacher,* pp. 180–182.

Scarcella, R. (1990). *Teaching language minority students in the multicultural classroom.* Upper Saddle River, NJ: Prentice Hall.

Scarcella, R., & Chin, K. (1993). *Literacy practices of two Korean-American communities* (Report No. 8). Santa Cruz, CA: The National Center for Research on Cultural Diversity and Language Learning.

Schecter, S., & Bayley, R. (2002). *Language as cultural practice: Mexicanos en el norte.* Mahwah, NJ: Lawrence Erlbaum Associates.

Solomon, Z. (1991). California's policy on parent involvement: State leadership for local initiatives. *Phi Delta Kappan, 72,* 359–362.

Suárez-Orozco, C., & Todorova, I. (2003, Winter). The social worlds of immigrant youth. *New Directions for Youth Development,* pp. 15–24.

Taylor, D., & Dorsey-Gaines, C. (1988). *Growing up literate: Learning from inner-city families.* Portsmouth, NH: Heinemann Publishers.

Torres-Guzmán, M. (1991). Recasting frames: Latino parent involvement. In M. McGroarty & C. Faltis (Eds.), *Languages in schools and society: Policy and pedagogy* (pp. 529–552). Berlin: Mouton de Gruyter.

Torres-Guzmán, M. (2004). Language, culture, and literacy in Puerto Rican communities. In B. Pérez (Ed.), *Sociocultural contexts of language and literacy* (pp. 111–135). Mahwah, NJ: Lawrence Erlbaum Associates.

Trueba, H. (1998). The education of Mexican immigrant children. In M. Suárez-Orozco (Ed.), *Crossings: Mexican immigration in interdisciplinary perspectives* (pp. 251–275). Cambridge, MA: Harvard University Press.

Trueba, H. T., Moll, L., & Díaz, E. (1982). *Improving the functional writing of bilingual secondary school students* (Contract No. 400-81-0023). Washington, DC: National Institute of Education.

Tse, L. (2001). *"Why don't they learn English?" Separating fact from fallacy in the U.S. language debate.* New York: Teachers College Press.

Valdés, G. (1996). *Con respeto: Bridging the distances between culturally diverse families and schools.* New York: Teachers College Press.

Valdés, G. (2000). Bilingualism and language use among Mexican Americans. In S. McKay & S. Wong (Eds.), *New immigrants in the United States* (pp. 99–136). New York: Cambridge University Press.

Wong Fillmore, L. (1990, May 1). *Latino families and the schools.* Remarks prepared for the Seminar on California's Changing Face of Race Relations: New Ethics in the 1990's. Sponsored by the Senate Office of Research. State Capitol, Sacramento, California.

Yao, E. L. (1988). Working effectively with Asian immigrant parents. *Phi Delta Kappan, 70,* 223–225.

7

Assessing English Learners

OVERVIEW

Assessment is perhaps one of the most familiar and perplexing endeavors in teaching. All new teachers have at least 16 years of experiences being assessed, tested, and evaluated in English; yet most have only scant experience designing and conducting assessment for fully proficient English students, and precious few, even those with years of teaching experience, know how to assess English learners for language *and* for learning. Moreover, classroom assessment has become increasingly more complex with the introduction of standards-based instruction.

This final chapter invites you to become more knowledgeable about ways to assess how well English learners in your classroom are improving in English and performing over time on specific content area assignments (MULTIPLE WAYS OF ASSESSMENT TO OPTIMIZE ACADEMIC LEARNING PRACTICES, AFFILIATIONS AND CONNECTIONS TO WIDER ACADEMIC COMMUNITIES OF PRACTICE). Your classroom assessment needs to be fair (not biased against non-English-speaking children) and valid (measuring what it says it is measuring). Moreover, your classroom assessment needs to show that your students are making progress toward academic practices in language and the content areas. Lastly, your assessment needs to address local and state learning standards.

Like it or not, since the passage of No Child Left Behind Education Act in 2002, all states require standards-based instruction for and periodic assessment

223

of language arts, science, math, and social studies. States with high English learner student populations have also begun to develop K–12 English-language proficiency standards with descriptive criteria for different levels of proficiency and different grade levels. You can view your state's language proficiency standards by looking them up on the Department of Education Web site. In many of these states, the English-language proficiency standards have been aligned with existing language arts standards, which are in turn tied to high stakes tests, salary increases, and contract continuances (Poyner & Wolfe, 2005). It is important to gain a good working knowledge of the standards required in your school so that you can show parents and others that your students are meeting the standards. More importantly, you need to be able to provide a strong rationale for the multi-ple assessments you use to demonstrate learning and be able to resist policies and practices that place English learners in jeopardy of being held back from continuous learning (PROMOTION OF CRITICAL CONSCIOUSNESS). Accordingly, the goal of this chapter is to provide you with an overview of assessment practices and issues, including the use of standards for assessment purposes.

We begin by looking in on Julia, who meets up with Jake to chat about assessment over coffee. Like many teachers today, Julia is faced with decisions about how to incorporate standards and assessment into classroom routines with minimal distraction from the way students engage in learning activities. Julia has her own stance about assessment but wants to hear what Jake has to say about it, with the hope that she can find better ways to assess her students' learning.

Episode Seven: Julia and Jake Meet to Chat About Testing

The 5-year school improvement plan at Bruner Elementary includes a revision of the assessment and evaluation plan for all teachers. Since the beginning of the year, teachers in both the bilingual unit and all-English classrooms have been required to take a series of workshops and training to improve instruction for and assessment of English learners. This week Julia attends a workshop on ways to document student progress toward the state standards and how to showcase the progress in students' portfolios. After the workshop, she calls Jake to invite him for coffee to talk about some of the issues she has with the standards.

Jake listens to his phone messages as soon as he gets home from school on Friday. *Cool. There's a call from Jules.* He calls her immediately.

"Hi, Julia, it's me. I got your message. I would love to meet for coffee this evening. How about if I swing by and pick you up around 8?"

"I'll be ready. Hey, do you mind if I bring some of my students' portfolios so you can see what I am doing?"

"Please, I would love to take a look at them." Jake hangs up the phone and heads for the shower.

On the drive to the coffee shop, Julia tells Jake that she has reservations about putting information on the district's English-language proficiency standards in student portfolios. "I don't mind standards, but my students do so much more than the ELP standards call for. Plus, the criteria they use for the different skill areas are based on a fragmented isolated view of language. You know me. I see language and literacy as holistic and functionally tied to communities of practice."

"I know what you are saying," says Jake. "I agree that the ELP standards are pretty lame. I have aligned them to the existing language arts standards, which use richer criteria. Then, I use those criteria to show what students are doing and where they are heading."

"That's a great idea," Julia says. "Is the principal cool with that?"

"Mrs. Turner encourages us to be creative," says Jake with a wink.

Inside the coffee shop, they grab a table near the back of the shop, where they can continue the discussion. Julia pulls out her student portfolios. "I think I do a pretty good job of providing lots of evidence that students are making progress. Take a look at this student's portfolio. I have *process* information to show development over time of oral and written abilities, along with some of the student's *best works,* with her explanation for choosing the work. And I have started to put in information about ELP standards."

"I like how you have everything so organized and documented. I make up a standards sheet, where I list all of the ELP standards for my grade level, and then I provide a general description of where the student is and where he or she needs to be. This is a good place to use descriptors from the language arts standards. They are almost the same as the ELP standards, but they are written from a more holistic, integrated perspective."

"I think I can do that, Jake," says Julia, jotting down a note to herself to make up a Standards sheet.

"I know you can, Julia. And, you'll see, it is not that difficult once you get the hang of it," says Jake, as he sips his coffee. "Actually, that's the easy part. The hard part is doing the assessments. I just don't care much for testing, but I am trying to learn how to do it right so I can show off how talented my students really are."

Julia and Jake continue their discussion about assessment, comparing notes and trading tips.

Sharing ideas with fellow teachers who share your stance toward children and teaching is one of the best ways to make improvements in how you do assessments in your classroom. Let's continue this conversation by looking into the assessment of spoken and written language abilities.

LANGUAGE PROFICIENCY ASSESSMENT

Assessing how well a student uses English to speak socially and in academically desirable ways, and assessing whether the student is becoming more proficient in spoken and written language over time, is no easy feat. Most schools rely on standardized and norm-referenced language tests to determine a student's spoken and written language proficiency levels (Haley & Austin, 2004). Standardized tests are constructed by large testing businesses, such as Harcourt Brace and Educational Testing Service. They are designed for easy scoring and speedy administration, and they provide you with little information about what students can do with spoken and written language in your classroom. Most standardized tests are norm-referenced, meaning they compare your students' scores against a population of students with which the test has been standardized. You have little control over the use of these types of language-proficiency tests, but you can spend some time preparing your students to take tests wisely and efficiently, and very often you can be involved in the scoring of the spoken and written language sections of these tests.

There are many types of classroom assessment that yield multiple samples of student language abilities, which you can then align to English-language proficiency standards as well as other academic accomplishments and showcase in each English learner's portfolio. The following sections offer assessment activities for spoken and written language that you can use to demonstrate student learning. There are two good rules of thumb to follow in using any of the assessments discussed below:

1. What you assess should resemble what happens in your classroom. When your students are familiar with the assessment activity, the results are likely to be trustworthy.

2. What you assess should provide you with information about progress toward your classroom goals, one of which should be language and content area standards. Knowing how well your students are doing means not only how well they are performing as members of communities of practice, but also how well their performance relates to learning standards associated with the school domain communities of practice.

We begin with ways to assess spoken language for social and academic purposes.

ORAL LANGUAGE ASSESSMENT

One of your major responsibilities in working with English learners is to enable these students to communicate meaningfully using spoken language for social and academic purposes. As we have seen throughout this book, conversations, inquiry, and discussions using appropriate content area terminology and ways of speaking are fundamental for active participation in learning communities and for the creation of membership identities in these communities. Accordingly, you will need to select assessment activities that fully represent the range of oral language tasks you expect students to use while participating in myriad classroom activities. Table 7.1 presents a number of oral language activities you can use to assess and document how well your students are progressing in classroom spoken English.

Note that each assessment activity is general enough to use across the content areas, and for each type of activity you can elicit specialized vocabulary that you may have been studying or that you wish to assess in particular.

Oral Interviews

You can conduct oral interviews with individuals or with pairs of students at all levels of English proficiency. Oral interviews resemble discussions and conversations about literature and content presented in Chapter 4 (the Karen Smith Model, Instructional Conversations, and the Joan Tough Model). Oral interviews enable you to elicit and assess descriptions, information, and students' opinions about topics that have been discussed in class or topics that are generally familiar to the student. Your goal in conducting an oral interview is to engage a student in a comfortable conversation that reaches the upper limit of the student's spoken abilities. You should have a list of guiding questions that are appropriate to the language proficiency and age of the student being interviewed.

To rate the interview, you can use either a holistic or a more analytical scale. With a holistic scale, you can rate the student from 1 to 5 on listening, speaking, vocabulary, use of language functions (descriptions, explanation, opinion, suggestions, recommendations, etc.), and fluency of expression. A more analytical scale might include rubrics specifically concerned with grammatical structures, specialized vocabulary, fluency, and speaking. You can also use a simple checklist of language skills to show that the student is or is not using certain vocabulary, language functions, or grammatical structures. Whatever rating method you adopt, it is best to wait until after the interview to rate the student.

Descriptions and Storytelling

For beginners and intermediate-level English learners, you can use picture cues to assess narrative abilities and descriptions of people, objects, and events. With picture cues, you can elicit story vocabulary and literary talk

Table 7.1

Oral language assessments for the classroom

Assessment Activity	Format	Language-Proficiency Level	English Language Proficiency Indicators
1. Oral interview	One-on-one	Beginning, Intermediate, Advanced	• Describing people, places, events, and things • Asking for and giving information • Asking for and giving an opinion
2. Descriptions and storytelling using picture cues	One-on-one	Beginning, Intermediate	• Describing characters • Narrating story • Giving information • Giving an opinion
3. CD/cassette tapes	One-on-one, groups, whole class	Intermediate, Advanced	• Listening for gist • Listening for specific information • Listening for and giving directions
4. DVD chapters	One-on-one, groups, whole class	Beginning, Intermediate, Advanced	• Describing people, places, and events • Asking for and giving information • Asking for and giving an opinion
5. Information gap dialogue	Pairs	Beginning, Intermediate, Advanced	• Describing items • Asking for and giving information • Asking for and giving directions
6. Story recounts	One-on-one	Beginning, Intermediate, Advanced	• Describing characters and events • Asking for and giving information • Summarizing
7. Role-playing, simulations	Pairs, small groups	Beginning, Intermediate, Advanced	• Greeting/leave takings • Asking questions • Asking for help • Agreeing/disagreeing • Asking for and giving opinions • Asking for and giving advice • Asking for and giving directions • Persuading • Encouraging
8. Oral reports	One-on-one, small groups, whole class	Beginning, Intermediate, Advanced	• Describing events • Explaining events • Giving information • Asking for information

Source: From *Authentic assessment for English Language Learners: Practical approaches for teachers* by J. M. O'Malley & L. V. Pierce, 1996, New York: Longman. Adapted with permission.

about stories. Using picture cues for descriptions and storytelling is important because it prepares English learners for the standardized language tests, all of which use picture cues to elicit spoken and written language about stories and descriptions.

The pictures you use for stories and descriptions should be appropriate to the age and interest levels of your students. You can collect all sorts of pictures from magazines and books. Look for pictures that enable students to make vivid descriptions and/or tell an interesting story using the pictures. Descriptions and stories with more characters and characters of the same gender are more difficult than descriptions and stories with fewer objects and easily distinguishable characters. For example, if you have a picture of three little girls playing on a swing set, and one of them points to a butterfly, which lands near another girl who doesn't see the butterfly, this will require more referential and explicit language than if there is only one little girl and a butterfly.

Using picture cues is similar to conducting an oral interview. However, you will need to keep your talk to a minimum, because your goal is to get the student to produce as much language as possible for as long as possible. For beginners, you may need to ask *yes/no* questions and invite students to identify the names of people and objects and talk about colors, sizes, and locations. To rate the descriptions and narratives, you can use the same kind of holistic or analytical scoring system with rubrics for the various levels of proficiency.

It is a good idea to develop a picture file to correspond as closely as possible to the activities you have for classroom themes. For example, Julia has a whole range of pictures of elephants from India and Africa, as well as elephants in U.S. zoos. She keeps story pictures and pictures with other objects so students can tell a story using the pictures. You can organize your pictures alphabetically or by themes. You should laminate your best picture stories, and keep your alternatives in plastic file slips.

CD/Cassette Tapes

Use CD/Cassette tapes of authentic language use to assess listening abilities. You can make your own recordings of news, music, weather, announcements, and instructions. For younger children, you might use an iPod or a similar device to record the sound of songs and fun activities from children's television programs and then burn your own CD for classroom use. You can use the CD or cassette tape for individual learners, small groups, or the whole class to assess for understanding the gist, specific information, directions, and descriptions. For children in the upper elementary grades, you can use CD/cassette recordings of songs to assess what the song is about and what certain words might mean in the context of the song. Product commercials are also fun to use in assessing the ability to listen for important information and to evaluate a commercial for its truthfulness.

DVD Chapters

You can use DVD chapters and clips of a few moments from a movie to assess various aspects of speaking and listening. With DVD chapters, you can select the clips and even decide on the speed. As you preview the clip, you can think of questions and vocabulary that you want students to generate upon viewing the clip. Show the DVD clips and then have students tell about the people, places, and events they remember. They can also ask questions and give opinions about the clip. Have students predict what will happen next, and what happened before, in the clip they watch.

There is video software available that allows you to piece together your own DVD clips. You can then present events out of order and have students describe the appropriate order using narrative sequential discourse, using words like *first, next, then,* and *finally.* Some video software also enables you to make your own movie clips and burn them onto a DVD, which you can then use for assessment purposes as outlined above. With your own movie clips, you can focus attention on key vocabulary and discourse practices as they occur in your classroom. You can rate the students' understanding and spoken proficiency using the scales mentioned above.

Information Gap Dialogue

In this type of dialogue exchange, there are two people, one with information that the other person needs in order to complete a task. Typically, the information involves descriptions of pictures, maps, and/or real objects placed out of view of one of the participants. The dialogue consists of descriptions of objects using information about color, size, direction, location, and sequence. The dialogue occurs either between you and a student or between two students while you assess the interaction. If the information given is clear, the person receiving the information should be able to select the correct object, picture, or design, thereby eliminating the information gap. However, if the person on the receiving end of the information cannot select the correct object, picture, or design, the information giver has to rephrase the message with more explicit information. In preparing the information gap activities, make sure that descriptions are straightforward, requiring minimal analysis.

For younger learners, you can design treasure hunts or maps of the school and have students give one another directions to key locations. You can also ask students to label objects based on what they hear from you or their partner. In another kind of activity, students use LEGOs® to make a model and then describe it so that their partner can build an exact replica, using only directions given by the first student. Students can practice information gap dialogues using *Back and Forth: Pair Activities for Language Development* (Palmer, Rogers, & Winn-Bell Olsen, 1985). This book is full of reproducible pictures that students work on in pairs. You can also collect *Hocus Pocus* cartoons in the daily newspapers for use with older learners. These are two pictures that look very similar but vary on five or six details. The goal is for each student to describe the picture and, through dialogue, discover the differences in details.

To rate an information gap dialogue, you can devise a rubric for both the speaker and the listener. For the speaker, the rating scale should range from 1 to 3 on accuracy and clarity of the description. For the listener, the rating should focus on the ability to follow directions/instructions or the ability to select the described object, person, or event.

Story Recounts

This type of oral assessment always interacts with reading, especially a student's knowledge of story structure. To minimize the extent to which you assess story structure, you can direct the focus of interaction to descriptions of characters and story events that are familiar to the student. You can have the student select a favorite story, even a story he or she has written. The story should be relatively short and not contain vocabulary or concepts that make it too difficult to understand.

Students who can read should read the story silently; otherwise, you can read the story to them or play a cassette tape or CD of the story. Immediately afterward, ask the student to relate in his or her own words what the story is about. Keep prompts for more information to a minimum, because the goal is to have the student produce sustained talk about the story.

Rating a story recount is similar to other types of oral language tasks. Depending on the age and grade level of the student, you can develop a rating scale or checklist that includes various levels of ability for describing the setting, characters, sequence of events, range of vocabulary, problem identification, and problem solution (Gibbons, 2002).

Role-Playing and Simulations

Role-playing should be familiar to students because they are asked to take on roles in small-group work. For English learners, role-plays are a safe way to practice using English in multiple, socially appropriate ways. Simulations are role-playing situations that require interaction in order to solve a particular problem or to decide upon a group decision. Role-playing and simulations are worthwhile ways of introducing problem-solving to classroom activities. For example, in Julia's class, students devised a sociodrama (Scarcella, 1987), in which several students took turns playing the role of different animals (elephant, rhino, hippo) and a local farmer to develop a play about feeding areas and the farmer's rights. Students developed their own dialogue, practiced it, and then presented it to the class. Julia made sure that students incorporated greetings, leave-taking, and politeness formulas and worked with students on ways to agree and disagree.

For beginning students, role-plays can be simple, using questions for information and assistance. You can help more advanced English learners to develop dialogue for agreeing/disagreeing, giving opinions, offering advice, and recapping information. It is very important to give students ample time to practice their roles in pairs or with their simulation group. Cue cards with main ideas help students learn their lines.

Because much of the language in role-plays and simulations is rehearsed, you can rate students using rubrics that you have already developed, and give them credit for how well they take on the role of the character they represent.

Oral Reports

There will be times when you ask students to present their work on a project to the entire class or other audiences as an oral report. A good oral report relies on notes or cue cards the student creates to highlight important aspects of the material. Beginning English learners can present oral reports using artwork, posters, computer graphics, overhead projectors, and other visual support. More advanced students will need to rely more on written text as they report to the class, using PowerPoint presentations, overhead projectors, and the white board.

Preparation for oral reports is critical for students' success. They need clear guidelines on how long to talk, what to talk about, what areas must be covered in the report, and how the report will be evaluated. You can go over the scoring rubric with students to make sure that students are aware of the guidelines and what you will be looking for in the report. Moreover, you can prepare a check sheet, which lists the major components you want students to provide in their report. Remember that the purpose of an oral report is to present information to a known audience using a variety of sources and support for conveying the information. Accordingly, the assessment rubric should focus on how well the student conveys information and not so much on pronunciation and grammatical features. There are several questions that will help you organize your scoring rubric, including: Does the student present a central idea or theme that he or she researched? Are there details to support the main idea? Has the student prepared notes and used them for guiding the report? Does the student use visual support to express meaning?

WRITTEN LANGUAGE ASSESSMENT

Written language assessment includes ways of assessing reading and writing. In practice, reading and writing are inseparable from each other and from speaking and listening (Faltis & Hudelson, 1998). Written and oral language are always learned in a social context, and how children use written and oral language depends on the purposes of each within academic communities of practice. English learners who have already acquired academic literacy abilities in their home language should be able to show progress in reading and writing in English. Assessment of reading and writing should focus on authentic literacy activities and on how well students understand the purposes of reading and writing, which Gee (1989) refers to as *power literacy*. English learners who acquire this kind of literacy develop a deep understanding of the functions and uses of literacy in school and society; in doing so they are likely to identify with others who engage in reading for multiple purposes. Furthermore, to the extent that English language learners acquire powerful literacy, they also acquire an awareness of academic uses of language—how written language is used in the various academic content areas for conveying meaning through narrative, procedural, and expository text (Haley & Austin, 2004; Short, 2000). (See the section on self-assessment practices, later in this chapter, for ways to assess powerful literacy.)

Informal Reading Inventories

For this type of assessment, use passages from books and other authentic reading materials that are of varying levels of difficulty. It goes without saying that you should be constantly sharing good literature with English learners and talking with them about why it is good literature. Knowing what your students enjoy reading and what they find difficult helps you decide what kinds of reading passages to use in the inventory. Ordinarily, you begin with a reading passage that is relatively easy for the student and then increase the level of difficulty, using no more than three passages (Peregoy & Boyle, 2000). You ask the student to read the passage aloud and then ask informational and interpretive questions about the text, and have the student provide a summary of the passage. The interaction around the text should resemble the interaction you have with students when you are discussing readings in other settings. If possible record the readings using an iPod or some other unobtrusive recording device so that you can listen to the recording and at a later time assess the student's understanding and ability to talk about and summarize the text. Based on the student's reading strengths and needs, you can devise a plan of action to help improve where needed.

Running Records

Running records (Clay, 1993) are a form of miscue analysis (Goodman, Watson, & Burke, 1987), which focuses on variations from print that a reader makes during oral reading. Unlike miscue analysis, however, running records require little preparation. You will need a blank piece of paper with lines to correspond to each line in the student's text. You can sit next to or stand behind the reader and place a check mark on a blank line for every word a student reads correctly and record words the student reads that are not in the passage (word substitutions) as well as self-corrections. You can also jot down your observations concerning fluency (e.g., hesitations, sounding out strategies, and reading speed). Meaningful substitutions and self-corrections are indicators of good reading ability. Reading with expression also indicates that the student is making sense of text.

You can use student self-selected passages or you can select several passages based on your knowledge of the student's abilities and reading preferences. The text a student reads should be about 10 minutes long or less. The general rule is that if the student makes uncorrected miscues on more than 10% of the words in the text, the text is too difficult for the reader (Clay, 1993). Running records require little time and reveal much about a student's reading abilities.

Dictation

You can dictate reading passages that you use from informational reading inventories to individual students or to groups of students. It is best to read the passage completely once while students write as much as they can. Then reread the passage one more time so that students can fill in the blanks. Dictation assesses a student's understanding of written text, but as an integrative test, it also draws on listening. You can use lyrics to songs and text from movies as well.

Reading and Writing Checklists and Rating Scales

Checklists are simple descriptions of behaviors that you indicate with a *yes/no* rating (Herman, Aschbacher, & Winters, 1992). You observe a student in the act of reading or writing and indicate behaviors the student exhibits. For example, for reading, you might observe whether a student begins by making predictions, self-corrects while reading, identifies main ideas, predicts outcomes, and draws conclusions (O'Malley & Pierce, 1996). For writing, you might check to see if a student uses an organizer in pre-writing (list, outline, graphic organizer), makes a first draft, has others read the work, revises the draft (using more precise vocabulary and sentences), and edits the work for spelling, punctuation, and grammar. You can use this simple form of assessment to keep track of student behaviors over time—say, for instance, every 6 weeks.

Writing Rubrics

Writing rubrics divide writing abilities into various levels of proficiency. Using rubrics, rate each student on the basis of holistic, primary trait, or analytic scoring procedures (Haley & Austin, 2004). Holistic scoring relies on a variety of criteria that you look for in a student's paper and then assign a score according to whether or not a student shows evidence of indicators of proficiency within a rubric for a particular level. Typically, the rubrics include indicators for conveying meaning, organization and coherence of ideas, vocabulary usage, and mechanical aspects of writing.

Primary trait scoring is a type of holistic scoring that typically focuses on standards. Accordingly, indicators of proficiency within each rubric are linked to particular writing standards. For example, suppose a writing standard for 2nd-grade English learners set out that those students must identify, describe, and apply conventions of standard English in his or her communications. The primary trait that you would be looking for is whether and how well a piece of writing shows evidence of basic English conventions. The indicators would vary for beginning, intermediate, and advanced English learners with respect to quantity and quality of errors produced in the writing.

Analytic scoring enables you to score specific features of writing separately, and in doing so, you can provide more specific information to students about aspects of their writing development. For example, you can decide on indicators for Organization of Ideas, Writing Style, Sentence Formation, Grammatical Usage, and Mechanics. The indicators vary according to the score you assign the student across the writing features of interest (Hamp-Lyons, 1991). Some English learners prefer analytic scoring to holistic scoring because it provides them with specific feedback about their writing (O'Malley & Pierce, 1996). Whether you use holistic or analytic scoring, it is important to constantly review the rubrics to ensure that they reflect what the students are doing in your classroom.

Self-Assessment

English learners need multiple opportunities to assess their own reading and writing abilities. Self-assessment enables students to become aware of their strengths and where they need to place more emphasis, giving them power over their own literacy (Gee, 1989). Reading self-assessments can range from checklists of reading behaviors and rubrics to learning logs and reflection logs for older students (O'Malley & Pierce, 1996). Checklists and rubrics are ways for students to see for themselves what kinds of reading and writing strategies they use or don't use. Students can also use checklists to indicate all of the places and functions of reading and writing in their neighborhood and school communities (Bausch, 2003). Learning logs and reflection logs enable students to write how they feel about what they are learning and how well they understand what they are learning. Learning logs are useful for English learners who are hesitant to participate in discussions about reading and writing. You can ask students to reflect on what they learned, what helped them learn new words and ideas, what was easy and difficult to understand, and what they might do next time to improve their learning.

You can develop checklists for English learners to self-assess their writing strategies before, during, and upon completion of a writing assignment (Haley & Austin, 2004). For pre-writing self-assessment, students can pay attention to ways for developing a topic before writing about it. For example, students might be asked to indicate *yes* or *no* to the following statements as a way to self-assess helpful pre-writing strategies:

1. I have an outline of my ideas to organize my thoughts.
2. I have a semantic web of my ideas to organize my thoughts.
3. I talked with my classmates about my ideas.
4. I used different sources to help me develop my ideas.
5. I am interested in learning more about my ideas.

Then, during the composing phase of writing, the student might be asked to respond to these kinds of self-assessment statements:

1. I made a first draft of my ideas.
2. I used words that helped make my ideas clear.

3. I cut and pasted drawings or pictures into my writing.

4. I wrote as much as I could about my ideas.

5. I tried to follow my outline to organize my ideas.

6. I have a beginning, middle, and end that are easy to see.

Finally, upon completing a first or second draft, the student might be asked to respond to statements concerning final edits and revisions:

1. I checked with classmates to see if the paper made sense.

2. I checked to see if I stated my purpose clearly.

3. I added or took out parts to make the paper better.

4. I checked for spelling, punctuation, and grammar.

You will need to spend extra time ensuring that beginning-level English learners understand each of the statements providing scaffolds and home language support as needed.

A simple and effective way for English learners to self-assess is to use "traffic light" icons to label their written work green, yellow, or red according to whether they think they have good, partial, or little understanding for reading and whether they think what they have written conveys good, partial or little meaning (Black, Harrison, Marshall, & Wiliam, 2004). Likewise, you can have students use traffic light icons to indicate ease or difficulty of vocabulary and spelling words, as well as for ease or difficulty of Web pages used for gathering information.

PORTFOLIOS FOR ENGLISH LEARNERS

The best way to demonstrate that English learners are meeting state standards and showing improvement over time is through the use of portfolio assessment. This is especially the case when you teach using inquiry-based learning and organize learning around themes (Peregoy & Boyle, 2000). A portfolio is a purposeful, chronological collection of actual student samples of work in language arts and writing, designed to reflect student development in one or more areas over time (Haley & Austin, 2004). Ideally, you and your students work together to generate lists of written and artistic tasks, projects, or exhibits for agreed-upon learning areas that you wish to showcase. You can also design a portfolio that provides evidence of meeting language and content area standards.

In the classroom, you will need to think about English language learner standards in addition to content area standards. You are accountable for quarterly reporting about every English learner in your classroom. This means that you need to pay careful attention not only to how well English learners are participating in and affiliating with academic learning communities of practice, but also to how well they are improving or not improving in their English-language abilities. Portfolio assessment is *where* you document what you observe, what students understand and do, and how well they perform on language and content area activities in your class.

Portfolios can be highly reflective, emphasizing English learners' perceptions, interpretations, and strategies used in acquiring and applying knowledge. The main idea in portfolio assessment is for you and your students to collect, develop, and link students' work over time to show how and the extent to which multiple learning has occurred. When students select a sample of their work to be included in their portfolio, you might ask them to write a reflective statement explaining why the piece was important and why they chose it for the portfolio. You can also discuss with them orally why they chose to include a piece. This helps students develop self-assessment strategies as well as providing you with information about how they see themselves as learners in the class (Haley & Austin, 2004). You can have students do this every 2 to 4 weeks, or as needed. Some English learners may require help developing explanations for why they select items to showcase in their portfolios, but over time and with practice, all students should be able to give reasons for selecting materials.

In addition to student self-selected work, you can also place in the portfolio student's work that provides evidence of understanding as well as producing knowledge through computations, writing, art, and the World Wide Web. You might look for examples of invented spelling to show phonics knowledge, or you can include work that includes thematic vocabulary knowledge. In consultation with the student, you may also want to jot down why the work is important and how it shows growth and awareness of what is happening in class and in the community. Julia uses 2″ by 3″ Post-it® notes to keep anecdotal records of English learners' language development with respect to standards. She keeps a clipboard with index cards for each of her students. If she observes them figuring out the meaning of a word using a strategy she has discussed with the class, she makes a note of it on a Post-it note and sticks it to the student's index card for that day. Over time, she gathers the notes and writes out a summary of the indicators of performance for the various language standards and places the summary in the student's portfolio.

In addition to English performance, try to include evidence of students' critical understanding of social consciousness. For example, suppose your class has a discussion of historical and visual inaccuracies of the Disney film *Pocahontas,* based on Cornel Pewewardy's review of the film (Pewewardy, 1995). Later several of the students write on their own why the film negatively stereotypes Native Americans and uses racist terms such as *savages, devils,* and *primitive.* This work might be something that would be placed in the students' portfolios, along with many other samples of their critical writing abilities.

Last, make sure that you include English learners' self-assessments of language and content area abilities. Self-assessments show that a student is self-directed and can plan for future learning. You want your English learners to showcase those self-assessments to demonstrate a clear understanding of what they need to do when they use language for academic purposes in various communities of practice.

CONCLUSION

If your goal is to become the kind of teacher who can empower students, who questions the role of assessment in determining what gets taught and how it is taught, who wants to teach and assess against the grain, then you must learn to assess in ways that enable students to show their multiple strengths and knowledge bases. You have to believe that you can find ways to show that all students can be successful. You can achieve this goal by creating a classroom in which all students have multiple opportunities to learn, regardless of their language and cultural background. You can facilitate this goal by learning how to assess your students using a wide range of authentic assessment strategies that advocate for your students as learners in academic communities of practice. Likewise, you can learn to scrutinize the societal and educational contexts that legitimize assessment practices that potentially and actually disable students from learning (Cummins, 2000). Standards-based assessment is a reality for all teachers. You alone have the power to define how you interact with children and their communities and how much you will allow standards to inform what you do in your classroom.

ACTIVITIES

1. Ask your cooperating teacher for writing samples from a variety of English learners with varying English proficiency. Using the Stanford English Language Proficiency test or some other rubric (see O'Malley &

Pierce, 1996), rate the students' writing level and compare your ratings with classmates.

2. With a classmate, perform a running record (Clay, 1993) on an English learner reading a leveled book that is appropriate for the learner. Compare your record with your partner's record and discuss what the running record reveals about the student's ability to understand and make sense of the book.

3. As you visit classrooms as part of your internship and teaching experiences, pay attention to the extent to which English learners have access to equitable assessment procedures. Seek answers to the following questions:

   A. Do English learners have access to broadly conceived approaches of assessing language and academic content learning that are appropriate to their developmental level, age, and oral and written language proficiency? Do English learners have access to broadly conceived approaches of assessing special needs?

   B. Are the approaches to assessing language, academic content learning, and special needs non-biased and relevant to learners' needs?

   C. Do trained specialists give assessments?

   D. Are the results of these assessments explained to parents and the community in the language used by the parents and community members?

4. Make an appointment to sit down with your cooperating teacher or an experienced bilingual/ESL teacher and go over a student's portfolio. Find out how the teacher integrates district and state content standards with English-language proficiency standards and how these are documented in the portfolio.

REFERENCES

Bausch, L. (2003). Just words: Living and learning the literacies of our students' lives. *Language Arts, 80*(3), 215–222.

Black, P., Harrison, C., Marshall, B., & Wiliam D. (2004). Working inside the black box: Assessment for learning in the classroom. *Phi Delta Kappan, 86*(1), 8–21.

Clay, M. (1993). *An observation survey of early literacy achievement.* Portsmouth, NH: Heinemann Publishers.

Cummins, J. (2000). *Language, power, and pedagogy.* Clevedon, England: Multilingual Matters.

Faltis, C., & Hudelson, S. (1998). *Bilingual education in elementary and secondary school communities: Toward understanding and caring.* Needham Heights, MA: Allyn & Bacon.

Gee, J. (1989). What is literacy? *Journal of Education, 171*(1), 18–25.

Gibbons, P. (2002). *Scaffolding language, scaffolding learning: Teaching second language learners in the mainstream classroom.* Portsmouth, NH: Heinemann Publishers.

Goodman, Y., Watson, D., & Burke, C. (1987). *Reading miscue inventory: Alternative procedures.* New York: Richard C. Owen.

Haley, M., & Austin, T. (2004). *Content-based second language teaching and learning: An interactive approach.* Boston: Allyn & Bacon.

Hamp-Lyons, L. (1991). Scoring procedures for ESL contexts. In L. Hamp-Lyons (Ed.), *Assessing second language writing in academic contexts* (pp. 241–276). Norwood, NJ: Ablex.

Herman, J., Aschbacher, P., & Winters, L. (1992). *A practical guide to alternative assessment.* Alexandria, VA: Association for Supervision and Curriculum Development.

O'Malley, J. M., & Pierce, L. V. (1996). *Authentic assessment for English language learners: Practical approaches for teachers.* New York: Longman.

Palmer, A., Rogers, T., & Winn-Bell Olsen, J. (1985). *Back and forth: Pair activities for language development.* Englewood Cliffs, NJ: Alemany Press.

Peregoy, S., & Boyle, O. (2000). *Reading, writing and learning in ESL: A resource book for K–12 teachers.* New York: Longman.

Poyner, L., & Wolfe, P. (2005). *Marketing fear in American public schools: The real war on literacy.* Mahwah, NJ: Lawrence Erlbaum Associates.

Pewewardy, C. (1995). Why one can't ignore *Pocahontas. Rethinking Schools, 10*(1), 19.

Scarcella, R. (1987). Sociodrama for social interaction. In H. Long & J. Richards (Eds.), *Methodology in ESL* (pp. 208–213). New York: Newbury House.

Short, D. (2000). Language learning in sheltered social studies classes. *TESOL Journal, 11*(1), 18–24.

Index